Metropolitan Impact of Manpower Programs: A Four-City Comparison

Edited by
Garth L. Mangum
R. Thayne Robson

Olympus Publishing Company
Salt Lake City, Utah

Contents

List of Tables

iv

Acknowledgments

Many hands and minds other than those listed as authors were involved in this study. Alfred Zuck, Abraham Stahler, Ralph Walker, and Frank Stanard of the Office of Evaluation in the Manpower Administration, U.S. Department of Labor, suggested, financed, and shepherded it to conclusion. The openhanded policy of Malcolm R. Lovell, Jr., Assistant Secretary for Manpower, in making public all evaluation results, made publication possible. Officials of regional manpower administrations and state, local, and private agencies in each city were the primary sources of data and insights. The cooperation of individual respondents to lengthy questionnaires made the follow-up survey possible. None of these of course is in any way responsible for the conclusions, though the study could not have been done without their help.

In addition to those listed as authors for each section, Frank McLaughlin of Boston College and Harold Goldstein of Northeastern University participated in the Boston data gathering and reporting. Ralph Mecham and Kenneth Olson filled similar roles in Denver. Curtis Aller played a major role in the San Francisco-Oakland Bay area portion, and Jay Fantz, Miriam Johnson, Malcolm Ligget, Jack Walsh, Don Bullock, and Robin Hatfield were also involved in data gathering. Decision Making Information (DMI) was responsible for the follow-up survey under the direction of Hilda Barnes. Each of these is responsible as well as credited for his or her contribution, and the editors and authors express gratitude to them all.

v

Introduction

The manpower programs introduced during the 1960s — programs designed to enhance the employability and earnings of various disadvantaged groups in the society — have multiplied into an interdependent but amorphous complex in cities throughout the United States. With funds severely limited relative to this group's serious employment handicaps, eradication of which is the objective of all the programs, evaluation is continuously needed to ascertain that scarce dollars are being spent as efficiently as possible. The important question is not which manpower program has been most cost effective in achieving its objectives, but what combination of manpower services can make the greatest contribution, within given budgets, to alleviate the employment problems of the disadvantaged.

Manpower programs and services cannot be fully effective if they are not delivered to the appropriate clients with reasonable efficiency. However, these programs do more than contribute or fail to contribute to the employment and earnings of the enrollees. They create new and absorb trained and experienced staff who could also find jobs in other public or private institutions that use similar personnel. Participation in the programs inevitably affects the attitudes and services of public agencies, extant and new, which serve the disadvantaged.

If one is to know the real worth of the manpower programs, he must measure the total impact on the community. However, communities affect programs as well as being affected by programs. Each program was introduced into an existing economic, political, and social environment which strongly influenced the nature of the programs and in part predetermined their relative success or failure. Problems and circumstances also differ among communities and may require a different set of programs, services, or policies.

Given these considerations, Olympus Research Corporation (ORC), under the aegis of the Office of Evaluation, Manpower Administration, U.S. Department of Labor (DOL), began in 1968 an experimental "total impact" evaluation of all DOL-funded manpower programs in three metropolitan areas. The intent was to answer two questions:

(1) What is the total net impact of the entire complex of programs in each community? (In other words, in what ways do these communities differ today from the condition in which they would have been had there never been a manpower program?)

(2) In what ways have the differing economic, political, and social environments required differing policies or influenced the relative success or failure of the programs?

The purpose of the study was to evaluate the impact of past efforts, determining their worth and contributing to decisions for continuation, modification, or abolition. But the study had other potential contributions: Public manpower policy of the early 1970s was focusing its attention on a series of issues which involved local conditions and administrative competence to an unusual degree. Three areas of concern were determined:

(1) Of necessity, the impetus and design of the manpower programs had to come from the national level, but services are usually delivered locally to individuals; e.g., by instruments of state or local governments or by private organizations. The best designed program can founder on ineffective local delivery. It has also been discovered through experience that a design which looks good in Washington may be less effective in a particular locality. Despite the similarity among urban problems, the economics, politics, demography, and psychology of various areas differ substantially, and program administration, intentionally or not, will differ in response. This realization led many to the conclusion that planning and administration of manpower programs should be decentralized to states and cities. Whether that will be an improvement depends upon the capabilities of state and local administrators and the efficiency of agencies of their governments.

(2) As the nation began in the early 1960s attacking unfamiliar problems for a previously unserved clientele, a series of categorical programs emerged, each with its own limited services, eligibility rules, funding sources, and administrative patterns — though with overlapping clientele. To be served, the client must fit the program. Could not the many programs be decategorized into one, making available the full list of services to be tailored to individual needs?

(3) Throughout all of the manpower experience, it was still not clear how much of the unemployment and low income of the disadvan-

taged was attributable to their own lack of the requirements for employability and how much was the fault of biases and shortcomings in the institutions of the labor market. One thing was very clear: No matter how much was done for employability and for placement, neither could overcome the absence of employment opportunities.

Some light was shed on each of these issues.

In order to make the test of total manpower program impact as instructive as possible, ORC chose three metropolitan areas of widely differing characteristics. Progressing from the simple to the complex, we selected Denver as a medium-sized city of consolidated political structure, without reputation for overwhelming social and economic problems. Boston was chosen as a larger city, with its long history of action on the manpower front but with target areas essentially within a single political entity. The San Francisco-Oakland Bay area was selected as the most complex situation of multiple political jurisdictions encompassing a number of overlapping labor markets, having experienced ghetto riots and being the site of large expenditures of manpower funds.

From the first year's experience, it became clear that while information was being gathered to allow evaluation of the institutional impact of the manpower programs, little was being learned about the impact of the programs on the working lives of the enrollees themselves. For that reason, a follow-up study was added in 1969, 1970, and 1971 of the postenrollment employment and earnings experience of samples of enrollees in the various programs and cities.

Meanwhile, the programs and situations had not remained static, and all the relevant facts and all the needed insights into complex systems had not been achieved. The second phase continued the study of administrative relationships. It had the added advantage of following the programs through a period of softening labor markets, just as the first phase had experienced tight labor markets.

The central focus of the study was to be the total manpower system at the local level rather than individual projects, programs, or functions. With this in mind, ORC made an effort to build a complete inventory of the total volume of dollars spent, the individuals served, their characteristics, the number and type of projects, their service components, and their outcomes over four fiscal years. Difficulties were expected, but their full extent was not foreseen. Records were scattered, frequently incomplete, and always lacking essential information. The immense amount of time devoted to retrieving data which should already have been compiled subtracted from the time available for more subjective but more profitable data gathering and analyses.

With the advantage of hindsight, it is now evident that it would have been better to have settled for the information that was readily available and to have relied on estimates for the gaps. Attempts to gain information from Washington records on expenditures, client characteristics, and post-enrollment follow-up for the Manpower Development and Training Act (MDTA) and Neighborhood Youth Corps (NYC) programs were no more successful. During the second phase of the project, it was discovered that the already deficient national manpower data situation (it cannot be called a system) had further deteriorated, but fortunately the follow-up data offset those which were no longer available from federal sources.

A number of special studies were conducted; a history of the activities of each agency and the progress of each program were completed. Since the Work Incentive (WIN) program was just being introduced, its impact and the interactions of the welfare agencies and the employment service (ES) were the subject of another special study during the first phase. A series of in-depth interviews of employers participating in the MDTA–on-the-job training (OJT) program and the Job Opportunities in the Business Sector (JOBS) program was undertaken. There were interviews with community leaders to explore their perceptions of the impact of the manpower programs, with a special focus on the minority communities. There was a special study of the staff of the manpower agencies designed to produce information on their background, training, and patterns of job mobility. Other special studies were made of the impact of placement services on (1) relative postplacement earnings, (2) the quality of work stations, and (3) the employment impact of work experience programs and the National Alliance of Businessmen's NAB-JOBS program on subsequent employment and earnings of enrollees. All of these components cannot be included within the brief compass of this book.

For evaluation, the major lack in the original methodology was any knowledge of the impact of the programs on the subsequent employment and earnings of the participants. Without that there could be no real evaluation of the worth of a program or a combination of programs. We could talk of the quality of program administration, program linkages, needed improvements, and institutional impacts. These were valuable and necessary. Yet without some knowledge of the impact of program participation on the subsequent employment and earnings of enrollees, the study could not honestly be called an evaluation.

The follow-up survey met that need in part. It proved that on the average, despite a worsening economic climate, the enrollees were better off in every city and in almost every program than they had been before they enrolled. In some cities and for some programs, the change was spectacular. Since available resources precluded a control group for the study, the comparison was between the pre- and postenrollment experiences of the sample. Therefore, what would have been the situation of the participants had they never enrolled cannot be ascertained. One can only be certain that their gains, on the average, were far beyond prevailing trends in the economy. Even more significant than those results, the study proved that follow-up could be accomplished in ghetto areas at reasonable cost and with a high and statistically acceptable rate of return.

This book sets each metropolitan area in its social, economic, and political perspective. It traces the history of the introduction of manpower programs in each metropolitan area. It appraises the quality of administration for each program and for each functional grouping of manpower services. It assesses the impact of each program and functional service on the enrollees, the community and its institutions, and the labor market. It describes the methodology and displays the results of the follow-up study. It ends with (1) a judgmental evaluation of the total impact of all manpower programs and each program and functional service, comparatively, across the three metropolitan areas, (2) an identification of implications for current policy issues, and (3) recommendations for program and functional improvements.

Part 1
The Boston Experience

Morris A. Horowitz
Irwin L. Herrnstadt

The Old, the New, and the Other Boston

1

The nature, achievements, and shortcomings of Boston's manpower programs have been heavily influenced by an environment which involves the "old," the "new," and the "other" Boston. The old Boston is a composite of pride in its democratic heritage, its cultural tradition, and its continuing status as one of the world's most prominent centers for scholarship and learning and the less desirable image of conservatism, ethnic conflict, and political corruption. The term "the new Boston" has been coined to describe the recent resurgence of civic interest and a broadening of urban renewal activities. The "other Boston" is characterized by neither pride nor progress but by neglected neighborhoods of fearful and alienated people who live in the 50,000 housing units in the city (one in five) classified by the Boston Redevelopment Authority as either dilapidated or deteriorating, and whose children attend schools beset with problems.

Insistent demands for change have arisen in recent years — change in the school system, in local government and civil service law, in the tax provisions, and in the physical appearance of the city. But the city is reluctant to relax its commitment to the status quo. Progress is not absent, but it is limited and slow. Ironically, the same unique past that contributed to Boston's greatness is the most important factor in understanding the city's resistance to change.

New England Conservatism — Its Continuing Influence

Boston prospered during the reign of the Brahmins, as the blueblood Yankees came to be known. It was a historic port city during the clipper ship era and the focal point of the social ferment that swept the country in the late 1880s. From their Beacon Hill townhouses overlooking the Boston Common and from their brownstones at the lower end of Commonwealth

Avenue in Back Bay, the Cabots, the Lowells, the Peabodys, and Boston's other first families conducted their day-to-day business affairs. They kept a close conservative eye on the dealings of their banks, their law and real estate firms, and their family businesses. Yet, as Peter Schrag observes, the roots of Boston's difficulties can be found in this period.

> Although the city's capitalists helped finance several transcontinental railroads, they failed to develop one of their own, and thus Boston never became the great seaport that its geographical location might have made possible. The local conservatism — always aiming to keep family control of relatively small enterprises — ignored several major opportunities to bring heavy manufacturing industries to the city, directed the available capital to restrictive trust funds, and staffed the city's business . . . with the not-always competent sons of proper families.[1]

Furthermore, these Massachusetts patricians also kept a watchful eye on the management of public affairs and remained in active control of the Commonwealth until the Irish population had grown sufficiently to develop an effective apparatus—the Democratic Party—to challenge such control.

The Irish influence began in the 1840s, and by 1855 Boston's population was equally divided between Yankees and Irishmen. The Irish soon achieved a popular majority in numbers, but when allowed few opportunities in the business world, they turned to careers in civil service and in politics. In 1899, the Irish had gained firm control of the city. The Brahmins, forced to surrender their long-held domain, moved to the suburbs, to involvement in charitable organizations, and to continued control of the universities. But they still sought to maintain some leverage and voice in their city's affairs by transferring as much power as they could to the legislature, the governor, and various special commissions.

William V. Shannon has cogently described Boston's development, or perhaps more accurately lack of development during this period:

> This withdrawal and inertia of Boston's wealthy people and its business community conditioned the outlook of life of the Irish majority in the years 1900 to 1940. Because the city did not enjoy the economic expansion that invigorated other major cities, the Irish made very slow progress into the middle and upper classes. By the end of this period only four of the thirty directors of the Boston Chamber of Commerce were of Irish descent. . . . Ethnic and class lines almost exactly coincided. The majority who had the political power felt themselves distinctly separated from those who had the economic power, and the separation was not only along economic lines, as it would be elsewhere, but also along nationality, religious, and cultural lines. Moreover, the visible failure of the city to pro-

---

[1] Peter Schrag, *Village School Downtown* (Boston: Beacon Press, 1967), p. 27.

gress economically meant that the working class did not respect or have confidence in the business leadership even on the latter's own terms, that is, on economic terms. State Street could not reasonably assert that its stewardship of the economy had brought prosperity to the city.[2]

INDUSTRIAL AND OCCUPATIONAL TRENDS

Most of the economic expansion that the Boston area has experienced since the end of World War II has occurred outside the core city in suburban communities, especially along Route 128, the express highway circling Boston and referred to as "The Golden Arc." Until the recent economic decline, there were signs that the same kind of development was in store for Route 495, another express highway circling Boston approximately 15 miles farther from downtown Boston than Route 128.

Initially, a warehousing and distribution center, characterized by sprawling one-story buildings, the Route 128 area has become highly developed, with much of the land currently held by firms, both large and small, in the electrical-electronics industry. More recently, the area has been developing its own economy as these firms have been joined by shopping centers, service businesses, and motels. Boston now has only two-fifths of the metropolitan area's jobs with only one-eighth employed in manufacturing, compared to one-quarter for the entire standard metropolitan statistical area (SMSA). The city lost employment during the 1960s in manufacturing, transportation, communication and public utilities, and wholesale trade while gaining in finance, services, and government. The remainder of the metropolitan area experienced no losses while gaining in many of those industries where Boston declined.

These shifts in the location and composition of industry and population have combined to make life more difficult for Boston's disadvantaged workers. Industry and hence employment have become increasingly suburbanized. Manufacturing has declined relative to other industrial sectors, and its decline has been more rapid in the city than in the suburbs. The manufacturing firms remaining in the city are those which are more likely to have unskilled, low-wage jobs. The manufacturing jobs in suburban locations are more apt to be high-wage jobs frequently requiring higher levels of skill than those possessed by the typical disadvantaged worker. Finally, the growth in the other industrial sectors, such as finance, real estate, insurance, government, and educational and medical services, has occurred as readily in Boston as in the suburbs, producing a shift toward white-collar occupations with increasing requirements.

The results of this increasing demand for skilled professional and sub-professional workers and the decreasing demand for manual workers with

---

[2] William V. Shannon, *The American Irish* (New York: The Macmillan Company, 1963), cited in Schrag, *ibid.*, p. 30.

minimal skills have already begun to show up in the statistics. For example, early in 1969, when overall unemployment was still low, the employment service (ES) listed a total of 6,705 unfilled job openings, of which approximately half were in the professional-technical and the clerical-sales categories. Throughout the 1960s, the fastest growing category in the city had been professional and technical; clerical and service occupations also grew, but at a slower rate. Absolute declines occurred for operatives and laborers. Meanwhile in the suburbs, all occupational groups experienced growth, with white-collar and service occupations seeing the greatest gains.

TRENDS IN INCOME AND EMPLOYMENT

A high proportion of the poor of the Boston SMSA is concentrated in the city of Boston, even though Boston's living costs are among the highest in the nation. In 1970, mean household income was $14,794 in the SMSA, compared to $11,507 in the city of Boston. The $9,248 mean income of the nonwhite households averaged just 80 percent of that of white households. In 1968, 20 percent of Boston's households had less than $4,000 income, while 47 percent had incomes of more than $10,000. The SMSA meanwhile had a substantially smaller proportion in the lower category and a larger percentage in the higher. A 1971 press release of a U.S. Department of Health, Education and Welfare (HEW) report ranked Boston first among U.S. cities in the percentage of its people (15 percent) receiving welfare payments.

Of the unemployed and underemployed in selected poverty areas in 1966, the following analysis reveals that (1) of the unemployed 66 percent had not graduated from high school, and 34 percent had not gone beyond the 8th grade, (2) 37 percent of all family units were headed by women, compared to a national figure in 1966 of 21 percent, (3) 70 percent of the residents of these neighborhoods were nonwhite, virtually all of them black, and (4) 23 percent of the unemployed were 16 to 19 years of age.

Until the start of the economic recession in 1969, the Boston labor market was rather tight. The labor shortage classifications ranged from professional and clerical and sales jobs to a number of relatively unskilled occupations. Low pay and poor working conditions accounted for the apparent shortage of persons prepared to fill various unskilled, dead-end jobs. While many of these jobs went vacant, large numbers of disadvantaged workers in the heart of Boston were unemployed, working part time, or earning subsistence-level incomes. After 1969, many of the vacant jobs disappeared as the employment rate for the Boston metropolitan area rose from 3.2 percent in 1969 to 5.6 percent for the first four months of 1971.

However, conventional measures of unemployment misrepresent conditions for inner city slum areas. A 1966 survey found the unemployment rate in Boston's poverty area to be double that of the entire city. But when those working part time while seeking full-time work, those not seeking work though capable of and available for it, and those working full time for less than $60 a week were added to the conventional measure, 24.8 percent of the area residents were without minimally adequate employment.

POPULATION TRENDS

Despite the construction of luxury apartment houses which have helped induce some high-income people to move into the city, and despite the fact that sections of Beacon Hill and the Back Bay are still considered highly desirable downtown residential locations, the population of the city of Boston continues to decline. The 1960 central city population of 697,200 was 12.7 percent below that of 1950, and preliminary census reports for 1970 indicate another 10 percent decline during the 1960s to 628,200. Yet during the same 20-year period, the population of the Boston SMSA grew by more than 13 percent from 2,410,600 to 2,730,200. There is some reason to believe that this decline may have slowed or even halted about midpoint between the 1960 and 1970 censuses.

However, the aggregate population figures obscure important internal shifts in the composition of the population of both Boston and its metropolitan surroundings. First, the actual out-migration has been greater than the net figures for population change. The gross number leaving the city has been nearly double the natural increase which should have resulted from excess births over deaths. This has been true not only of the central city but to a lesser degree, of the fringe of cities and towns immediately surrounding Boston. By this standard, the core fringe 5 to 10 miles out from the city center has been losing gross population at about 10 percent per decade. At the same time, communities 10 to 15 miles out, ringed by the Route 128 inner belt circumferential highway, had an in-migration rate of 9.5 percent, while those communities 15 to 25 miles out, confined by the Route 495 circumferential highway, experienced an in-migration rate of 25.4 percent.

While Boston's total population declined 20 to 25 percent in the last 20 years, some sections of the city achieved significant growth. During the 1950s, considerable homebuilding took place in Boston's West Roxbury and Hyde Park sections (southwest of downtown Boston), where there had been substantial open land. In these districts, it was possible at reasonable prices to combine the amenities of suburban life with closeness and relatively convenient public transportation to the core city.

The concerns of Boston's out-migrants are the same as those of city dwellers across the country. They complain of crime in the streets and juvenile vandalism of both public and private property; they deplore the substandard housing; they are dissatisfied with inadequate recreational facilities and city services and the quality of the schools; they fear racial tension;

and they worry about the politics of city government and the degree to which citizen participation is blocked by the city's leadership.

ETHNIC COMPOSITION OF THE CITY

Ethnic neighborhoods and ethnic politics are still important in Boston. East Boston and the North End are clearly identifiable as Italian neighborhoods. They generally elect those of Italian descent to the legislature, although in recent years part of the North End has been included in a district dominated by Yankee and Republican Beacon Hill. Dorchester's Ward 14 has long been a Jewish neighborhood, but this has changed sharply in recent years, and in the 1970 election, a black was elected from the district as one of its two state representatives. There is a Chinese and Puerto Rican community, concentrations of Poles and Lithuanians, and groups of Syrians and Lebanese. Roxbury, North Dorchester, and the South End are predominantly black, although in parts of these neighborhoods, there are growing numbers of Spanish-surnamed people.

The Irish have dominated the city's politics and neighborhoods for most of the 20th century, with legislators of that descent for years representing all sections of the city except for a few Italian, Jewish, and Yankee neighborhoods. Until 1969, six of the nine city councilmen were Irish-Americans; by 1971, only the mayor and four of the nine city council members were Irish-Americans, while the others included three Italians, one black, and one Yankee. The elected school committee remained staunchly four of five in favor of the Irish.

As in most large northern cities, the most dramatic change in the ethnic composition in recent years has been the growth of the black population. The large net out-migration from the city, and the consequent overall population decline, also obscures a sizable in-migration of black and Spanish-surnamed people. From 40,000 in 1950 and 68,500 in 1960, Boston's nonwhite population grew by 70 percent to 116,300 by 1970. By 1969, blacks were 18 percent of the city's population — close behind the Irish-Americans who by then comprised only 22 percent of the city's population. In comparison, white Protestants were 13 percent, Italian-Americans 11 percent, and Jews 6 percent. There are no dependable statistics for the Spanish-surnamed population. One study estimates it at 25,000 to 40,000, with a school-age population of 5,000 to 10,000, of whom only 2,500 are in school, allegedly because of lack of bilingual instruction.[3]

Despite their 70 percent increase in 10 years, the proportion of blacks in Boston is still below that of any other major city in the Northeast. In additions, the black population is less concentrated than is normal for cities of its

---

[3] Joseph M. Cronin, *et al.*, *Organizing an Urban School System for Diversity: A Study of the Boston School Department* (Massachusetts Advisory Council on Education, October 1970), pp. 149–58.

size and region. In a survey published in 1971 of Boston's predominantly black area, 77 percent of the persons interviewed reported that some whites lived on the same street, and only 17 percent said that no whites lived on their street.[4] Whites, however, were a small minority in some of these areas, consisting principally of a residual group of older people. It was also found that among young black adults, 18 percent had at least one white friend among the five people closest to them. As might be expected, the integration in employment was much greater, with only 5 percent of young black adults working in places where there were no whites, and 70 percent working together with many or mostly whites.

Of the sample of Boston blacks, 71 percent were born outside the metropolitan area, often in rural areas of the Southeast. More than 70 percent of in-migrants arrived in Boston after their 18th birthday, and an estimated 60 percent of the black adult population in Boston in 1968 had arrived in the previous 15 years. Black nonmigrants had higher levels of education, were more highly skilled, and were more likely than the migrants to be in high- or medium-status occupations.

Blacks in Boston have found themselves in direct confrontation with the Irish-dominated political power structure, particularly in the school department. In 1970, approximately 30 percent of the public school population was black, in part because the black population is younger than the white, in part because of the large Catholic school system. As a result of the increasing size and militancy of the black minority, some slight inroads have been made against Irish domination of city government. However, citywide election of councilmen and school committeemen helps to perpetuate Irish political power. Mayor Kevin White appointed blacks to some important positions in his administration, and has maintained a sympathetic position toward the black community. However, he failed to carry the heavily Democratic city of Boston in his unsuccessful bid for the governorship in the fall of 1970 while running very well in the black wards of the city. This was interpreted by some to have been, at least in part, the result of a white backlash.

It was the 1969 elections which substantially changed the ethnic composition of the city council to four Irish, three Italians, one black, and one Yankee. The black, Thomas I. Atkins, ran second in the citywide election, as much to the surprise of his supporters as to his opponents (since his margin could have been achieved only with substantial white support), and was outvoted only by Louise Day Hicks who gained notoriety as a member of the Boston School Committee and now is a U.S. Representative from former Speaker McCormack's district.

---

[4] March Fried, *et al.*, "A Study of Demographic and Social Determinants of Functional Achievement in a Negro Population," a final report submitted to the Division of Research and Plans, Office of Economic Opportunity (Boston: Institute of Human Sciences, Boston College, January 1, 1971).

THE BOSTON SCHOOL SYSTEM

The Boston school system is a demonstration of the burden a once well-reputed school system can become if it fails to adapt to change. A description of the system is necessary to understand its current problems.

Three of the city's high schools — Boys' Latin, Girls' Latin, and Technical (for boys only) — draw their students from the entire city on the basis of competitive examination and are thus highly selective in their admissions policies. As a result, graduates of these schools do well in college admissions. However, in the 1940s, when Boston's population was much larger than it is today, admission to these three high schools was much easier for Boston schoolchildren. For example, many students were admitted to Boston Latin on the basis of their grade record without an examination, and tuition-paying students were admitted from suburban schools. Today, every student must take the competitive examination, and there are no seats available for non-Bostonians. Many factors help to explain this increase in demand for admission to the Latin schools, but the major reason is the declining reputations of many of the other Boston high schools.

Five other high schools — English High (boys), Girls' High, Boston Trade, Trade High School for Girls, and Boston High — also draw their students from throughout the city. English High, for many years the largest high school in the city, drew students from all over Boston, although it also was the district high school for the South, West, and North Ends. The school's reputation has declined in recent years. Since the original building was razed more than a decade ago, its students have been housed in buildings throughout the city.

Boston Trade offers a variety of courses primarily in the traditional crafts. Both it and Trade High School for Girls tend to be for students who cannot succeed academically. Boston High is a new school which grew out of a dropout-prevention effort. The school operates an imaginative work-study program and has developed close relationships with a large number of Boston employers. It has been widely regarded as very successful, and in 1970 the Massachusetts Advisory Council on Education recommended that its enrollment of 418 be expanded to 1,200 in the short run and to 2,000 or more in the long run.[5]

The remaining nine high schools (eight coeducational and one all girls) are district schools; although under the open-enrollment policy, anyone in the city can attend if seats are available. These schools offer college, business, and general curricula, and six of the eight coeducational schools have cooperative vocational courses for males as well. In addition, one of the schools offers a course on agriculture, though the emphasis in this program has increasingly been shifted to horticulture. The six vocational courses are specialized by schools atracting some 1,400 students from all over the city.

---

[5] Cronin, *et al., Organizing an Urban School System*, p. 202.

The vocational programs offered in the district schools apparently serve those students who complete them with reasonable success. In general, there are traditional vocational offerings — electrical, machine shop, sheet metal, wood working, and auto mechanics. Until recently, many of these programs had fewer slots than applicants, and as a result, the slots were filled on the basis of competitive examination. Students who failed the examination were put into the general curriculum which did little to prepare them for a specific occupation or higher education and which had a high dropout rate. At present, however, applicants to most of the vocational courses are admitted on a first-come, first-served basis.

Nearly half of the 22,000 students in the senior high schools are enrolled in occupationally oriented courses. Approximately 13 percent are in the trade schools and another 35 percent receive business and distributive education. Of the remaining 11,000 students, approximately 5,000 to 6,000 are in the Latin schools and in the technical school, leaving 6,000 to 7,000 students in the comprehensive high schools. Most of the latter students may be in college preparatory courses, but few go on to post-high school work.

The Boston School Department (BSD) has been allowed to take advantage of federal funds available for occupational education. Of $5 million in federal funds for occupational education allocated to Massachusetts in 1969, less than 1 percent went to Boston. Allegedly, the reason for this was the school department's failure to submit proposals.

The Boston school system faces some difficult education tasks in attempting to meet the educational needs of many of the poor, especially the minority poor in the city. Considerable controversy has developed in recent years concerning how well it is meeting this challenge. In 1964, the Boston NAACP released a report which showed that Boston ranked at the bottom of the list of comparable cities in terms of the number of its high school graduates admitted to college. Another study showed that as Boston children progressed in school from the 1st through 6th grades, they fell increasingly behind the national average in reading achievement, with the level of performance closely correlated with the income level of the school district.

On the whole, the reaction of school authorities to this report was defensive. Although changes are taking place, they probably are not sufficient to meet the problems these surveys uncovered. The school system has also been charged with neglecting the recent inflow of Spanish-surnamed youngsters from Puerto Rico. One organization has claimed that almost half of these youngsters do not attend school. The schools have insisted that there is no major problems.

The school system has not fostered creativity and intellectual brilliance as the chief educational objectives. This is not to say that the system lacks imaginative and stimulating teachers or that gifted students have been unable to obtain what they needed within the system. The system has mirrored the values of the majority of the residents (largely working or lower middle classes) in a city where the prevailing social class structure was largely accepted. A citywide survey of public school parents is an indication: When asked how much attention should be given to a long list of topics in the elementary schools, respondents most frequently mentioned five or six which were related to social control of the children (drug education, proper behavior, loyalty to the United States, preparation for jobs, good grooming). Controlling children's behavior was a recurring theme in the survey. Nevertheless, when parents were asked what they considered to be the primary goal of elementary schools, the most common choice was an inculcation of a desire for learning.[6]

In this context, the dominant and desired values of the school system have been the teaching of certain basic skills (the three Rs) and the inculcation of discipline and respectable behavior. Social and economic advancement was possible within such a context . . . but along well-established lines that did not disturb the existing class structure. Many of the teachers and administrators were drawn from the same working and lower middle classes as the parents of the students and thus reflect their values. As a result, the school system has tended to support the status quo. Although significant changes have begun to take place, the system has not been noted for innovation and has had difficulty adjusting to the demands of those unhappy with existing conditions.

Boston's Heritage

The politics of Boston have been the politics of the Irish who have provided nearly every major political leader since 1916. Boston is a Roman Catholic, Democratic city which has not voted for a Republican president or mayor since the mid-1920s. The career choices of the Irish had been largely restricted to civil service and politics. As other groups entered the city, the Irish became ardently and defensively possessive of their political domain in much the same way that the Yankees had clung to their ruling economic status in the late 1880s. To a large degree, the Irish have been successful.

From 1913 to 1949, Boston's politics were dominated by James Michael Curley who possessed the only machine-like organization the city has ever known. Most of his power and support came from thousands of people who thought of him as the "mayor of the poor," who felt strong personal loyalty to him because he "understood" them and their needs. Whereas the ward boss of the previous decade had provided them with jobs, food, coal, and other basic necessities of life, Curley talked of parks, playgrounds, schools,

---

[6] *Ibid.*, pp. 25–28.

and hospitals. The fact that he was twice jailed for various indiscretions made little difference; the people adored him. Murray Levin emphasizes, however, that even then Boston was not a "machine" city in the ordinary sense of the word:

> He [Curley] was unable to transfer the allegiance of his machine to any other candidate. Boston politics is thus highly personal politics, almost feudal politics, and elections are fought in highly personalized terms. . . . In Boston's situations, politics become highly fluid and depend very much on the candidates.[7]

The continuing appeal of such "personal politics" has been evident in every major city election since Curley's days. An example is the election of John F. Collins over John E. Powers in 1959. Powers was a strong favorite to win the mayoralty; he had created the image of a longtime public servant whose record demonstrated his honesty, integrity, and ability to deal with legislators; he had a broad base of public support and had been endorsed by everyone from the state's Republican leaders to Senator John F. Kennedy. Yet he lost to Collins, a candidate with little organization, who emphasized his role as the underdog and his lack of association with the professional politicians, and who based his campaign on an appeal to the "little people" to help him stop "power politics." The great furor caused by Louise Day Hicks in the mayoralty race of 1967 is another example of this phenomenon.

From the days of the shift from Yankee to Irish control, Boston has been at the mercy of its suburbs and the remainder of the state. The municipal powers vested by the departing Yankees in the legislators, the governor, and the various special commissions have continued to haunt and hinder Boston. Of the people who live in the metropolitan area, 75 percent reside outside the city where, according to Levin,

> Disgusted with inefficient government and a high tax rate, suburbanites feel that Boston deserves no consideration from the Commonwealth until Boston sets its own house in order. Underlying this sentiment is the knowledge that the suburbs will have to pay for any relief which is granted to the city.[8]

An example is the handling of the large annual deficits of the Massachusetts Bay Transit Authority which links Boston and its suburbs. Only 44 percent of the people using the service are residents of Boston, yet the city pays 62 percent of the debt and is allowed only 38 percent of the vote on the Transit Authority's advisory board. Similarly, the state legislature apportions the cost of maintaining some roads, recreational facilities, and water supply in the metropolitan area among the Greater Boston com-

---

[7] Murray Levin, *The Alienated Voter* (New York: Holt, Rinehart and Winston, 1960).

[8] *Ibid.*, p. 7.

munities, with Boston paying the entire amount assessed to Suffolk County, even though Boston is only one of four municipalities in the county.

Boston's tax base has shrunk with the steady addition of nontaxable property and the loss of business establishments, while the cost of government has continued to rise rapidly. The property tax remains virtually the only source of revenue. Yet the city cannot secure relief from the state legislature. In the past, the relationship between the city and the state was further complicated by the fact that Republicans dominated the legislature while Democrats held the city. However, for several years now both houses of the general court have been dominated by Democrats, and Republican governors have only been elected by appealing to people who normally vote Democratic.

URBAN RENEWAL

The eight years during which Collins served as mayor were critical for the city. He was determined to bring Boston out of its 30-year slump. Before his administration, a large renewal project had begun in what was then Boston's West End. Boston had the good sense to take advantage of the aid available through the Housing Act of 1949 and the slum clearance amendments of 1954, but unrealistic planning created a morass of social problems.

The project had been six years in the planning, more than enough time to arouse disgruntlement at the federal, state, and local levels. When the Boston Redevelopment Authority finally was established by legislative act in 1956 and began operations in October 1957, the bitterness increased immeasurably. Although the Redevelopment Authority moved ahead with physical renewal, it neglected the needs of the area's residents. When razing operations finally began, 9,000 residents of what had been a closely knit, working-class community of the West End were summarily displaced, with little consideration given to their relocation. Expensive, high-rise apartment buildings replaced walk-up tenements, with the residents of the latter having no voice in the planning.

The ensuing public outcry made it clear that the city could not afford to let this happen again. Realizing this, Collins imported Edward J. Logue, a redevelopment expert who had made a name for himself in Hartford. Together Collins and Logue began to plan for greater citizen participation in future redevelopment activities and to emphasize rehabilitation of existing structures as well as razing and renewal. Their efforts led to the creation of the Boston Community Development Program (BCDP), which later became Action for Boston Community Development, Inc. (ABCD), an organization whose history and purpose are discussed more fully in chapter 2.

Urban redevelopment became the symbol of the Collins administration. From 1960 to 1967, Boston was allotted more than $180 million in federal urban renewal funds, the largest single amount given to any city in the nation. Two-thirds of the money went for large-scale, rehabilitation-oriented, residential urban renewal.

When Kevin White took office in January 1968, he vowed to continue building "the new Boston." However, in addition to the physical needs of the city, he stressed the psychological needs of the residents and the necessity of making city government both responsive and responsible to the neighborhoods as well as to downtown. Therefore, while plans for physical renewal have continued, more typical of White's approach were the establishment of neighborhood service centers, popularly called "little city halls," the opening of the mayor's office downtown for 24-hour service to the city's residents, and the establishment of "Summerthing," a citywide recreation program emphasizing outdoor musical, dramatic, and dance performances. His intent has been to provide stronger lines of communication between the people and their government and to gather around him a "cabinet" of knowledgeable men as personal staff and field officers.

The *Boston Globe* commended Mayor White on this fundamental change in the management of the city's business:

> Mayor Collins' hiring of Edward J. Logue to run the Boston Redevelopment Authority — with a high salary and a new combination of powers designed to make the job attractive — was a critical breakthrough for Boston. But Collins never really followed his own precedent after the Logue appointment. Collins' department heads were uneven as individuals, and, as a corporate brain trust, nonexistent. . . . There may be as many as six or eight White recruits who have Logue's intelligence and energy. Very few of them have been handed the awesome power that was assembled at the BRA for Logue; yet the concern for innovation and insistence on quality that John Collins focused on the BRA has, in White's first year, been spread much broader across the spectrum of city departments.[9]

Political commentary in the same paper, however, has suggested that the mayor failed to develop support among the business and financial community whose leaders had backed Mayor Collins.

As the existence of this "cabinet" attests to White's effort to decentralize city government at the policy-making level, the establishment of the little city halls testifies to his efforts at the neighborhood level. Currently, such centers exist in 10 different neighborhoods, and as might be expected, the problems differ somewhat from one center to the next. The work is not especially dramatic; rather its value lies in those minor services performed which, over time, add up to major improvements. Perhaps most important of all is that the centers provide tangible evidence to Bostonians that "downtown" cares about their problems.

---

[9] *Boston Globe*, March 9, 1969.

A Summing Up

This chapter has reviewed those features of the Boston social, political, and economic environment important for an understanding of the magnitude of the city's manpower problems and the tasks facing the implementation of federal manpower policy in the city. While the total population of the city has declined, the number of poor and nonwhites has grown. These changes have been accompanied by a decline, on the average, in the educational and training levels of Boston's residents. The typical immigrant to Boston in recent years has been nonwhite, southern, and without industrial experience.

As nonwhites settled in more and more sections of the city, whites moved to the suburbs; housing became more dilapidated and social services deteriorated. Many businesses also sought new locations in the outlying suburbs. As a result, many of the better jobs open to the less educated are no longer in the city but in areas difficult to reach from downtown. At the same time, new jobs within the city have been white collar, requiring additional years of education that the city's newcomers often lack. In these factors, Boston differs little from other major cities.

When the federal manpower programs came to Boston, the staffs were confronted by serious employment problems and, as will be shown in the next chapter, by state and local agencies with serious shortcomings. They also found a city which, after a century of stagnation, was beginning to come alive, a city whose business community was taking steps, if only haltingly, to participate in its affairs and whose academic institutions were beginning to feel an obligation to help solve municipal problems. Moreover, they found a progressive political leadership ready to face the challenge.

Boston's
Manpower Institutions
2

The economic conditions of Boston established the need for manpower programs; the social and political environment shaped them and in many ways, predetermined their impact. The critical influences were (1) the conservatism of ES and the public school system, (2) the already existing manpower commitment of Boston's community action agency (CAA) — ABCD — and (3) the demographic and employment trends of Boston's population and economy. Just as the city's institutions have channeled and often hampered the impact of the manpower programs, those programs have wrought major changes in the institutions which have participated in them.

THE MANPOWER DEVELOPMENT AND TRAINING ACT

Though funding via the Manpower Training and Development Act (MDTA) became available in September 1962, the first MDTA institutional course did not begin in Boston until January 30, 1963. In all of fiscal year 1963, there were just 10 projects with only 321 enrollees. In the entire state of Massachusetts in 1963, there were 50 projects with "slots" for 712 persons. Critics attributed the delay in initiating MDTA institutional (classroom) programs to the cautiousness of such established public agencies as the Massachusetts Division of Employment Security (MDES), the Massachusetts Department of Education, and BSD. A conservative MDES staff, they alleged, found it difficult to accept training as a goal because it reversed their accustomed role of referring applicants who could meet employers' hiring specifications. The Commonwealth's archaic civil service regulations (which, for example, still give veterans absolute preference) and low MDES salary scales hampered the recruitment and retention of bright young secondary school and college graduates. Many of the staff were old-timers with memories of the insecurities and loose labor markets of the 1930s, who therefore gave priority to satisfying employers' require- ments rather than making applicants more employable through MDTA training. Moreover, performance traditionally had been measured by the number of placements, not their quality, and this quantitative criterion had determined promotions, appropriations, and size of staff.

In turn, BSD was allegedly handicapped by tradition-bound personnel who held narrow views of the role of education, opposed change, and denigrated vocational training. Although increases in school expenditures required the approval of the city government, the fact that the school sys- tem was directed by a five-man school committee elected at large on a non- partisan basis, rather than being appointed by the mayor's office, meant that it marched to a different set of political drums. Vocational educators in the state's Department of Education were unwilling or unable to bypass local school authorities or pressure them to respond to MDTA, probably because of a disinclination to stir ill will when the institutional benefits might be slight. Only after pressure from the governor did MDES and the Department of Education begin stirring.

Initially, all the institutional MDTA courses in Boston were single projects, given in the late afternoon and evening in sites scattered around the city and nearly always located outside poverty areas. Only one 1963 class, an after-school-hours course for electronic technicians, was given in an inner city school, Boston Technical High School, apparently because it had the necessary facilities and not because of any special effort to accom- modate the disadvantaged.

By 1964, harsh experience with disadvantaged enrollees having mar- ginal work experience and inadequate education had led to the develop- ment of multi-occupational Skills Centers throughout the country. These were designed for trainees who lacked the labor market exposure to make wise occupational choices, who were difficult to evaluate by customary test- ing techniques, and who required basic education, prevocational orienta- tion, and counseling. In the fall of 1964, such a center was opened in the Daniel Webster School in East Boston. The site was chosen because the school had been abandoned and was empty. The neighborhood was a low- income, working-class, Italian-American section. The national decision had not yet been made to concentrate manpower efforts on the disadvan- taged. The choice of location undoubtedly seemed sound, but it was re- sented by the black community who maintained that East Boston, and with it the school, were "off limits" to them because of racial conflict and that such entrance requirements as a high school diploma effectively barred them from most courses.

MDTA institutional training remained the only manpower program of meaningful size in Boston until the start of the Concentrated Employment

Program (CEP) in mid-1967. MDTA's importance subsequently declined relatively and absolutely as funds were diverted to CEP and later to the National Alliance of Businessmen-Job Opportunities in the Business Sector (NAB-JOBS) program.

THE BIRTH AND METAMORPHOSIS OF ABCD

The most important of the local "prime movers" in Boston's manpower effort has been ABCD and its CEP administrator. The magnitude and pivotal nature of ABCD's role justifies an extensive treatment of its history.[10]

A product of the "new" Boston's ambitious urban renewal effort of the early 1960s, ABCD represented a hitherto unknown coalition of the city's Irish political leaders, civic-minded Yankee businessmen, and private social agencies. These groups were disturbed by the social blight and malaise of their city. They envisaged urban renewal as offering the chance to reverse the process of social decay and ABCD as the cutting edge of this social rejuvenation.

Phases of Development

ABCD has passed through four phases in which its structure and goals were shaped by the need to adapt to the interests of outside sponsors. The first phase, from early 1961 until the summer of 1962, was spent groping for an organizational form and a substantive program and searching for continuing financial support. During this period, ABCD considered itself responsible for "social planning" and "community organization" as the social counterpart to the physical planning of the Boston Redevelopment Authority. Although neither of the roles ABCD identified for itself was precisely defined, by the end of this initial period, most of the agency's small staff were engaged in encouraging local residents of three high-priority urban renewal areas to participate in the renewal planning process.

This period ended with the advent of financial support from the Ford Foundation and the President's Committee on Juvenile Delinquency. The need to satisfy Foundation and federal priorities recast ABCD from the social arm of urban renewal into an anticipated catalyst for reforming and reorienting the city's public and private institutions.

The second phase, beginning in the summer of 1962, was a 15-month planning period during which the temporarily funded ABCD, now defining its role as one of "action research," had to give concrete substance to its program. ABCD was to design small-scale demonstration projects susceptible to scientific evaluation and to induce other agencies to implement them,

---

[10] The early history of Action for Boston Community Development is based upon key participants and upon Stephan Thernstrom, *Poverty, Planning and Politics in the New Boston: The Origins of ABCD* (New York: Basic Books, Inc., 1969).

thereby reforming themselves. ABCD gradually and intentionally disengaged itself from community organization as it became absorbed in devising experimental projects and negotiating working relationships with participating agencies.

The final months of this second phase coincided with the beginnings of phase three, lasting until early 1965, as ABCD became directly involved in the supervision of a limited number of projects serving three inner city target areas. One project was the agency's first introduction to manpower, a large-scale youth employment and training project awarded in the fall of 1963 by the U.S. Department of Labor (DOL). Another was a set of four programs already being implemented by BSD under ABCD's Ford Foundation grant.

The final phase began in 1965 with an influx of funds from the Office of Economic Opportunity (OEO) that financed two large Neighborhood Youth Corps (NYC) projects but, more importantly, thrust ABCD into community action and paved the way in 1966 for a heavy commitment to manpower development.

The successive changes in the role of ABCD reflect an almost uncanny pliability and willingness, for the sake of organizational survival, to accept programs offering financial support. Although this adaptability has made institutional survival possible, it has not ensured the security of specific individuals and undoubtedly has made it difficult for staff members to develop a long-run commitment to the agency. Instead, the organization has been the means by which able, ambitious, highly motivated ghetto residents have been able to move up the occupational ladder into a quasi-professional and managerial white-collar world.

ABCD as a Manpower Agency

The CAA concept of the Economic Opportunity Act (EOA) was modeled upon the Ford Foundation and the President's Council on Juvenile Delinquency experiences in the inner city; such cities as Boston, already involved, had a head start with the new OEO. As a result, just as the Foundation funding was phasing out, ABCD became one of the original NYC sponsors and Boston's official CAA (which met the "maximum feasible participation of the poor" requirement by reluctantly adding community representatives to its board of directors).

By mid-1965, ABCD was deeply involved in antipoverty and manpower programs, but the sudden infusion of new funds and responsibilities caused the organization to suffer an acute case of administrative indigestion, almost to the disaster stage. Financial and administrative irregularities led DOL to freeze ABCD's funds and the Ford Foundation to send in a review team. One consultant for the review team was Mitchell Sviridoff, then executive director of Community Progress, Inc., in New Haven and later a Ford Foundation vice president.

The upshot was the appointment of Sviridoff's own New Haven manpower chief, Boston-born George Bennett, as ABCD's executive director in April 1966. Bennett brought with him others of his experienced New Haven manpower staff and largely imported and imposed the ready-made New Haven manpower program. The move prevented the imminent collapse of ABCD's manpower division, but by excluding both local Bostonians and nonwhites, reinforced ABCD's negative image in the black community.

The key element in the new manpower program was a series (eventually 13) of neighborhood employment centers (NEC) that were to furnish a "comprehensive system" of referral and other employment services to ghetto residents. ABCD's work preparation programs were to give applicants the preparation needed for "stable employment." The new manpower program was to be an integrated system of services within easy reach of young inner city males and be open to them until they were ready to become permanent members of the labor force. The NEC network was to be the link between applicants, ABCD's work preparation programs, and steady employment.

ABCD justified its NECs and other manpower projects on the grounds that MDES offices and MDTA training sites were inaccessible to the ghetto residents, that stringent educational requirements barred those most needing help from MDTA institutional programs, and that there were no prevocational orientation, training, and work experience programs to improve the employability of youths and adults lacking a history of continuing labor market participation. It was also asserted that ghetto residents distrusted both MDES and BSD, the two institutions responsible for administering MDTA programs. MDES was alleged to be employer, not worker oriented, and to offer blacks only menial, low-wage, dead-end jobs; BSD was alleged to be "racist" and responsible for an unrewarding educational experience that had not brought decent jobs within reason. Nevertheless, Bennett was able to partially heal the rift between ABCD and MDES enough to arrange for the stationing of ES administrators in ABCD headquarters and placement interviewers and vocational counselors in the new NECs.

INTRODUCTION OF THE CONCENTRATED EMPLOYMENT PROGRAM

By the middle of 1966, Boston had the following manpower programs: (1) regular ES offices, as well as Youth Opportunity Centers (YOC) in Jamaica Plain and in East Boston, (2) MDTA institutional training, with its own Skills Center, offering both skills training and basic education, (3) an EOA work experience and training project with an estimated 2,200 enrollees (chiefly women) assigned to public agencies, (4) two MDTA–on-the-job training (OJT) contracts of 250 each, one held by ABCD and the other by the New Urban League of Greater Boston which were to sub-contract with private and public employers, (5) NYC in-school and sum-mer programs conducted by BSD for about 1,100 enrollees, and (6) ABCD's NECs, its out-of-school program for 250 youths, its Job Corps recruitment of another 250, and a foster grandparents program. The stage was set for CEP the following year.

CEP was introduced nationally in the spring of 1967 with the purpose of concentrating limited funds on a few target areas in order to have an identifiable impact and to centralize administration to interrelate the exist-ing programs in target areas. The model for CEP was JOBS-NOW, a YMCA-sponsored Chicago program which enrolled youthful members of street gangs, gave them two weeks of orientation in grooming, use of the transportation system, etc., and placed them with cooperating employers. However, with no funds or other incentives to attract employers, the CEPs became merely providers of routine manpower services. In theory, the CAAs were to be the sponsors of CEP and ES the provider of manpower services.

ABCD was in a strong bargaining position when it proposed itself as Boston's CEP sponsor. It was Boston's official CAA, with a tradition of community participation, and experienced in operating manpower and related programs. It already was operating five NECs in what were to become the target areas. They were natural devices for coordinating services because of their common listing of job openings and their access to ABCD programs. The only major manpower program that was not part of the ABCD system was MDTA institutional training.

DOL officials in Washington generally took a dim view of ABCD, in part because of the 1965 debacle and in part because its NYC program had found so few takers in Boston. Some felt that ABCD had lagged in develop-ing that program and that it was channeling excessive resources into central office staff and its downtown headquarters. For its part, ABCD chafed at what it considered insufficient freedom in staffing and operating its pro-grams. Nevertheless, there was no alternate sponsor for CEP in Boston.

DOL awarded ABCD a CEP $4.1 million contract in July 1967, allow-ing ABCD to expand its NYC program and to add New Careers and adult work crew (AWC) programs.

The unique feature of the Boston CEP were the orientation centers. Because it had been thought that the MDTA Skills Center and the school system were not providing adequate opportunities to the residents of the contemplated CEP areas, federal negotiators acceded to ABCD's proposal that it establish training centers. However, the federal officials, concerned about both the unfavorable reactions of public school officials and the cost of lengthy training courses, compromised with 15 weeks of "orientation," 13 weeks of which were actually entry-level skills training.

The first CEP contract called for the orientation and training of a minimum of 3,400 residents from six target areas and for placing in "meaningful, reasonably paid" jobs, a minimum of 2,400. The NECs were expected to place half in private industry jobs and the remainder in manpower programs. MDES was to continue its role in the NECs. Contrary to usual CEP practices, MDTA institutional training was not included.

Two of the target areas, Roxbury and the South End, are black ghettos; three others, Dorchester, Jamaica Plain, and Parker Hill-Fenway, are areas into which many blacks and Puerto Ricans have been moving because of overcrowding or dislocation by urban renewal. The South End also has had a sharp influx of Puerto Ricans in the last five years. The remaining area, South Boston, is the only predominantly white area.

Spending of the $4.1 million provided by the initial CEP contract had begun slowly but had accelerated until by the end of the year, weekly spending was consistent with an annual rate of more than $8 million. When the contract was to be renewed, the new regional manpower administrator (RMA) offered to continue the $4.1 million level but was told by Washington to cut this by $3.7 million. The money of all first-year CEPs was to be reduced in order to extend CEP to other cities. ABCD began to build community support by informing its advisory councils, NECs, and delegate agencies that DOL's proposal would require them to cut back operations by a third. All agreed they would rather shut down Boston's manpower programs than face the wrath the expected reductions would generate in the neighborhoods. Meanwhile, ABCD continued to spend at the rate of about $120,000 a week, even though the CEP contract had expired.

The experienced ABCD staff were not political novices. At that time, the Speaker of the House represented most of Boston's poverty districts in Congress. ABCD representatives flew to the Democratic national convention in Chicago to contact him, and he in turn got a commitment from the Secretary of Labor for $5.6 million. ABCD was allowed to commence spending as if it had $5.6 million for the full year, but only $4.1 million was allocated. The day of reckoning did not arrive, however, because ABCD's spending rate slowed and the money lasted the full year. But it took a new regime in Washington with stronger backing for Regional Manpower Administration decisions to build credibility for the office.

Meanwhile, opposition was mounting in the black community to white domination of ABCD and to the centralization of power downtown. Nonprofit neighborhood corporations, called "area planning action councils" (APAC), are part of ABCD's internal structure. These were demanding a stronger voice in the operation of the NECs and in determining overall ABCD policy just when the RMA was charging that too much money and effort was going into placating them. In the midst of all this, ABCD's white director resigned, taking with him eight of the top manpower staff. His resignation further exacerbated the high turnover rate which had always afflicted ABCD along with most CEP agencies. A review in the spring of 1969 showed that three-quarters of ABCD's staff had been with the agency less than two years. Many then in important posts had held unimportant jobs in ABCD a year earlier.

A new black director who had come up through the ABCD organization was able to still some of the internal conflict, but at a price. The previous director had been in a position to snare money, partly because it was available and partly because of his personal relations with Washington manpower officials. In contrast, his successor had to concentrate on using available funds more efficiently in the face of pressures for further decentralization and the growing appetites of the APACs and other community organizations. Pressure was also mounting from the Spanish-surnamed community for a larger role in ABCD and a larger share of its resources for programs to be controlled by the Spanish-surnamed. However, the New Haven group, though never completely acceptable politically, had been able to establish a reasonably integrated and efficient set of programs which continued without them.

At this point, Boston's manpower scene was jarred by a bizarre event which brought unfortunate publicity but had no serious consequences for local manpower programs. A private firm formed to provide services to antipoverty and manpower programs had proposed a training project for 500 automobile mechanics as part of a national project, but the project had not been funded when the firm was unable to show evidence of community support. An executive of the firm thereupon formed his own company, obtained financial backing, and produced endorsements from the heads of a number of spontaneous and unfunded private neighborhood organizations who had formed a consortium. Later it became apparent that the endorsements had involved assigning major portions of the training to these organizations. Training was just beginning when two consortium members were arrested for killing two of the others and a third person over money supplied by the program's financial backer. A fifth member was soon jailed on narcotics and gun possession charges. Four of the five consortium members had previous records for assault and armed robbery. ABCD had not been involved, DOL had honored no invoices to that time, and no public funds had been lost. There was a brief flurry of nationwide attention before the event receded from view with what were apparently no long-range political repercussions.

Two other renegotiations of the CEP contract and the subsidiary ABCD-MDES subcontract are of historical interest. The first of these began in the summer of 1969 and continued throughout most of the winter. Agreement was not reached until February 1970, with a six-month contract beginning March 1 and expiring the end of August. The parties had to implement new nationwide CEP guidelines that seemed to call for assumption by MDES of all manpower services in addition to the establishment of employability development teams which were to take responsibility for developing individual employability plans with the CEP enrollees. The critical negotiation thus was over the ABCD-MDES subcontract. Settlement of that was impossible without the RMA's clarification of what he was prepared to accept. In turn, the RMA had to convince Washington that the Boston CEP was unique and should not be subjected to the same subordination to ES as primary deliverer of manpower services, which was the national policy. CEP funding levels produced little trouble, ABCD apparently recognizing little could be done to reverse that decision. Concern with this issue was so high that little protest occurred over a further cutback in ABCD's CEP funds.

Incorporation of the new guidelines into the subcontract was the vital issue. ABCD feared that MDES might absorb the NECs, and possibly replace their indigenous staff with MDES staff. ABCD waged a political battle, supported by letters and telegrams from local supporters to Washington, protesting the impending evisceration of the agency. ABCD maintains that this campaign and the agency's ability to appeal to key legislators in Washington were responsible for preventing disaster. The RMA, however, denies that ABCD's action was successful — since it never was his intention to surrender ABCD's programs to MDES because of the community roots of the NECs. On the other hand, MDES feels that Washington failed to support it and the federal guidelines which MDES interprets as making it responsible for manpower services in CEP, a responsibility it could not abandon without Washington's explicit approval.

Most of the issues remained unsettled until the CEP contract was again renegotiated during the summer of 1970. Ultimately, however, a reasonable accommodation was accomplished, with ABCD still responsible for the overall manpower program in the target areas, while MDES personnel remained stationed in outreach centers in the ABCD-controlled NECs, performing most of the counseling and staffing the employability development teams. The dual responsibility will always be troublesome, but the working relationship is viable.

In June 1966, ABCD's manpower division staff had shrunk to 15 or less. By 1971, the manpower budget of $5.7 million from the CEP contract and $1.6 million for 10.5 NECc plus other activities from OEO for 10 of the NECs accounted for more than a third of the organization's expenditures, and the division has a staff of more than 450. There were 13 NECs, nine of them in the six CEP areas. In addition, ABCD is responsible for four orientation centers, three operated by ABCD and the fourth subcontracted to the Opportunities Industrialization Center (OIC), Boston's version of a Philadelphia-based, national, black, self-help organization.

The remainder of the ABCD manpower action consists of sponsorship of AWC, NYC, New Careers, and MDTA-OJT programs.

Some criticism of ABCD's administration of manpower programs is justified. Its staff turnover has been high, its administrative processes at times erratic, and its early record keeping of questionable reliability. But ABCD filled a critical void left by ES, the Boston school system, and vocational educators. MDES was distrusted by ghetto residents, had no permanent offices in poverty areas, and had no specific plans to move into these areas. The Boston school committee and local vocational educators also seemed uninterested or incapable of reaching the disadvantaged. MDTA programs and vocational high schools seemed designed, at least initially, to attract the better educated and motivated. The original MDTA Skills Center, despite its courses in basic education and communication skills, was poorly located and depended upon MDES for recruitment and placement; only ABCD and OIC provided outreach or intensive follow-up service.

ABCD opened NECs and orientation centers which provided outreach and part-time follow-up for indigenous individuals who could relate to the hardcore unemployed. It well may be that ABCD's swift move simply beat MDES and the vocational educators to the punch. However, the older organizations had had several years to respond but had not done so. Moreover, ABCD undoubtedly was a catalyst, stimulating other agencies to take positive steps. ABCD stepped on a number of toes by moving into jurisdictions other agencies claimed but had not occupied.

Advent of NAB-JOBS

NAB was organized under the leadership of Henry Ford II after President Lyndon B. Johnson's January 1968 appeal to private employers in 50 cities to employ 500,000 hardcore unemployed over the next 3.5 years. The Boston goal was 18,000. At the same time, the President proposed using federal funds to support businessmen implementing the JOBS program.

The major goal of NAB was to encourage industry to hire individuals whom they ordinarily would not employ and to demonstrate that many of the hardcore unemployed could become productive workers through industry's initiative. Prestigious businessmen were appointed as NAB regional and metropolitan chairmen. On-loan business executives directed by a full-time, loaned, executive "metro director" were to contact employers to obtain pledges to hire the disadvantaged.

The NAB-JOBS program has contract and noncontract components. The noncontract component is for firms that pledge to hire and train the hardcore unemployed without using federal funds. The contract component is for firms requesting federal funds to underwrite the added costs of recruiting and training those designated as disadvantaged by the CEPs or ES, according to a prescribed definition.

The contract phase of NAB-JOBS began in Boston early in 1968 and by July, contracts had been negotiated with 15 firms and two consortia of firms in the Boston labor market area. By mid-1970, 60 contracts had been awarded under these programs.

The Boston JOBS program experienced initial difficulties probably not too different from those of other cities. There were no patterns or guidelines from Washington. The assignment was new, and no one knew how to go about fulfilling it. A regional chairman and a metropolitan chairman for NAB were appointed, even though Boston was the only city in the region. Boston's first metro chairman was from an old Boston family; the first metro director was unable to devote the time needed for the program. Unacquainted with ghetto politics, both men tended to listen to the most strident voices and rejected ABCD as not representative of the poverty community. ABCD was informally excluded from making referrals or giving technical advice about contracts.

On the noncontract side, job pledges were to be obtained by volunteer solicitors recruited from local businesses. The solicitors differed greatly in ability, experience, status, and the amount of time they could give. Their lack of training led to confusion about the meaning of a pledge. It could vary from a vague promise to take some hardcore unemployables at some indefinite future time to a specific promise based on a company's actual needs in the immediate future. Six MDES personnel stationed in outreach centers were responsible for converting pledges into specific job orders as well as for recruitment and referral. Job orders were to be circulated to the NECs and to MDES. A lag of two or more weeks between the solicitors' visits and those of the job developers allowed employers to back out. Many "freebie" (noncontract) pledges thus could not be delivered.

Probably as critical as these organizational problems was the initial distrust between ABCD and MDES personnel, supposed partners in a joint endeavor, as well as between ABCD and NAB. The distrust between MDES and ABCD was due in part to a difference in styles of operation. The ES staff apparently lacked confidence in the competency of ABCD personnel. ABCD personnel claimed that ES personnel assigned to NAB-JOBS withheld crucial job details. Kept in the dark and in turn lacking confidence in MDES, staff in the NECs refused to refer applicants for fear that they would be sent to poor jobs or those already filled, thus discrediting ABCD and the NECs. Even when requested to refer individuals to contractors, ABCD often was reluctant to do so on the grounds that the jobs were undefined and therefore unacceptable. ABCD became convinced that individuals certified by ES were not so severely disadvantaged as those ABCD would have referred.

In addition, pressure for results from NAB headquarters in Washington led to hastily written contracts, sometimes by individuals unfamiliar with the essentials of a good manpower program. Jobs, whether dead end or not, frequently were included without being investigated, and essential supportive services were sometimes overlooked. ABCD's exclusion from the contractual process precluded a critical review of the contracts or the chance to counsel those negotiating them.

The appointment in October 1968 of a new metro director signaled a reversal in policy on NAB-JOBS contracts and in attitude toward the black community. The new director had been successful in a similar program in the Midwest where he was well regarded by black activists. He was responsible for a rapprochement with ABCD and for emphasizing the quality rather than the quantity of job opportunities in NAB-JOBS contracts, sharing ABCD's opinion that poor jobs would discredit the JOBS program in the black community. This concern with quality downgraded the noncontract phase of the program.

ABCD representatives were introduced at early stages of contract negotiations so that they could informally screen contracts and explain their services to business representatives. ABCD also was given responsibility for recruiting to ensure that the disadvantaged were referred to contractors. Subsequently it has assumed a greater role in assuring that the quality of funded contracts is maintained. Both ABCD and the Work Incentive (WIN) program now are given the chance to make referrals during a limited period before the orders are distributed more widely.

The apparent inability of the MDES unit to develop jobs from employers' pledges led to the transfer of this function to the business volunteers in the fall of 1969. In addition, in September of that year, Boston's NAB entered into a technical assistance contract with DOL, which enabled NAB to employ staff to help firms interested in the JOBS program prepare contracts and implement them. Since the only experienced personnel available were ABCD staff, NAB, by hiring them away, in effect bought a partnership with CAA and CEP.

In January 1970, a new Boston metro chairman was appointed, and the metro director was retained. The new chairman appears to be participating to a greater degree than his predecessor in the day-to-day operations of the program. The focus of the program has not changed. The critical handicaps of Boston's NAB, as shown later, are the small number of committed employers and the small number of jobs which the emphasis on quality imposes.

Providing Access to Jobs

Boston's manpower training programs, like those in other areas, soon demonstrated that providing skills was only the first step in getting the disadvantaged into satisfactory jobs. Jobs had to be found, their requirements matched with the abilities of the applicants, and the job and applicant brought together. In most places matching people and jobs is the responsibility of the public ES and various private charity agencies. Boston has the advantage of two public agencies, MDES and the NECs, as a check on each other's effectiveness.

Under the best of circumstances, placement is not easy. Despite the introduction of a Job Bank, which circulated among ES offices and CAAs a daily printout of job orders, there is no single listing of all existing job vacancies with detailed descriptions of job duties and requirements. There is no single inventory of persons seeking work or of specific and detailed education, experience, training, and abilities of these persons. The problem becomes considerably more complex when the focus is upon disadvantaged persons and the hardcore unemployed. The supply side of the labor market becomes almost impossible to quantify. Even before such persons can be offered training for specific skills or jobs, they must be located, convinced that they can be helped, and oriented to the world of work. In addition, they must be convinced that not only can they learn a skill, they can obtain employment in "acceptable" jobs which will raise them out of poverty.

On the demand side, obtaining a list of job orders to be filled is far from sufficient, even for those who have been rehabilitated and trained. Job development is a critical factor. Employers must be convinced that they must lower or change their hiring standards or restructure jobs in order to make it possible for the disadvantaged to succeed in meaningful jobs in the labor market. Employers must be willing to ease some of their standards of performance and conduct, at least temporarily, in order to permit the disadvantaged persons to succeed.

Before 1962, ES offices in Massachusetts, as elsewhere, operated primarily as labor exchanges and the staff as administrators of work tests for unemployment and insurance claimants. In its job placement functions, MDES focused its attention upon filling jobs that were listed voluntarily by employers. Credit for a job placement was given to a local office only when a referred applicant was hired by an employer who had filed a job order. The emphasis was on servicing employers who were willing to file job orders with MDES. As established government agencies which had functioned under the same rules for more than 20 years, no state ES in 1961 could have foreseen the drastic changes that were on the horizon. When the changes occurred, these agencies found it difficult to adjust, and many still have not accomplished the transition.

Inadequate staffing, relatively low wages, and the rigidities of state civil service systems, as well as vested interest, added to the problems of MDES's adjusting to its new role under the Area Redevelopment Act of 1961 and MDTA in 1962. These two acts added such responsibilities as conducting surveys of area training needs, developing training policies, selecting and referring individuals for training, and placing them after they are trained.

RESPONSE OF MDES TO MANPOWER PROGRAMS

Until the implementation of CEP and the Human Resources Development (HRD) program in 1967, the "new" manpower efforts of MDES were confined to its responsibilities under MDTA. Since then, a succession of responsibilities for the disadvantaged has been thrust upon MDES. In some cases, it responded well; in others, unenthusiastically.

Relationships between MDES and state vocational educators have been reasonably amicable and cooperative, despite feelings of some in MDES that the Division of Vocational Education (DVE) has exercised an unwarranted veto over MDTA courses. Relationships between MDES and BSD on the one hand and ABCD on the other have been mutually frustrating at times and marked by suspicion and latent hostility. Nevertheless, a *modus vivendi* has existed between MDES and ABCD, dating at least since a "cooperative agreement" was reached just before the establishment of the first NEC in September 1966. The agreement gave MDES a limited labor market role in poverty areas and paved the way for ABCD sponsorship of CEP. It barred MDES from establishing its own offices in what were to become target areas, though there is some question whether ES offices would have been welcomed even if they had been opened there. Under CEP, the cooperative agreement became the basis for a formal arrangement between both institutions by which MDES became a subcontractor to ABCD, stationing placement interviewers and employment counselors in the NECs and administrators in ABCD's central office.

The underlying source of the acrimony probably was the abrupt entry of ABCD into a manpower void left by MDES and state and local vocational educators. MDES had made no special efforts to recruit and counsel the disadvantaged, or to develop meaningful employment opportunities for them. Vocational educators for their part made no independent effort to provide in accessible locations prevocational training that would equip the disadvantaged with work habits and fundamental skills essential to finding and keeping decent jobs.

The HRD Concept

The HRD concept began on a demonstration basis in Chicago in 1965 and was adopted as a part of national ES functions in August 1966. The goal of HRD was to reorient ES from an employer-oriented screening agency to an applicant-oriented agency that accepted the responsibility for developing the job potential of individuals who needed help. ES was to concentrate on the hardcore unemployed and underemployed in urban slums, emphasizing services to improve the employability of and find suitable jobs for youth, older workers, the handicapped, members of minorities, and the urban and rural poor. These services were to include special counseling and testing, instructing in appropriate work habits, referring to occupational training, and maintaining contact with the worker after he was employed to help him adjust to the workplace.

The HRD effort had a slow start in Boston, receiving a mixed reception by MDES staff members and only lukewarm endorsement of top administrators. Staff members sensed a lack of urgency in the regulations emanating from Washington and were uncertain as to the national commitment to the program. Some resented the shift in the major focus of their organization, which now required more positive action than merely attempting to fill job orders as specified. It was feared that years of effort to improve the image of MDES would be wrecked and that both workers and employers would come to see MDES as a "welfare agency" and a refuge for the incompetent and unmotivated. The diversion of resources to HRD meant that MDES would be that much less an all-round employment service — since it must cater to groups whom private agencies would not find profitable to serve. Others in MDES saw the new program as an opportunity for obtaining additional resources to make available more intensive service to all applicants. Still others saw it as an opportunity to shake up the lassitude of the average ES employee and to push the agency into the mainstream of current manpower problems.

The formal aspects of the program were implemented without much enthusiasm. In Boston, the two YOCs — one in Jamaica Plain and the other in East Boston — became the principal offices for HRD. The Jamaica Plain section was Irish, rapidly turning black, and the other was a working-class Italian section. Under the present ES "full service" policy, although still identified as YOCs, they are now open to applicants, irrespective of age, and make their own placements. As a result of their earlier reputation, the YOCs are more likely than other offices to attract disadvantaged youth entering or reentering the labor market.

In addition, ES placement interviewers were stationed in the NECs where all activities were to be considered HRD. In the regular ES offices, the interviewers were to identify on their records HRD applicants and were to give them whatever special services were available and needed by the applicant. Although the HRD program was announced in February 1967, it was not until May 1967 that DOL circulated official criteria identifying those eligible for HRD treatment. Significantly, the criteria omitted the need to be poor to qualify for "intensive employability services." It was not until the new eligibility criteria of February 27, 1968, that a person had to be impoverished. The original criteria were broad enough to encompass *anyone* with unusual labor market problems; and even under the new tighter specifications, MDES has encouraged a liberal interpretation of who is eligible under the criteria.

From the start, and even after the new criteria, placement interviewers were free to determine who was entitled to special HRD services. The discretion at this level has made for inconsistencies in handling like individuals both among offices and possibly within the same office. It has also allowed continuation of a loose definition of "disadvantaged." Nevertheless, a liberal interpretation of eligibility can be defended. It can be preventive in its effect and can help salvage someone before he becomes a hopeless problem.

Although some new facilities and staff were provided for HRD, the policy was to reallocate existing staff. Special efforts are at the expense of other MDES clients. Nevertheless, the diversion of scarce resources to HRD activities makes sense. It means helping within limited resources those who most need it, letting those with more marketable skills and acceptable characteristics fend for themselves in the labor market.

Originally, there were no special arrangements to prepare the staff to deal with HRD clients; there was no extensive outreach, nor any particularly distinctive handling of people. Nor were there special training programs to help placement interviewers and counselors. While some internal staff training occurred, there was no intensive program to orient the employees to the problems of the hardcore unemployed. The MDES administration considered it a normal function of the line staff to train continually. The only sensitivity training offered the staff were addresses about minority viewpoints by minority group leaders. As professionals, they were expected to know how to handle the disadvantaged . . . a false premise since the HRD concept meant an abrupt about-face in attitudes and methods. Accustomed to years of trying to please employers, MDES personnel now had to help applicants increase their worth to employers and persuade employers to adjust hiring specifications and job requirements. Yet it was useful to make workers employable only if employers could be convinced that their needs would be satisfied in the process, an especially difficult task with those employers inclined to use MDES as a last resort.

The MDES data indicate that more than two-fifths of its office activities were devoted to HRD clients, and MDES is moving to a goal of three-fifths. Its data also indicate that the number of nonwhites using its regular offices far outnumber NEC applicants. However, there are no figures showing how many of the nonwhites served by MDES offices actually are at a serious disadvantage in the labor market. The average number of job development contracts per applicant has been greater for HRD than for non-HRD applicants; the placement rate for HRD applicants has not been significantly different from those for the others.

Over time the HRD concept seems to have had an impact on the staff members of local offices; some local offices seem to be making special efforts to develop jobs for specific disadvantaged applicants. Managers of local offices are constantly urging and persuading interviewers to refer their hard-core unemployed and disadvantaged applicants even though they do not quite match the employers' job orders. The interviewers are being urged to forget the MDES traditional cost-effective approach that tried to minimize the amount of time spent per placement. Efforts are made to convince employers to lower their hiring requirements. Favorable labor market conditions before 1969 to 1970 made this approach more feasible than in the looser markets afterward.

The counseling background, business experience, and willingness to innovate by the office manager are major explanations for the attention given hardcore unemployed applicants by this office. In addition to the philosophy of the office manager, the redirection of emphasis can be explained by his ability to train new counselors and other personnel in accordance with his ideas. These counselors are fresh out of school and bring with them a contemporary empathy to the hardcore unemployed and minority groups. Moreover, their professional style is still relatively flexible and open to suggestions about servicing the hardcore unemployed. A continuing weakness of the HRD effort is the sparse resources available for extensive outreach or supportive follow-up, despite a recognition of these needs by local offices.

Minority Placement Activity

As the principal manpower service agency, ES is involved to some degree in almost every manpower program. Of some concern is the effectiveness of regular ES offices in placing minority group applicants, especially blacks. A record of job placements of nonwhite applicants has been kept since October 1967. Nonwhites comprised 20 percent of all regular office placements in fiscal year 1969 and 24 percent in fiscal year 1970. The bulk of the nonwhite placements was made by the industrial and ES offices. In fiscal year 1969, about 20 percent of all nonwhite placements were in the industrial office and about two-thirds, chiefly domestic and other casual service workers, in ES. In the next fiscal year, the proportions changed substantially, with the industrial office accounting for nearly 40 percent and ES for a somewhat greater proportion. The importance of these two offices in serving nonwhites is indicated by the fact that about half the placements by both were nonwhites in fiscal year 1970.

As a result of having MDES placement interviewers stationed in the NECs and the orientation centers, ES has records of placement activities in these field offices of ABCD. These records provide the opportunity to compare the placement of nonwhites by the NECs and the regular ES offices in Boston. During the period October 1967 through April 1969, a total of 2,457 nonwhites were placed by the NECs, while the regular ES offices placed 15,337 nonwhites. The occupational distribution differed significantly. Slightly more than a fourth of the NEC nonwhite placements were clerical; 22 percent were low-level, miscellaneous occupations; slightly more than 10 percent were nondomestic service occupations; approximately 13 percent were benchwork occupations; and another 6 percent were machine trades. If one classifies domestic and nondomestic service jobs as either dead end or at the bottom of the occupational ladder, then the NECs have done better for the nonwhites than have the regular ES offices. Still the regular ES offices serve many more nonwhites than do the NECs, despite the more favorable location of the latter, their outreach efforts, and their more empathetic and "culturally" attuned staff.

Role in Manpower Programs

In addition to its counseling, testing, placing, and other traditional responsibilities (including the additional emphasis of HRD), MDES plays a substantial and key role in every manpower program. The MDTA institutional program identifies training occupations, with reasonable expectations of employment and eligible people needing training. It has full responsibility for the MDTA-OJT program, now called "JOBS low-support program." It shares responsibility for administration of WIN with the Massachusetts Department of Public Welfare. MDES has an agreement with the Massachusetts Rehabilitation Commission providing for mutual cooperation and full responsibility for the supplementary training and employment program for unemployed enrollees of manpower training programs.

At one time, MDES personnel were stationed in the NAB-JOBS clearinghouse where they handled job development and trainee certification. At present, the ES role is limited to recording the program activity in a job center in NAB headquarters.

The "employability teams" determine whether the recipients of the aid to families with dependent children program, referred by the state welfare department, are eligible for WIN; if so, they enroll them, develop employability plans specifying training needs or help, arrange for training, and then make the appropriate assignment. MDES also has the responsibility for job placement, after training is completed, and both statistical and supportive follow-up.

In explaining the program's slow start, MDES staff claim that the welfare department was slow in sending people; the department claims that it was prepared but that delays in federal funding of the MDES-WIN employability development teams prevented the staff from processing its referrals. Although the ES teams initially were underutilized, this situation no longer exists.

The agreement between MDES and the Massachusetts Rehabilitation Commission calls upon ES to refer all handicapped applicants to the ES office for determination of eligibility and possible treatment, and for the rehabilitation offices to refer the rehabilitated to MDES for placement. However, referral to MDES is voluntary by the Commission who has handled its own placements in the past and probably will continue to do so.

MDES referrals to vocational rehabilitation, however, are in the interest of MDES — since it probably would have difficulty placing more handicapped applicants.

As a result of the 1966 cooperative agreement between ABCD and MDES, the latter agreed to station central administrators in ABCD headquarters and placement interviewers and vocational counselors in ABCD's NECs. The agreement was later extended to the orientation centers as they developed. MDES also agreed to operate the teletype system that links the NECs and MDES to a central Job Bank. As ABCD added NECs and later with the creation of employability teams, the number of ES personnel stationed in other offices increased. Under the 1971 CEP subcontract, however, ES counselors were removed from the orientation centers, and in addition, responsibility for job development was shifted to ABCD.

The Employment Service and the Community

Even if more resources were devoted to HRD and to training MDES personnel, the reputation MDES is said to have among the ghetto residents would have to be overcome. During interviews, ORC learned from a black "moderate" that ES "hasn't done the job. If they had, [our organization] wouldn't be here." He feels that ES is interested "only in bodies and numbers, not soul." He believes that his organization develops "the entire individual" and that it is the responsibility of that organization "to our community and our people [to] counsel the whole man . . . not part of him."

Black spokesmen can recite a long list of grievances: no outreach capacity, no job development, no offices in low-income areas, little or no vocational counseling or guidance, middle-class white attitudes ("prejudices") that preclude "understanding" of low-income blacks, an inability to relate to the poor as distinguished from the unemployed, impersonal treatment ("no soul"), stereotyped views of blacks as suitable only for menial, dead-end service work or manual labor. These criticisms no longer are justified, but it will take time, effort, and good deeds to convince blacks that this characterization of MDES no longer is valid.

Despite such adverse judgments, MDES personnel have performed commendably in helping staff ABCDs, NECs, and orientation centers, even though MDES placement interviewers and counselors have received no intensive training for this role. Although the first MDES placement interviewers assigned to the NECs and orientation centers were carefully screened volunteers (and thus properly motivated and given a two-week orientation), those now assigned to ABCD work are drafted and learn on the job. Assignments to ABCD now typically come from the ranks of recent hires. The MDES explanation is that their experienced staff no longer volunteers for service in ABCD because of its public attacks on MDES.

MDES personnel in the NECs and orientation centers seem to be accepted and effective (although the latter have been unhappy about the failure of ES personnel to develop jobs or perform active follow-up). Possibly part of the explanation for the comparative success with the MDES people stationed in other areas is that the NEC supervisor, who is an ABCD employee, can have an unwanted MDES staff member removed. At the same time, MDES has been willing to heed such requests as well as those of its personnel who want to return to regular office assignments.

Serious friction developed early between MDES and OIC, apparently for ideological reasons. As a self-help organization, OIC could not accept the assignment of white professionals. Apparently job performance and competency were not the real issue, although OIC spokesmen will insist that white professionals could not and cannot relate to impoverished blacks. The fact that those assigned were middle aged, middle class, and female may have had much to do with the conflict. Nevertheless, five of the eight MDES staff originally assigned to OIC were withdrawn, leaving only three responsible for dispensing MDTA stipends.

An extreme view has been that MDES has neither the resources nor the temperament to reach those who need help most. However, this evaluation of MDES is not necessarily accurate today. Not all the failure to open employment offices in poverty areas or to aggressively serve the disadvantaged can be blamed on inertia or indifference. There is evidence that various external factors prevented ES from showing its full mettle . . . not the least of these were limited federal financing of the HRD program and the unusual speed with which the, by then, amply financed ABCD opened NECs in poverty areas. Moreover, MDTA originally did not include outreach services or contemplate the training of the disadvantaged ghetto resident.

Probably as significant as any of these limitations was the early exclusion of MDES offices from what became CEP target areas, the result, it has been claimed, of an understanding reached in Washington in 1964 or 1965 between the DOL office responsible for establishing the YOCs and the first ABCD executive director. According to one not unbiased version, this understanding gave ABCD the exclusive right to recruit and refer residents of its turf. MDES was restricted to the periphery of Boston's poverty area.

There also is the performance of the ES personnel stationed in other areas to demonstrate that, given the chance and proper conditions, they can serve the disadvantaged well, and in poverty areas. Most of the criticism of MDES seems to come from nonwhites. It is not a foregone conclusion that disadvantaged whites feel the same way. Finally, ES has established, often on the initiative of local staff, a number of outreach stations in or adjacent to ghetto areas and has begun to add indigenous neighborhood aides. More important is the perceptibly sensitive attitudes of local office managers in a number of offices that are used extensively by low-income blacks and Spanish-surnamed, such as the industrial and ES offices and the Jamaica Plain office. These local office efforts have been supported by area and state MDES administrators.

NEIGHBORHOOD EMPLOYMENT CENTERS

The NECs function similarly to ES offices. The NECs have job and program openings for persons who walk in looking for employment or training. If an applicant is ready for work, or insists upon a job immediately, NEC will try to place him rather than refer him to a program.

The NECs appear to serve large numbers of people. According to ABCD's records, in fiscal year 1970 the NECs handled more than 27,000 applicants (of whom roughly half were new), referred approximately 19,000 either to jobs or programs, and placed about 4,000 in jobs and more than 2,000 in programs. Their placement effectiveness has been sensitive to business conditions, falling from 44 percent of job referrals in fiscal year 1969 to 29 percent in the deteriorating labor markets of fiscal year 1971.

The employability development teams introduced in 1969 to 1970 have modified the internal structure and focus of the eight NECs in the seven CEP areas. In the past, informal teams discussed individual cases as needed. Now anyone deemed not "job ready" is supposed to be assessed, counseled, and provided other services as necessary before being assigned to the appropriate CEP program. A majority of applicants probably will be job ready and not enrolled with CEP teams or will require only counseling before being referred to jobs. However, team members constitute half or more of the nonclerical staff of their NECs.

A primary difference between the NECs and the ES offices is supposedly the former's outreach efforts. Certainly more outreach is performed by the NECs than by ES, but the total amount is modest and probably not critical for obtaining disadvantaged applicants. The NECs are most in need of entry-level positions that offer training on the job and the opportunity for advancement. This need in turn requires a large number of job developers making business contacts. The NECs do not have sufficient staff for extensive job development, nor can it be done effectively by them individually. Until 1970 to 1971, centralized job development was under the direction of ES staff assigned to ABCD Central but is now being handled by ABCD on a more decentralized, but coordinated, basis.

Placement services for applicants in NECs outside CEP areas and for job-ready applicants in CEP-NECs are provided by ES personnel stationed in other areas and by ABCD staff functioning as informal teams. With the employability development teams, an applicant is supposed to be either job ready or not and is assigned accordingly. However, the limited slots in CEP programs and the large number of applicants mean that in reality much the same kind of individuals have been served by the so-called "job-ready side" of the CEP-NECs as by the employability development teams. The dilemma facing the CEP-NECs, then, is who among a relatively homogeneous group will receive the special help and program assignments offered by the employability development teams, and who will not. In the non-CEP-NECs, of course, this conflict is absent.

While the capabilities and effectiveness of NECs differ, all try to help job applicants develop realistic vocational goals. Referrals are made to stopgap jobs to tide applicants over while they are waiting for a more appropriate job or a program opening.

The location of the NECs and their reputation for helping the disadvantaged attract persons with employability handicaps that make placement almost impossible. Some of these difficulties include severe drug addiction, serious prison records, mental retardation, and inability to speak English. Applicants with such problems may be referred to other agencies, and those who speak only a foreign language to English as a second language (ESL) courses, some of which ABCD conducts.

In addition, many women with school-age children need jobs with special hours. Such work is hard to arrange, and the majority of the women with these requirements are not placed. Unless a woman insists, the NECs normally will not place her as a chambermaid or waitress. They also hesitate to place any applicant on a job that pays less than $2.00 per hour. The rationale is that such low-paying jobs have little or no significance to the firms and therefore are likely to be menial or dead end. In addition, a weekly paycheck of less than $80 is not considered adequate for an adult with dependents.

The problem of job finding is delayed for those in work and training programs, including the 15-week orientation and training courses in the orientation centers. Job development by the orientation centers and the trade connections of orientation center instructors give the training program an advantage in matching men and jobs.

MDES-NEC COMPARISONS

While there undoubtedly is overlap in the clientele and services of ES local offices and the NECs, the extent cannot be measured. Individuals eligible to apply for jobs and training available in the NECs also are eligible to apply at ES offices; and the latter, under the HRD program, theoretically are in a position to offer some of the same services as ABCD. However, the following differences do exist.

(1) Many people who apply at the NECs are not likely to go to ES offices. The reputation of ES and its staff has not been as good as it might be among the hardcore unemployed, particularly if they are nonwhite. ES civil servants are considered to be staunchly

middle class, with little awareness of, or sympathy for, the needs of those living in the ghetto. The NECs serve a larger proportion of younger, inexperienced nonwhites, while ES offices serve a higher proportion of older, more experienced ones.

(2) ES offices are physically located outside hardcore poverty areas, at best on the fringe of the ghetto. Their location makes it somewhat difficult for the ghetto residents to visit them and also implies a certain sense of social distance between ES personnel and the people they must serve.

(3) ES has become involved in a limited way in outreach, primarily by stationing staff in poverty areas and by the recent hiring of a limited number of neighborhood aides. Many of those applying at the NECs have been drawn to them, directly or indirectly, by neighborhood workers performing outreach.

(4) ES offices still are likely to be more concerned with finding a job for the unemployed, in contrast to the NECs' greater interest in improving the employment level of their applicants. The NECs pride themselves in their efforts to lift people out of menial jobs, or into training programs that make better jobs feasible. Nevertheless, these differences can be exaggerated.

(5) ES typically completes its service for an applicant when he is placed on a job; in contrast, the NECs have counseling and other services to make sure that a person sticks to the job.

The conclusions one can draw are that ES and ABCD constitute two separate job placement systems with different clientele. The ES-HRD clientele are probably more like the ES regular applicants than they are like ABCD's applicants. Second, both ES's and ABCD's job placement activities are meeting the special requirements of their respective clientele. ES has the advantage of long experience in job placement. Over the years, certain ES staff members have developed a rapport with personnel directors of particular companies that permit job development for individual applicants.

ABCD's placement system is relatively new; its employer contacts are more likely to be in the inner city or downtown Boston. In addition, NEC applicants are likely to want jobs in the inner city for a variety of reasons, including the difficulty of commuting to a job far from the city. Thus the job placement activities of ABCD tend to be limited to jobs within the city or within reach of the local transit system, whereas the better jobs have been emerging in suburbs 5 to 10 miles away from the center of Boston.

The placement process has clearly improved as a result of the HRD activities of ES and the placement efforts of the NECs. However, most of the disadvantaged have probably not yet been touched by either of these programs. Many who have been placed find themselves on the same kind of menial, dead-end jobs that were always available. Nevertheless, the situation is improved over the past. But despite the step-up in activities of these two organizations, their total placements are relatively small compared to those hired through other channels.

Direct Job Placement

Samples were drawn randomly of half the persons placed on jobs by local ES offices and by the NECs during April and May 1970 in an effort to answer the question: Do job placement programs by themselves upgrade the job level of disadvantaged individuals? Those sampled were applicants identified as HRD by MDES and as disadvantaged by ABCD and placed directly in jobs without intervening training or other programs. The last job held prior to placement was compared with the one on which they were placed.

The MDES sample contained 602 disadvantaged persons; the ABCD sample, 573. Some of the demographic characteristics of the two samples differed. The median age of 25.2 years and the 71 percent males in the MDES sample both were significantly (statistically) higher than the corresponding measures of 22.6 years and 65 percent in the ABCD sample. The ethnic composition of the MDES sample was 40 percent black and 13 percent Spanish-surnamed; that of the ABCD sample, 42 and 16 percent, respectively. The difference in median years of education in the two samples was slight and not statistically significant (11.16 years for the MDES applicants and 11.3 for the ABCD). In general, ABCD served younger people, more females, and more blacks and Spanish-surnamed (ethnic groups most likely to be disadvantaged and poor).

The wages earned on both the job before and after placement were obtained for only 466 of the 602 in the MDES sample. The MDES group on the average suffered a modest wage reduction of $0.064 an hour. Moreover, the spread of their wages before placement was much wider than that after placement (a standard deviation of $0.697 compared to $0.484). Apparently MDES referred applicants to a much more uniform pool of jobs than that from which they had come.

The results were just the reverse for the 496 in the ABCD sample of 573 who reported two sets of wages. This group received a wage increase of almost $0.15. Again, the range of wages before placement was greater than that afterward (a standard deviation of $0.773 compared to $0.546).

Both agencies seemed to be placing people either in similar jobs or in jobs paying much the same wage of about $2.30 per hour. However, the older MDES group originally earned much more per hour than the ABCD group (approximately $0.20 more). Hence, the ABCD group gained when it obtained an average wage of $2.31 on its postplacement jobs, while the MDES group lost when it averaged an almost identical $2.30 an hour.

In the MDES sample, blacks were the chief losers; in the ABCD sample, the Spanish-surnamed gained the most. Before coming to MDES, blacks reported the highest hourly earnings, Spanish-surnamed the lowest — for a difference of $0.32. After being placed, blacks earned only $0.07 an hour more than the Spanish-surnamed who were still at the bottom. Similarly, the Spanish-surnamed earned the least and blacks the most before coming to ABCD. After placement their positions were reversed (see Table 2-1).

Multiple regression equations, with number of dependents, age, and years of education as independent variables, explained little of the variation in the level of postplacement wages or of differences in wage change. The only statistically significant coefficient was that of education, and then only for a few groups. Where there was a significant relationship, it was direct with respect to wage level but not with respect to wage changes. These results confirm our earlier findings that the smallest gains, if any, tended to be made by those with the highest beginning wages.

In conclusion, ABCD's placement activities appeared to reach and best help one of the most disadvantaged groups; namely, the young, poorly educated, low-paid black or Spanish-surnamed person. MDES was less likely to attract as young or as poorly paid a group and consequently offered its applicants relatively less than what they had before.

MANPOWER PROGRAMS AND THE PLACEMENT PROCESS

The effectiveness of placement efforts can be determined only by an extended follow-up of persons referred to jobs. The criteria for determining effectiveness should include the continuity and stability of employment, the wage level and its progression, the status of the job and advancement, and such subjective factors as job satisfaction. Length of time on the initial job may not be relevant if this job leads to something better.

TABLE 2-1

Average Wage after Placement and Placement Agency
(By ethnicity)[a]

	MDES		ABCD	
Ethnicity	Wage after Placement	Wage Change	Wage after Placement	Wage Change
Black	$2.27	$0.20	$2.32	$0.07
Spanish-surnamed	2.20	0.05	2.41	0.28
Other white	2.35	0.00	2.28	0.18
Other nonwhite	$2.42	$0.08	$2.08	$0.02

[a] Data collected by Olympus Research Corporation.

Most of the statistical follow-up of job placements is done by ABCD, OIC, and NAB. Follow-up by ABCD has been spotty, due principally to the limited resources available to devote to the difficult task of locating numerous individuals placed in different establishments in different parts of the city. Unlike NAB and OIC, many of ABCD's placements are independent of training or work programs.

The comparison of MDES and ABCD direct job placements for a two-month period in the spring of 1970 indicates that these two organizations serve a somewhat different population. However, both seem to refer their applicants to similar jobs, as measured by their entry wages.

The existence of manpower programs has increased the job-finding resources available to the disadvantaged. Before 1962, formal placement (except that in private hands) was limited to the activities of ES offices. At that time, ES saw as its principal function that of filling specific jobs that employers had listed voluntarily with local offices; applicants were screened in terms of the requirements of these jobs. Little effort was made to develop new jobs, recruit hardcore unemployed, alter hiring requirements, or improve the qualifications of applicants by orientation, education, or training.

The new manpower programs probably have improved the supply side of the man/job-matching process. Basic education and orientation are available in most manpower programs. The number of slots in training programs are too limited, relative to need, but substantial numbers of people can be given skills. Most programs have been able to fill their authorized and funded slots. On the demand side, however, success has not been that obvious. Here, manpower agencies have been relatively unsuccessful in developing a range of meaningful jobs for the hardcore unemployed. Despite the efforts made, there has not been widespread success in convincing employers to adjust the hiring requirements of entry classifications to permit greater employment of the hardcore unemployed.

The placement function involves the meshing of demand and supply. Manpower programs in Boston have made placement services more accessible to disadvantaged persons. These programs have led to greater involvement by MDES on behalf of the disadvantaged and brought neighborhood employment centers into ghetto areas. In terms of the quality of services, ABCD's NECs became available to groups with highly unfavorable employment experiences, and placed them in jobs which were a substantial improvement. MDES, having chiefly available jobs comparable to those available to ABCD, could not improve the employment of the average applicant who had better prior employment and earnings than ABCD's average applicant. The message is clear . . . ES can only place applicants in jobs that exist — it has no meaningful leverage on the labor market.

Training and Jobs for Boston's Disadvantaged

3

A number of factors suggested that the solution for many of Boston's manpower problems could be found in training programs. These factors were the weaknesses of the school system (including its vocational offerings), the inflow of southern blacks without industrial skills, an employment structure shifting toward higher level service and white-collar jobs, and until the current recession, a tight labor market with complaints of labor shortage.

As in other cities, Boston launched its training effort with no clear idea of the problems associated with training the disadvantaged. No one knew the number of people in need of training nor the levels of expenditure necessary to serve them. Nor had anyone explored the full extent of their educational handicaps and uncovered the difficulties of designing programs to fit the characteristics and needs of differing groups. Experience was necessary to discover the gap between the existing capabilities of disadvantaged job seekers and the requirements of attractive jobs and then learn that the gap often could not be closed by short-term, remedial training programs. Finally, it took time to realize that there was a difference between having the skill for a job and gaining access to it.

MDTA INSTITUTIONAL TRAINING

The MDTA institutional training program in Massachusetts and in Boston had a slow start. It briefly was the dominant program, until funds were siphoned off for CEP and for incentives to employers to hire the disadvantaged. Funds for the statewide program reached a peak of approximately $12 million in fiscal year 1966 and then declined. The peak in Boston was reached in 1966, when $5.3 million were authorized, falling thereafter to $2 million as funds were diverted to CEP and JOBS (see Table 3-1).

TABLE 3-1

MDTA Institutional Training in Boston

Fiscal Year	Enrollments	Completions	Approved Funds (thousands)	Expenditures (thousands)
1963	321	201	$ 381.4	$ 337.6
1964	1,847	1,370	2,326.7	2,242.7
1965	827	711	1,187.7	1,052.9
1966	2,356	1,848	5,344.9	4,316.7
1967	1,051	907	1,043.8	804.9
1968	1,084	792	1,750.7	$1,282.3
1969	695	619	1,533.4	NA
1970	835	430	$2,086.5	NA

NA = not available.
Source: Boston School Department and Massachusetts Division of Employment Security.

The basic responsibilities for the MDTA institutional training program are in the hands of MDES and the state DVE. It is the responsibility of MDES to identify occupations in which there is a "reasonable expectation of employment" and to determine if eligible people are in need of such training. Next, it is the responsibility of DVE to locate the facilities, establish the curriculum, and administer the specific courses. In Boston, DVE has delegated its authority to the Boston school committee. As a result, most MDTA institutional training courses are offered in the physical facilities of the public school system, and the instructors are state-certified vocational teachers often drawn from Boston schools.

Handicaps of Boston's MDTA Program

The basic problem of Boston's MDTA institutional training program has already been identified. It has been reasonably successful in training white, middle-class unemployed and underemployed persons, especially those who have drive and motivation and need only training. However, the program was not geared originally to reach disadvantaged persons, especially nonwhites dwelling in the slums of the city. Despite the later addition of courses in basic education and communication skills, the location of these classes still hampered the participation of minority groups living in low-income areas.

In early 1966, the Boston coordination team of the President's Committee on Manpower investigated and seriously indicted Boston's manpower programs. The team noted that the virtually autonomous Boston school committee clung to bygone concepts that were instrumental in blocking millions of dollars of funds needed for school construction, that the

Massachusetts civil service law was generally recognized as one of the most restrictive in the nation, that BSD and the civil service law crippled the operation of federal manpower programs, that MDES was hampered in recruiting an adequate number of competent staff to carry out its manpower responsibilities, and that DVE unwisely relied on the city's school department for facilities, equipment, and instructional staff for MDTA programs.[11] The team went on to note that training facilities were available on a part-time basis (often in undesirable locations), that renovations and installations of equipment took many months and required clearance through as many as 60 administrative levels, and that courses were being staffed for the most part by moonlighting teachers because full-time teachers on MDTA institutional projects were ineligible for tenure. The shortage of counselors was dramatized by the Boston school system's requirement that guidance counselors must first have five years of general teaching in the Boston schools. There was apparently reluctance by DVE to contract with private institutions for facilities, equipment, and programs. Indicative of its lack of commitment to the program, DVE, as reported by the team, had filled only eight of the 16 job slots authorized for MDTA programs.

The establishment of multiservice Skills Centers which provided counseling, prevocational training, basic education, and skills training in a wide variety of occupations had been strongly urged by the Washington manpower administrators as the most efficient way of training the disadvantaged. In 1964, after much discussion, it was agreed to try to establish such a training program in one building in Boston. Since the Daniel Webster School in East Boston was empty and available, it was chosen for conversion into a Skills Center. Well over half of the enrollees were concentrated in programs in East Boston in 1966 and 1968 through 1970.

East Boston is distant from black neighborhoods in an area blacks enter with some uneasiness, while the school itself is difficult for outsiders to find. Continued limitation to this facility until late 1970 had much to do with the low enrollment of nonwhites, which has consistently been about one-third of Boston's MDTA enrollees.

Although space requirements, speed of conversion, accessibility to public transportation, and availability apparently dictated the choice of the school, it is indicative of the tenor at the time that no serious thought was apparently given to the reactions and needs of the black community. The choice was not necessarily an intentional slight but simply an unawareness at the time of the special problems of the inner city. The standard argument justifying retention of the school was that using public transportation to travel beyond the black ghetto was a necessary part of vocational preparation, if blacks were to work outside their own community. The repeated

---

[11] President's Committee on Manpower, "Boston Coordination Team's Report" (June 1966), mimeographed.

defense of the choice by BSD spokesmen has only served to harden attitudes. However rationalized or justified, the choice of the Daniel Webster School remained a symbolic sore point. It was as a substitute for an accessible training center that ABCD developed its own 15-week Skills Centers in its orientation centers.

In addition to its extensive use for skills training, the Daniel Webster School has been the focal point for projects in basic education, employment orientation, and communication skills — all courses intended solely for the disadvantaged. However, the enrollees have remained primarily white, with a rising proportion of Puerto Ricans for whom the basic education and communication skills have been especially important.

After considerable pressure from minority groups (especially the Spanish-surnamed), community agencies, and the mayor's office, an additional Skills Center, a satellite of that in East Boston, was finally opened in the fall of 1970 in the South End, a low-income, racially mixed area of blacks and Spanish-surnamed migrants.

Even though free to choose any facility they deem appropriate, state vocational education officials prefer to rely upon the vocational education departments of local schools. The argument is that training by uncertified teachers represents a lowering of standards, while using nonpublic facilities is wasteful duplication that leaves existing plant and classrooms underutilized. It also encourages interagency rivalry for students.

Results of MDTA Institutional Training

It is difficult to accept with equanimity the casualness with which record keeping and reporting of data are treated by many manpower programs. Figures of costs, enrollments, and completions were not available for many projects. Even the funds expended — by program, by city — are not available from one central place and must be painfully reconstructed at the local level. Data on the results of programs by city are becoming more difficult rather than easier to obtain. Some improvements may have occurred at the national level, but local figures on MDTA have not been available since 1968.

Of the nearly 7,000 persons for whom enrollment was authorized in MDTA institutional programs in Boston between July 1, 1966, and December 31, 1968, demographic characteristics are available for 6,000 enrollees. Project records are available for only 2,160 enrollees who completed the programs; of these, follow-up reports on employment experience during the first year following completion of training are available for only 592. Though more limited in time, more representative data are available from follow-up surveys made for this study covering a sample of persons enrolled in all Boston manpower training programs between December 1969 and February 1970 and are summarized in Table 13-4 in part 4 of this book.

The figures indicate a concentration in clerical occupations for which market demand has been strong. However, there is a decided minimum of trainees in manual occupations with prerecession-reported labor shortages, such as the machine trades, repair of electrical equipment, and structural work.

Using a sample of projects for which all data are available, we see that the actual costs for a week of training per trainee who completed his program averaged $86 in fiscal year 1966, $76 in fiscal year 1967, and $92 in fiscal year 1968. The dropout rate, with the number of persons who started the program as the base, fluctuated around 30 percent in fiscal years 1963 through 1966, reached a low of 23 percent in fiscal year 1967, and rose to 41 percent in fiscal year 1968.

The total amount of time employed during a full year is a better measure than persons employed at a point in time. On the average, four of five trainees were worked at least 75 percent of the time during the year after they had completed training. The nonwhites did as well as the whites. There was a direct but not marked relationship between years of education and percentage of time employed . . . the greater the education, the larger the proportion who worked close to 100 percent of the time.

Employment may be considered an end in itself, but the primary reason for concern with unemployment is the impact on family income. Both proportion of available time worked and the earnings from that work are necessary to determine income. A significant indication of the benefits of MDTA training is the earnings of participants before and after training. Based on 768 institutional and 121 OJT reports for 1966 to 1969, the median wage rose by $0.49, or 30 percent. Nonwhites did somewhat worse than whites (a $0.44 compared to $0.49 increase). The increase was substantial, but the question of representativeness of the observations remains.

Not all MDTA completers' earnings rose after training. Of the total 1967 MDTA institutional trainees, 31 percent showed an earnings decrease from year before to year after completion of training, while 9 percent changed.

The ORC follow-up survey offers a more dependable measure of results for those enrolled in MDTA and other training programs during December 1969 and February 1970. Enrollment was at a low ebb, and the sample was approximately 50 percent (most of them in the Daniel Webster School but others individually referred to private schools). Their characteristics are recorded in Table 13-4, part 4. The mean wage rate of MDTA enrollees was $0.41 an hour higher after training than in the last 36 months before training and $0.30 higher than the last 12 months before training. Despite the deterioration in the labor market, the MDTA enrollees in the sample worked about the same average 70 percent of the available time after training as they had done before (see Table 13-5, part 4). As chapter

13 explains, upward wage trends, even during the existing economic recession, may have accounted for something like $0.12 per hour of the wage gain. It is uncertain whether the MDTA enrollees would have been above or below the trend in absence of the program.

The indications are that MDTA served a group in a somewhat better labor market position, as indicated by their pretraining earnings compared to those in other training programs. However, it made a substantial favorable contribution to their subsequent employment and earnings. The route to MDTA enrollment is through ES referral. ABCD's NECs make their training referrals to the orientation centers when slots are available. Disadvantaged persons are more likely to come to the NECs than to ES and are thus less likely to be referred to the MDTA programs.

Skills Training in Orientation Centers

Under the sponsorship and financing of CEP in the fall of 1967, ABCD's manpower division established two orientation centers and delegated to the OIC the running of a third. A fourth center was opened in July 1968 designed exclusively for graduates of NYC, although this restricted use was soon abandoned. These centers, especially geared to youths and adults with limited skills and spotty or nonexistent work histories, offer skills training for entry-level jobs along with supportive services designed to aid the enrollee until she or he is successfully established in a job. In most cases, the program is limited to a maximum of 15 weeks for any enrollee, with the equivalent of two weeks of orientation to the requirements of the world of work and the remaining time for training in such skill areas as upholstery, electronics, welding, floor and ceramic tiling, drafting, auto body repair, auto mechanics, typewriter repair, offset printing, clerical, telephone operator, keypunch operator, office machines, and data processing. In addition, the orientation centers offer courses in adult education and in ESL, as well as a special keypunch course for the Spanish-surnamed.

No specific skills or abilities are required for enrolling in the orientation centers, but the income level of the applicant must fall below the poverty line. The program is especially designed for the disadvantaged who are living in specified CEP-designated slum areas of the city. Since the training is supported from MDTA funds, adult enrollees receive the usual MDTA stipend which varies with the average unemployment compensation payment in the state. Young enrollees with more than one year of work experience get the same stipend. Those with less experience get $20 a week. A transportation allowance is also provided if applicable. To qualify for the stipend, the enrollees must spend 30 hours a week at the center.

While in training, the enrollee is given supportive coaching by ABCD counselors stationed in the orientation centers. With the establishment of employability development teams, responsibility for counseling also has devolved on the team which is located in the trainee's NEC of origin, rather than in his orientation center. This physical separation precludes day-to-day personal contacts between a trainee and team members, mitigated in some cases by the presence of the NECs and teams in the same building as the orientation centers.

The employability development teams supposedly provide a superior diagnostic device for determining an individual's needs and choosing an appropriate program for him. In practice, unresolved questions over the administration and control of the teams have hindered complete implementation of the team concept, especially with respect to team caseloads and improvement of selection and referral techniques. However, the use of the team has provided a different bonus: Since the teams are more responsive to DOL control than the ABCD staff, their existence allows the Regional Manpower Administration to know who is receiving CEP-financed services.

In three years of operation from July 1967 through June 1970, the three orientation centers operated by ABCD and the one subcontracted to OIC had a total of 3,737 enrollees. Of this total enrollment, 866 were still enrolled at the end of June 1970, while 2,871 had terminated. Nearly three of five of the 2,009 trainees who terminated from the three ABCD-operated centers during the three years were placed in training-related jobs. Dropouts from the ABCD-operated orientation centers accounted for 35.7 percent of all terminations, with another 5.6 percent transferred to other programs or centers. OIC placements were 67.4 percent of its 899 terminations, with dropouts at 30.5 percent and transfers at 4.3 percent. However, OIC placement figures may include some persons placed without their having attended training programs. For the four centers together, placements were 61.1 percent and dropouts 34.1 percent.

The average orientation center enrollee was younger and had slightly more education than the average MDTA enrollee. He was twice as likely to be male and black, less likely to be a head of household, more likely to be on welfare, and just as likely to be Spanish-surnamed.

The average orientation center enrollee did not gain in employment stability. He had been employed 63 percent of the time during the 36 months before training and 75 percent of the time during the last year before training. He was employed 76 percent of the time after training. However, his improvement in earnings was substantial since his pretraining average hourly earnings were $1.78 and $1.88, while his earnings after training averaged $2.45.

The orientation centers have trained a relatively small number because, ABCD has argued, of funding rather than capacity constraints. As of 1969, the three ABCD-operated centers had a maximum of 210 slots based on the amount of stipends available, but capacity for 333 according to course openings. ABCD claims that its centers could enroll and train more than 700 people at any one time but were restricted to 400 at the full-stipend level. The ABCD centers had an annual flow of 1,242 enrollees, including a 25 percent turnover allowance.

The job placements of graduates from some courses have been less than satisfactory, and this has hindered enrollment. Other programs, such as clerical, auto repair, and data processing, have almost always been filled when they begin. The decisions as to which courses will be taught have been based upon informal labor market surveys conducted by ABCD. However, as in most other organizations, certain rigidities exist. When a program is instituted, it is difficult to convince the administration of ABCD that the course should be dropped. There are, of course, economic considerations, such as investment in equipment, space, and instructors, which must be considered along with applicants' interests and demand in the labor market when the decision is made to drop or add a course.

Since many of the training instructors and other staff personnel are indigenous to the community, they readily develop a rapport with the trainees. The staff seem to make concerted efforts to keep each trainee in the program and to have him succeed despite the special problems of disadvantaged slum dwellers. In a number of instances, the orientation centers have worked out special arrangements for the hiring of trainees directly by companies. For example, one company interviewed clerical trainees in the fifth week, and those who were chosen were put on the company's payroll immediately. They continued their training at the Skills Center for five more weeks, and then went into the company, receiving a raise, and were given more training under the company's MDTA-OJT contract.

Another interesting and highly successful program has been developed with the United States Postal Service. The trainees were referred directly from the NECs. Those accepted into the program went to an orientation center for two weeks and then on to a job as a postal clerk or mail handler in the Boston postal annex where they worked about 36 hours a week on a swing-shift arrangement. During this time, they went to the centers for two hours a day to receive basic education. After 90 days, the trainees were allowed to take the civil service examination, and if they passed, were given permanent jobs.

Factors responsible for this success were work orientation in the context of a specific job; classes specifically designed to prepare trainees for a noncompetitive civil service examination; stable, relatively high-paid employment at the end of orientation, with the promise of permanent civil service status and a substantial wage increase on passing this exam; intensive coaching; strong support from Boston area postal authorities, including a willingness to be open minded about enrollees with unsatisfactory backgrounds; and a capable project administrator with substantial administrative freedom.

The training programs in the orientation centers are not geared to turn out highly qualified craftsmen. Training programs of considerably greater length than 15 weeks would be necessary. But within the constraints of the centers' operation, they manage to hold a significant portion of their trainees, all disadvantaged, through the training program and also manage to find jobs for most of those who terminate. While the total numbers are not especially large, the overall impact seems to be significant.

The best possible estimate of the costs of putting a disadvantaged person through the training program in an orientation center is approximately $1,100 to $1,200 per enrollee, including the stipend. This estimate means that the weekly cost per trainee is approximately $80, not much different from the weekly cost per MDTA institutional training, though the number of weeks average a little more than a third as long. A comparison of costs, however, should not be the principal basis for judging the relative merits of those two training programs. Unlike the MDTA training program, the orientation centers are geared specifically and solely to training the disadvantaged — people who need a wide variety of supportive services and special help in addition to training — if the program is to succeed.

The follow-up study found OIC enrollees to be 80 percent black and 10 percent Spanish-surnamed, but with more education than either ABCD or MDTA enrollees. Like ABCD's training, OIC's trainees were younger than MDTA's.

TRAINING WELFARE RECIPIENTS UNDER WIN

From a delayed start, the Boston WIN program has constantly struggled to keep its slots full. In the beginning, the program had to be explained to already overworked caseworkers who then had to locate the aid to families with dependent children recipients for whom WIN participation was mandatory and to present the program to those for whom it was voluntary. Adequate numbers of appropriate referrals have continually been a problem because of heavy social worker caseloads and dependence on voluntary participants. Other reasons were sketchy or nonexistent medical histories of potential enrollees, the reluctance of some social workers to urge their clients into an experience that may not be successful, and insufficient day-care facilities which only now are being increased.

Boston had 1,600 WIN slots in fiscal year 1970, and ES estimated that it would need 3,700 aid to families recipients to fill these slots. In mid-1970, there were 21,704 aid to families recipients and another 9,613 families and individuals on general relief. Potentially, in any one year, less than a fifth of the aid to families heads of households could become involved in the program.

Through March 1971, a cumulative total of 7,193 persons had been referred to the WIN program, and 4,106 (57.1 percent) enrolled, of whom 2,354 (57.3 percent) had been terminated. Just 226 (5.5 percent) of the enrollees had been employed for more than 100 days, the period designated to cease follow-up. At the end of March 1971, there were 109 others in jobs.

The word "enrollee" has a specific meaning under WIN. It includes anyone who has met with his ES-WIN team after referral by the welfare department and has formally agreed to participate, even if only awaiting placement in training, school, or directly on a job. Compared to CEP enrollees, higher proportions of WIN enrollees were females (60.1 compared to 39.0 percent), white (48.5 compared to 26.9 percent), and at least 22 years old (75.4 compared to 57.1 percent). However, there was little difference in educational attainment. In both cases, roughly two-thirds had not finished high school.

Originally there were eight WIN teams in Boston, composed of five members each; two more were added in the summer of 1970, and a third in December. The membership of the teams had been increased to six in May 1970 when WIN undertook its own two-week orientation, previously subcontracted to ABCD. Two of the new teams were specially staffed and located to serve the large number of recently arrived Spanish-surnamed residents. The Boston WIN program also is responsible for a work sampling center manned by eight ES personnel and available not only to WIN enrollees but to CEP as well. The 11 MDES-WIN teams have considerable leeway in the choice of the training programs for their participants.

Basic education was contracted with BSD at two sites, one predominantly black, the other with large numbers of Spanish-surnamed. Skills training has been contracted with private schools, private firms, and other training institutions. Limited use has been made of MDTA courses and facilities, primarily because of their inflexibility and until recently, the necessity of waiting for the start of the next training cycle. The WIN teams prefer to refer enrollees to private training facilities on an individual basis. Little use has been made of OJT with private employers, but enrollees have been placed in work experience slots as custodians, typists, and housekeepers in public agencies. Despite the 1970 federal policy to make greater use of special work experience projects, few have been developed.

There were only 87 WIN enrollees in the Boston follow-up sample, of whom 75 percent were female and 89 percent were heads of households. Nearly three of five were members of minority groups, and almost two of five were blacks. Of the 54 who were contacted after training, only 26 had found jobs, most probably because the others had left the labor force. However, the mean wage rate of those who found jobs was approximately $0.57 higher than before enrollment. They were employed two-thirds of the available time following enrollment, compared to one-half to three-fifths of the preenrollment period. If we couple the higher wages with the steadier employment, we find that those who sought for and found jobs after training were rewarded with an average annual earnings increase of $1,300 to $1,500 (see chapter 13 in part 4 of this book).

The most important potential pool of enrollees has been mothers with dependent children. Their participation is voluntary in Massachusetts, and the shortage of child-care centers has prevented many from being enrolled in WIN or from completing the program. A mother can be reimbursed for payment to an individual baby-sitter, but reimbursement requires a bill for submission to the welfare department. Often a baby-sitter is a relative or neighbor, so that submitting a bill may be impractical. MDES claims its WIN teams have had to reject many mothers as inappropriate referrals because of the lack of child-care arrangements. As of February 1971, contracts had been made with 19 day-care facilities with 636 slots, all in or near inner city poverty areas.

Another possible constraint is that while voluntary participants can drop out without any change in their welfare benefits, there is some uncertainty on the part of potential enrollees about the promptness with which payments will be resumed. According to social workers, there is a general reluctance of aid to families with dependent children recipients to leave a secure world they know for one they do not. Women are unsure that the training or experience they receive will equip them for jobs that pay enough to make the disruption and effort worthwhile. In addition, social workers say that some women see training as a relief from the tedium and boredom of the home but have reservations about entering the labor force on a permanent basis.

The major constraints still seem to be locating enough eligible welfare recipients who will become permanent members of the labor force. Until more enrollees are terminated by employment, it will be difficult to judge the overall effectiveness of the teams and the programs. There has been some uneasiness on the part of the Regional Manpower Administration over the program's failure to develop work experience positions and the heavy reliance on institutional programs.

As the data above indicate, large numbers have been enrolled and placed in components, but comparatively few have completed the program in a job. As for training, it is clear that the WIN program has a definite advantage in its ability to choose among alternatives. It may select any realistic training program for an applicant, pay his tuition, and send him to the best private or public institution available in the area. It is likely, therefore, that many participants in WIN will receive training superior to that given participants in other manpower programs. The question is whether the potential population to be served includes significant numbers of people who become permanent and self-supporting.

The Impact of Boston's Training Programs

Over the four fiscal years 1966 through 1969 about $17 million, including stipends, were spent on basic education and skills training for adults and out-of-school youth. With those funds, some 12,000 persons were enrolled in programs. Data are unavailable to estimate the number who completed training, but a possible 7,000 remained in training long enough to have gained useful amounts of skill. Of these, about 5,600 found jobs. The success rate of those who completed the programs appears to have been better than 75 percent for the more advantaged MDTA trainees and 60 percent for the central city orientation center trainees. ABCD and OIC enrolled the most disadvantaged persons and brought them the greatest increases in employment stability and earnings.

WIN enrollees consisted primarily of welfare mothers, less than half of whom were employed after training, probably because most of the others were unavailable for work. But for those employed, the continuity of employment and the gain in earnings were impressive. The postenrollment employment stability and earnings of MDTA enrollees were comparable to the other programs. However, the MDTA group was less likely to be of minority background and had more favorable pretraining earnings and steadier employment. Therefore, their gains from enrollment were relatively less. There is no question, however, that all the Boston training programs resulted in substantial gains for those who participated and were available for work afterward.

Job Creation in the Public Sector

Federal manpower programs began with the assumption that the mismatch between a person and a job could be corrected by changing the person. It followed that if the supply of jobs were adequate, the unemployed or underemployed could reach good jobs through remedial education. Some EOA programs implied that the structure of the labor market and employer hiring practices might also be culpable. Experience has shown the initial assumption of manpower programs was an oversimplification.

Completion of a training program is only a "hunting license" to seek a training-related job. It cannot guarantee the existence of a job nor the certainty of access to it. A large proportion of unskilled and semiskilled jobs requires no particular skill but only a willingness to submit to industrial discipline and put forth physical effort. Many entry-level jobs can be handled by those without education and skills but who are blocked from entry by artificial "credentials traps" and prevented from advancing by rigid job structures. Programs to make enrollees more employable were also developed.

Neighborhood Youth Corps (Out-of-School Program)

There are three NYC programs: (1) a full-time, out-of-school program for idle youths, 16 to 18 (formerly 16 to 22), mostly high school dropouts, (2) a part-time, in-school, job-creation program for youths attending school, and (3) a summer employment program to supplement the in-school program. The goals of each have changed periodically.

ABCD has been sole sponsor of the out-of-school program in Boston since the original contract in 1965. The program was augmented in 1968 with CEP money so that there are two out-of-school NYCs following somewhat "different drums." Declining federal interest in NYC and the program's uneven record locally have led to a steady whittling down of slots from 1,000 in fiscal year 1965 to 177 today.

ABCD program administrators, following what they considered federal instructions, initially saw NYC as a feeder in which youths would remain a short time until placed in other manpower programs, such as Job Corps or MDTA. In the first year, most NYC enrollees were assigned to work stations in public and nonprofit agencies. ABCD has never resorted to private industry, despite the October 1966 EOA amendments authorizing its inclusion. Initially, there was no remedial education or skill preparation and little counseling. The staff had to concentrate on developing work sites and maintaining contact with enrollees in scattered locations.

It was not until the spring of 1966, when the NYC role was understood to be one of encouraging youths to return to school in addition to imparting proper work habits, that DOL approved ABCD's proposal to include an experimental education component which could lead to a high school general education development (GED) diploma. The educational component was subcontracted to Northeastern University's new Laboratory School, designed specifically for dropouts, where NYC enrollees spent from six to eight hours a week without compensation.

By 1967 to 1968, work crews under indigenous supervisors began replacing work stations. There still was no skills training, and a local attempt in the spring of 1968 to incorporate it was short lived. By then attention had returned to providing work experiences on job sites, but close enough for effective supervision.

One of the largest providers of work experience had been the Boston Navy Yard, under Project Value, a federally established program for which NYC provided stipends while other federal agencies provided work as "hosts," without being compensated for costs. Project Value represented a breakthrough with its promise of a job for those successfully completing the training. In the spring of 1969, there were 115 Navy Yard slots in such areas as clerical, welding, and painting, and as computer aides. However, there probably were no more than 35 enrollees at any one time. After nine months of work experience, enrollees were eligible for civil service status on a noncompetitive basis. A chronic problem was the threat of cutbacks at the yard. A similar arrangement under Project Value existed at Hanscom Airfield. Project Value was terminated in 1970.

At the end of August 1969, the educational component was terminated by DOL which claimed that under revised NYC guidelines, it no longer had funds for such a project. A 1970 policy shift in Washington produced new guidelines that redirected emphasis from work experience to skills training and remedial education. Work crews were to be discontinued and the number of slots cut. The change was considered more likely to increase youths' long-run employability. ABCD's attempt to implement the new design had to overcome strong staff opposition, leading to the replacement of the program director and other key personnel.

In 1970 the NYC design reallocated money from stipends to instructional staff and more intensive supportive services, raising yearly expenditures per enrollee by nearly a fifth, from $2,800 to $3,400. The more expensive program was made possible by a reduction in slots in 1969 and in the size of stipends in 1970. Enrollees were limited to those aged 16 and 17 and a basic stipend of $36 for 32 hours, a substantial cut from the previous $1.40 an hour. In contrast, the CEP-financed positions continued to be open to 18-year-olds and to offer a stipend of $1.60 an hour. Unrestricted by national guidelines, ABCD had paid higher stipends to enrollees in its CEP-NYC on the grounds that the comparatively low regular NYC stipend was a serious impediment to recruiting. However, the differential had been used to minimize absenteeism in the remedial education class where attendance was not paid. Youths were recruited into the lower paying regular program and rewarded for good school attendance by being "promoted" to the better paying CEP component.

A small sample of NYC trainees in the program during at least one of the four calendar years, 1967 through 1970, indicates that the average participant was 17 years old, single, with less than 9th or 10th grade education. Slightly more than half were male. In 1967, about half the trainees were black and another 10 percent Spanish-surnamed (nearly half still are black, but the percentage of Spanish-surnamed has risen). The program experience of almost half the trainees was clerical; that of the remainder was scattered among a variety of skills. A quarter of the sampled trainees found clerical jobs after training; a fifth returned to school. Typical hourly pay before a trainee entered NYC about equaled the minimum wage; after NYC was completed, it was about $2.00. Other data suggest that only a small percentage of all enrollees since 1967 have been placed in permanent jobs.

On paper, the restructured program offers such improvements as individual employability or training plans, skills training in fields currently in demand and with future potential, and links to other training programs.

These features, combined with 12-week cycles, are expected to permit periodic reappraisal of individual plans and a reinforcing sequence of education, training, and work.

Despite the added flexibility and scope for individual treatment, the design incorporates institutionalized instruction for youngsters, with a deep antipathy toward formal schooling, an artificial classroom work environment in most skill areas (except where the ingenuity and trade contacts of individual instructors permit deviations), and the need to continuously integrate new enrollees (because of the inevitable high turnover) while giving old ones more advanced instruction. NYC has the difficult task of retaining the interest for up to two years of trainees whom primary labor market employers find unacceptable because of age, inexperience, and attitudes. The critical — and probably still the scarcest component — is a staff capable of maintaining control, instilling realistic expectations toward work, imparting acceptable work habits, and offering progressively more challenging and intriguing experiences for often alienated and hostile youngsters and increasingly for Spanish-surnamed youth from a peasant culture who usually are illiterate and do not speak English.

The reasons for NYC's past failures have been numerous: the growing lack of enthusiasm in Washington, unrealistic and shifting federal goals, the former meaninglessness of work crew activities, the exclusion until now of skills training, low stipends, and locally after the first year, weak, inexperienced staff members. A persistent and possibly basic weakness has been insufficient money to provide the intensive services probably required to help the severely disadvantaged youths ABCD deliberately and correctly enrolled. With the recent changes in program director and program design, and the added money for staff, serious efforts are under way under some capable personnel to strengthen the program.

Despite the program's uneven history, NYC work experience has given some youths enough discipline and skills to obtain meaningful, steady work — but probably not the large majority. Still, the program has provided youths with income and a better appreciation of the working world. Counseling, the change in attitude it can produce, and new values instilled by remedial education . . . all contribute to a youth's employability. The latest shift in NYC should have favorable consequences for improving employability. NYC now is trying to do more than develop good work habits; it also is trying to equip youths with a marketable skill and the core of a basic education. The additional resources per trainee for education, counseling, and supervision have the potential for improving the quality of the program services.

Neighborhood Youth Corps (In-School Program)

The goal of the in-school program has been to prevent youth from poor families from dropping out of high school by providing constructive part-time jobs that offer working experience and income. Enrollees are limited to 15 hours of work a week, at a stipend of $1.60 an hour (formerly $1.45). Most work only 10 hours a week. The program functions 42 weeks a year; it currently has 496 slots and a staff of five administrators and 16 part-time supervisors. Most NYC sponsors have been private, nonprofit agencies, although CAAs, public schools, and other public bodies have participated.

Until the end of fiscal year 1966, the in-school and the summer programs were contracted jointly to ABCD and BSD; from mid-1967 until June 1970, BSD was sole sponsor of the two programs. ABCD was assigned both programs in June 1970, allegedly because of too few minority group members in staff positions (especially senior positions), the neglect of youths from severely disadvantaged backgrounds, and meaningless and menial work. APACs or their youth activities centers now recruit for the in-school program.

One reason for the unpopularity of NYC programs in Boston has been poor work assignments. The current ABCD director of the in-school program has concentrated on improving the kind of jobs, apparently with some success. After ABCD became sponsor of the in-school program, a number of custodial and other menial jobs were dropped. According to ABCD, since June 1970, all the job slots in both the in-school and summer programs have been filled, suggesting the improved attractiveness of both programs, although the weakened state of the labor market must have had a role.

Enrollees now work as laboratory technicians, nurses' aides, tour guides, and clerks, as well as with local community groups organizing youth councils. The in-school program shares many of the work sites of the out-of-school program. Public and private nonprofit agencies are the chief employers; the largest is the Veterans Administration Hospital. After completing high school, many enrollees have been employed permanently by these agencies.

There are no reliable data showing the success the in-school program has had in reducing school dropout rates. However, the program does provide income, which probably represents a substantial contribution to the well-being of the families of most of the enrollees. Greater efforts are now under way to include youths from more disadvantaged families.

However, many of the jobs continue to be "make-work," despite recent efforts to develop meaningful positions. Many positions were especially created for the program, a fact frequently known to enrollees. It may be unfair to generalize about the work experience of all those who have passed through the in-school program; some undoubtedly had worthwhile assignments which taught them something about the working world. The campaign to improve the quality of jobs is still relatively new; an evaluation of the results would be premature.

Summer NYC Program

BSD's handling of the summer program has been criticized by ABCD and black groups who charged that enrollees were mainly whites from areas generally not considered impoverished, that some program supervisors were "political" appointees from outside poverty areas, that there was discrimination in hiring, that many slots remained empty, and that many jobs were make-work. After ABCD became sole sponsor in the summer of 1970, enrollments reached 2,100, surpassing the allotted 1,812, even though funds from the mayor's office no longer supplemented the NYC stipend of $1.45 an hour. The summer program was shortened from 10 to nine weeks in order not to reduce the number of participants. About half the approximately 2,100 enrollees in the summer of 1970 were male, slightly more than half black, and about a quarter Spanish-surnamed. Slightly more than 60 percent were in families receiving welfare assistance. In the summer of 1968, when the program had 1,300 slots, there was difficulty finding youngsters whose families met the poverty criteria and who were interested in jobs at $1.30 to $1.40 an hour for 32 hours a week. City funds raised the rate to $1.80 an hour and extended the work week to 40 hours, with the result that about 1,000 youths were enrolled. The types of jobs changed somewhat after ABCD took charge, efforts having been made to improve their quality and include jobs of interest to youths. The jobs are similar to those of the in-school program — the largest single employer being the Veterans Administration Hospital.

Summer Youth Employment Programs

In an effort to keep the young people off the streets during the summer months, especially in poverty areas, a special summer employment program (generally without federal funds and sponsored by the city) was conducted in 1967 through 1969. This program is separate and distinct from the NYC program.

In the summer of 1967, the program was run by MDES which placed 2,500 youths in various jobs in the private sector. During the summer of 1968, the program was run by the mayor's office through ABCD. Some 3,000 letters were sent to local employers, resulting in approximately 350 replies which led to from 1,200 to 1,400 openings, averaging about $1.90 an hour. Placements in the private sector were handled by the NECs and similar agencies; those placed included a high percentage of disadvantaged youths and blacks.

In 1968, the city of Boston hired approximately 450 youngsters for such work as raking leaves and cleaning bathhouses at $1.80 to $1.90 an hour. Most of these openings were given to the NECs, but when word leaked out that the city was hiring, most of the jobs were filled directly by City Hall. When the 1968 NYC summer program could not fill its slots, the city added $0.40 an hour to the $1.40 federal stipend.

The federal government provided another 800 jobs for the 1968 summer youth employment program, mostly in the post office and Boston Navy Yard. The NECs received none of these listings because of a decision by the federal executive board of the Civil Service Commission that MDES also assume the placement function. The state government generated about 40 jobs in the Boston area. There were some 300 unverified job placements in the private sector and an additional 200 unverified job placements by the Commonwealth of Massachusetts. All told, it is estimated that the program provided jobs for approximately 3,000 youths. However, youths are ordinarily hired every summer, and the state agencies may have taken credit for every job, not just the increment.

In 1969, a similar summer program was undertaken, this time administered by NAB. As early as the first week in July, approximately 3,500 young men and women were employed under the program — approximately 1,650 in private industry and 1,850 in government agencies. While most of these jobs undoubtedly served a useful function and most would have existed anyway, employers appear to consider the expenditure as a social investment.

Some jobs have been created under the program, particularly those added to public payrolls. Most, however, probably have emerged at the expense of white middle-class youths who found it more difficult to find summer employment. From the viewpoint of a social investment, public and private employers and the displaced middle-class youths have provided income to youths from disadvantaged families and have bought peace in the streets.

Each summer since 1966, ABCD also has administered an OEO-funded, two-month program for in-school youth, aged 14 and 15. Enrollments have averaged more than 700 in the last few years. OEO's desire for more "meaningful" activities led to the conversion of the program in 1970 to a year-round activity for 250 youths, with no change in a funding level averaging $759,000 a year. The age limit was raised to 25, effective 1971, to accommodate those expected to participate in contemplated youth business enterprises.

Fully converted in 1971, the program is administered directly by the APACs which recruit and employ youth from their respective neighborhoods. As a summer program, it has employed a field staff of college students and has functioned much like the centrally directed NYC summer counterpart for older students. As a full-year, APAC-directed program, it is expected to provide improved work and other experiences. It is felt that the APACs, chronically shy of money, are not likely to use the youth purposelessly. Enrollees will average 15 to 20 hours a week over the year, 10 when school is in session and up to 30 during the summer, receiving $1.60 an hour instead of the former $1.25.

Title V Program

The Work Experience and Training (WET) program, under Title V of EOA, seems to have been one of the least known of the various antipoverty programs. The city of Boston's Title V program was launched in February 1965 through the planning efforts of Boston's welfare department and the state director of WET. The aim of the program was to provide work experience, education, and training for recipients of all categories of public assistance. Emphasis was placed on recipients of aid to families with dependent children.

The local projects functioned as 100 percent federally funded experimental units in the city's welfare department. Each unit was headed by a work training supervisor who was immediately responsible to the local director of public assistance. There was one work training specialist for every 60 trainees and a special unit for program direction and consultation.

Training arrangements with various sponsoring organizations covered a broad range. At one extreme, arrangements were made with public and private employers to take on enrollees as employees and give them "free" OJT. At the other extreme, contracts were made to pay trainee tuition in existing schools; e.g., secretarial or hairdressing. Other arrangements were made to meet the need and the interests of specific individuals. Title V funds met the enrollees' training expenses, such as lunch, car fare, and child care. When possible, child care was purchased from existing day-care centers. However, many women were denied access to WET because child-care facilities were lacking.

New Careers

Despite the rather widespread national publicity about New Careers and its philosophy, there has been relatively little understanding of the program in poverty areas of the city. As part of CEP in Boston, New Careers recruits through the NECs. Participants must come from a CEP target area, meet the poverty guidelines, be at least 22 years old, and have finished no more than one year of college.

The program is funded by DOL to provide disadvantaged persons with training and careers in the field of human services. New Careers contracts with state and local social service agencies to pay all or most of the costs of work training during an enrollee's first year. During the second year, New Careers pays half the costs, while the agency pays the remainder. In Boston the program requests prospective training agencies to submit job descriptions for an enrollee's first, second, and third years in order to demonstrate the existence of career ladders. Such agencies must guarantee the enrollee a job at a specified level after he has succssfully completed the program which runs for two years. Enrollees are encouraged to finish earlier in order to make the limited number of slots available to more applicants.

In Boston, enrollees have been paid $2.00 per hour since January 1970 for a 40-hour work week, a rate the employing agency can supplement. The program provides: (1) two weeks of formal orientation or training tailored to the needs of the enrollee and the agency, (2) courses ranging from basic to college level, including a special ESL class for 30 enrollees, (3) counseling and guidance to assist enrollees in adjusting to the new white-collar work environment, and (4) periodic group sessions where enrollees can express their opinions and discuss their expectations.

From the program's start late in 1967 through 1970, a total of 741 individuals have been enrolled. For the period 1967 through 1969, slightly more than half the enrollees completed the program. The typical completer was 30 years old with 12 years of schooling. Slightly over half were women; two of five, single; and a large majority, black. About 10 percent of the noncompleters left because of insufficient pay, another 10 percent because they found a better job or returned to school, and about 25 percent because of personal problems or need to care for the family.

As New Careers enrollees, the trainees have worked as teacher's assistants, youth workers, community and recreation aides, health aides, and dental assistants, averaging $2.00 an hour. Posttraining jobs have included community aide, recreation aide, youth worker (about 33 percent), teacher-instructor (6 percent in 1967, but 33 percent in 1969), and community developer (about 10 percent). Posttraining wages have ranged from $2.70 to $3.00 per hour.

The small number of enrollees is not too relevant. New Careers philosophy is to skim those from the hardcore disadvantaged who show the potential to advance into paraprofessional and professional positions. The success of the program must be gauged by the career ladders that are developed and the ability of a significant number of enrollees to climb them. The major obstacle has been an inability to create meaningful ladders. Agencies are ready to accept enrollees as aides to teachers or to social workers but not to develop definite promotional steps upward to the professional level. There are institutional barriers, such as rules of union and professional societies, as well as legal barriers, such as civil service and licensing regulations, which limit the creation of career ladders.

New Careers in Boston has bought a number of white-collar positions in white-collar environments for a small number of disadvantaged persons, generally from the ghetto area. Few New Careers trainees have made the step to the professional level. However, many will continue holding a white-collar job, which is a step forward from the typical job previously held. The New Careers program carves out white-collar-entry jobs, but upward mobility beyond them has been difficult. For a significant number of enrollees, the title of the program is a misnomer, although New Careers has improved the employment situation of many enrollees.

Adult Work Crew

The AWC program in Boston, funded entirely by CEP and known nationally as Operation Mainstream, provides work relief for older workers and at the same time tries to open purposeful jobs that will be a major source of rehabilitation. In many ways the program, started to help people with sporadic or nonexistent work histories, is similar to that of NYC, except that its enrollees are usually much older. Eligibility is limited to chronically unemployed poor persons at least 22 years old.

In Boston priority has been given to older workers, those with no reasonable prospects for full-time employment or training under other federal programs, and those who have completed such programs but have not been placed permanently. Included have been drifters, alcoholics, drug addicts, and former mental patients. According to AWC supervisors, at least 90 percent of the enrollees have police records, chiefly for drunkenness or related reasons; many also have medical problems, psychological problems, or both. During 1967 through 1969, all the enrollees have been males averaging about 40 years of age, single or living alone, with 10 years of education. About half have been whites.

All the program's 100 slots generally are filled, although 20 to 25 persons leave the program each month. Enrollees receive $1.60 an hour and work 35 hours a week, but weekly take-home pay for a single person is about $47. An average of about 20 attend the program's basic education classes for 2.5 hours each morning before going to their work sites. Time spent in school is also paid.

From 1967 through 1969, a total of 786 persons had some contact with the program; 136 never appeared at the work site after their initial interview. Approximately 320 worked at a site but left without being permanently placed. Two AWC supervisors suggested that no pay during the first two weeks was a reason enrollees left within two weeks. A total of 220 enrollees have been placed on permanent jobs after being in the program from two weeks to two years.

At the start of the program in 1967, participants worked on work crews doing rehabilitation or maintenance work on buildings, land, parks, recreation facilities, and community facilities in urban renewal and other low-income neighborhoods. By mid-1970 work crews had been eliminated in favor of specific jobs at a work site, and efforts have been made to provide OJT. As a result, enrollees have had the chance to learn basic skills as mechanic repairmen, maintenance men, landscapers, clerks, nurse's aide technicians, and construction workers. Work sites have included the Veterans Administration Hospital and Boston's state hospital and nursing homes, the parks department, the fire and police departments, and ABCD. Those who left the program for work have been employed as maintenance men, cooks, kitchen helpers, clerks, and social work aides.

Since a large percentage of the enrollees have been alcoholics, and many have had police records or have been in mental institutions, it is recognized that not all AWC participants can be trained for jobs in business, or if trained, can keep them. Many participants cannot hold jobs; in general, their work records are such that few companies would be willing to give them a chance. However, the program does provide enrollees an income, and many of the activities would not have been performed, or at least not performed as frequently, had not the program provided the service free. Moreover, a significant minority (possibly well over a third) of the enrollees obtained and kept meaningful positions. In addition, AWC records show that during the three years beginning in 1967, about one-quarter of the enrollees found jobs on their own or were placed on jobs while in the program. The 25 percent job-placement rate of enrollees is commendable.

Subsidizing Access to Existing Jobs

Many elements enter into the subsidizing of existing jobs. The different programs adopted and applied in Boston attest to this fact. The MDTA-OJT and NAB-JOBS programs are but two that we will discuss in the following paragraphs.

The MDTA-OJT Program

The OJT program got off to a very slow start in Boston as it did nationally. Many employers were reluctant to participate, and unions were concerned that OJT programs for unemployed workers might lessen job opportunities for their members. In addition, there existed the problem of the statute requirement that OJT projects supplement but not replace existing training programs. The basic purpose of MDTA-OJT was to reduce, by public subsidy, employers' reluctance to train workers. However, the program could reimburse employers only for training costs . . . training allowances could not be used as wage subsidies because of political and union opposition and because of prevailing wage laws. Relatively few employers seemed to find the average reimbursement of $25 a week for supervisory time, wastage, and other training costs a sufficient incentive to train workers on the job. Companies also considered it burdensome to deal with the "red tape" involved in government programs.

When the labor market began to tighten in 1964, MDTA-OJT became increasingly attractive to employers. A number of national trade associations became contractors for large numbers of MDTA-OJT slots and then subcontracted them to their member firms around the nation. By 1966, OJT enrollments had increased from the 6, 12, and 19 percent of the three preceding years to 29 percent of funded MDTA enrollments. An administrative goal of 50 percent was established for fiscal year 1967. This decision accompanied one allocating two-thirds of MDTA efforts to training those facing the greatest disadvantages in the competition for jobs. Unfortunately, as employers were pressed to increase their participation in the OJT program, the proportion of the disadvantaged who were enrolled fell rather than rose in Boston as elsewhere.

Although the data are scarce and conflicting, records show a cumulative total of just 865 slots between October 1965 and August 1968. These were authorized in separate agreements with three companies, one union, the Boston-Masonry Joint Apprenticeship Training Committee, ABCD, and the New Urban League of Greater Boston, for an overall approved cost of $536,800. ABCD received 250 slots in September 1966 under its original CEP contract and the Urban League 200 in February 1967 as part of a national contract. The Urban League's role was to have been that of a broker (an intake and referral unit) for OJT programs operated by small employers.

Despite the availability of more lucrative NAB-JOBS contracts, in July 1969 there were still seven active OJT contracts with more than 600 slots and with at least 168 current enrollees plus an unknown number in the Urban League's 300 slots. The best estimate that could be obtained was that a cumulative total of 825 persons has been enrolled in OJT programs since 1965. At least one of the seven contracts began October 1968 (with the Lemuel Shattuck Hospital), and two others (with the Massachusetts Restaurant Association) were funded in 1969 to run until 1972.

Two local contracts have unique features. One, with the Massachusetts Bay Transit Authority for 120 slots, was to train transit operators. The first group of 26 trainees began in May 1969, and by early August, all 120 slots were filled. The contract was completed in September 1969. The second was with the AVCO Corporation in Roxbury where 88 minority group employees received upgrade training for a variety of comparatively skilled printing and white-collar jobs. The original contract came to approximately $5,000 per trainee, though actual cost data are not available.

An important criticism of OJT and probably one reason for its declining emphasis has been uncertainty about whether trainees were actually disadvantaged. Despite MDES certification and the MDES goal for fiscal year 1968 that 45 percent of OJT enrollees be HRD referrals, most of the enrollments occurred before there was any measurable definition of the disadvantaged.

There also has been doubt about the extent to which systematic training occurred under the OJT contracts and the degree to which those hired differed from those who would have been hired without the subsidy. These doubts are probably fully justified concerning the subcontracts with small employers through the Urban League and the restaurant association, though evidence is lacking. The situation for the larger firms is mixed.

It is not feasible with present information to evaluate MDTA-OJT programs in Boston. Clearly, some workers who went through OJT acquired skills for specific occupations. However, for most such trainees, the program meant a job rather than training. Also, since many OJT contractors required new hires to have certain levels of basic education, and perhaps skills, the program was not oriented to employing the disadvantaged. It is generally agreed that the OJT program did not serve an appreciable number of disadvantaged persons and that the training provided was of minor consequence.

Little attention has been given to the funding of new OJT programs in Boston since the start of the JOBS program. ABCD decided to drop its contract in response to this shift in policy. The average outlay per OJT trainee was approximately $650 for 26 weeks. The annualized figure for JOBS is about $3,000, or $1,500 for a 26-week period. But the OJT program did not require that all its trainees be disadvantaged, and in the Boston area, it was estimated that the percentage of disadvantaged was nearer 45 percent. In addition, during most of its history of OJT, the definition of disadvantaged was loose, and certification was sometimes treated casually. Under the JOBS program, certification of the disadvantaged, though not always dependable, receives greater attention and care.

In 1970, administration of the low-support programs was shifted from NAB to MDES. Only a few small contracts had been written, and MDES was still unsure about how to avoid conflicts with the JOBS-70 program over possible contractors.

NAB-JOBS Program

The contract phase of NAB-JOBS began in Boston in 1968. In all the contracts combined, fewer than 2,000 slots were to be filled over about a three-year period. The value of these contracts was $6.2 million, or roughly $3,100 per slot. The average number of slots in the later contracts was considerably less than those contracted earlier in the program, and the costs per slot lower as well. A number of the earlier contracts contained low-wage, dead-end jobs, and this may be a major reason that retention increased from 53 to 59 percent. However, ABCD's exclusion may have meant that disadvantaged blacks had less chance of entering the program or, if enrolled, of receiving the services that help retain the disadvantaged.

When the later contracts were written, much greater attention was given to the quality of the jobs and supportive services in the contracts, despite the downturn in economic activity. Detailed demographic and biographic data were obtained for 281 trainees employed by five contractors. The typical trainee was a young unmarried black male who previously had earned less than $2.00 per hour on an unskilled job. These data also show better retention rates for (1) females, (2) whites, (3) married persons, (4) those over 25 years of age, and (5) those whose starting pay on a NAB-

JOBS position was at least $2.00 an hour. About 80 percent of the trainees remained employed at least nine months.

In all but its earlier contracts, Boston's retention rate appears to have been better than that of the country as a whole, reflecting credit upon the effort to upgrade contract quality. On paper, the noncontract component of the Boston JOBS program has been by far the largest. A total of 236 noncontracting firms pledged 5,133 jobs under the program and hired 1,600 individuals. NAB data indicate that as of January 1970, about 1,000 of the noncontract hires were still employed.

There is, however, considerable lack of confidence in the validity of the figures reported by the "freebies." Some employers pledged their turnover, but not specific vacancies. The NAB office estimated that about half the pledges never became job orders. An estimated four pledges were needed for each job. There also has been concern about double counting. A brief check by the Boston NAB office indicated that the actual hires by a sample of firms were about 40 percent of the figures reported. Moreover, some firms had reported off-street hires as placements, without evidence that these individuals met the criteria for certification as hardcore unemployed. If these criticisms are valid, actual placements by noncontract firms may be as low as 600.

On the other hand, by late 1969 a large Boston firm included among the "freebies" reliably had hired 175 direct referrals from an OIC training course over the previous 20 months and had conducted its own programs to hire the disadvantaged and minority group members. If this experience is not unique, there may be more activity by noncontractors than the Boston NAB figures indicate.

There are no data on the characteristics of noncontract hires. Undoubtedly, many firms that made pledges to NAB put forth some effort to employ more blacks or disadvantaged workers regardless of race. No new jobs were created, but to some extent the disadvantaged might have filled vacancies which would have gone to others. Nevertheless, the conclusion of many manpower observers in Boston is that the noncontract pledges redistributed jobs very little. It was these dubious results that persuaded the current metro director of NAB to concentrate his relatively scarce administrative resources on contracts. By 1970 these had become the principal focus in Boston, accompanied by a campaign to write contracts with better provisions.

Nearly every JOBS contractor made some changes in hiring requirements, recruiting methods, testing, orientation procedures, worker training, ways of supervising, disciplinary rules, and supervisor training. Over half the contractors had hired additional staff to provide special training or counseling services. Some of the contractors had used the program to hire more blacks as part-time staff, but most did not appear motivated by the desire to create a better image. Most of the contractors insisted that social conscience was an important reason for their involvement, although some indicated that they were motivated by labor market pressures.

Most of the contractors who normally hired the disadvantaged used their JOBS contracts either to take on larger than normal numbers of risky recruits, make greater efforts training them, or both. Most of the contractors who did not normally hire the disadvantaged had had intentions of doing so, and JOBS contracts probably induced them to take the step. Compared to contractors' existing work forces or regular hires, those hired under JOBS contracts were more likely to be black, to be less educated, to have poorer employment experiences, and to have criminal records. The Boston experience suggests that JOBS contracts emphasize quality jobs and services.

Regardless of how well the contract payment approaches the actual cost of hiring the disadvantaged, to be successful, a NAB-JOBS contractor must make a basic adjustment in social attitudes, modify his hiring channels, and be willing to cope with higher absenteeism and turnover, as well as incorporate new people with different backgrounds and living patterns into his regular work force who may resent the intrusion. The employer has no way of judging the impact upon the productivity of his regular work force. It takes a management that is convinced of the correctness of its move to make a JOBS contract successful.

Impact of Boston's Jobs Creation Programs

The aim of Boston's jobs creation programs was to gain access for the disadvantaged to existing jobs or to create jobs for them. Many of the jobs created in the public or private nonprofit sector were socially useful but would not have come into being if the federal government had not subsidized them. In other cases, private enterprise was subsidized to employ disadvantaged persons instead of the nondisadvantaged who normally would have been hired. An effort was also made to develop new kinds of jobs by restructuring existing ones and opening them to the disadvantaged.

The WET program (Title V), terminated in 1968, proved to be a different avenue for providing income to welfare recipients, but failed in its goal of rehabilitation. The NYC, AWC, and New Careers programs all had the goal of providing preemployment opportunities or work experiences for either youths or adults. Except for New Careers, each of the programs also sought to provide jobs for specific groups of the disadvantaged in order to provide them with an income. Varying degrees of effort were given to furnishing jobs that would lead to upgrading or to more skilled positions. Again these programs offered different amounts of training, sometimes little at all, for meaningful jobs.

The New Careers program differed by concentrating principally on white-collar, paraprofessional jobs. It was assumed that with the proper experience and supplementary education, selected disadvantaged persons could be placed in newly developed career ladders leading to high-level paraprofessional jobs or to professional jobs themselves. The program has been unable to develop new occupations or the career ladders promised. So far, little data have been adduced to indicate the success of New Careers. The last reorientation of NYC gave top priority to education and skills training, but the results of this change are not yet available.

In-school NYC and the summer employment program are primarily job-creating programs. There has been little success in opening training positions and little concern with the long-run potential of the enrollees. These programs, looked at narrowly, have managed to put to work persons who under normal circumstances could not obtain employment . . . in effect, making the government their employer of last resort. The AWC program, dealing as it does with seriously handicapped older men, is partly job creating and partly an attempt to give enrollees existing jobs above the menial level.

Data on the MDTA-OJT programs are sparse; however, the program has served few of the disadvantaged. Unproved but likely, most employers have not provided meaningful training. Few MDTA-OJT contracts have been funded in Boston since the start of the NAB-JOBS program.

The JOBS program seems aimed in the right direction. Not only are jobs created through a federal subsidy, but there has been concern about their quality and potential for advancement of the workers. If the current policy of Boston NAB continues, disadvantaged persons should have better opportunities than they did under the earlier contracts. If judged by its size, however, the contract component of the JOBS program has had little impact.

Institutional and
Labor Market Impact of
Manpower Programs
4

A major determinant of the success or failure of manpower programs has been the competence and the philosophy of the organizations and personnel charged with their administration. These organizations were in turn affected and changed by the assignments they were given and the milieus into which they were plunged. These factors of cause and effect are critical elements in evaluating the total impact of manpower programs on the city of Boston.

As manpower programs have been introduced, modified, expanded, or contracted over the past few years, various agencies of government — federal, state, and local — have been affected differently. Some gained authority and power while others lost. Some grew faster than others. In addition, social and community organizations sprang up to help administer the different components of the manpower program. Some had contracts with government agencies and others with prime contractors. With government agencies and nongovernment organizations involved in a series of interconnecting and overlapping programs, the relationships were too complex to unwind. However, it is possible to describe and analyze some of the major organizations and their interrelationships and the impact these organizations and relationships have had upon the various manpower programs. The labor market impact is more difficult to describe simply because it has been so minor.

ORGANIZATIONAL STRUCTURES AND POLICIES

To some degree, description of the internal structures and policies of the Regional Manpower Administration and of MDES, ABCD, NAB, OIC, and other manpower agencies duplicates material in earlier chapters; nevertheless, a concise description at this point is necessary to clarify the interrelationships among these agencies and their impact upon programs.

Before mid-1968, the administration of manpower programs in Boston was the fragmented responsibility of a myriad of different bureaus and offices, each of which reported directly to its own headquarters office in Washington. After the launching of CEP in 1967, a representative of the Washington office of the Manpower Administration also was on the scene, but it was never quite clear who had coordinating responsibilities for the various programs. In mid-1968, an RMA was appointed for the New England region with headquarters in Boston and was given the principal responsibility for coordinating the manpower programs within the jurisdiction of DOL.

Since the Bureau of Employment Security, Bureau of Apprenticeship and Training, and Bureau of Work Training Programs, all part of DOL, still maintained their own regional offices in Boston, the authority of the RMA was limited and unclear. In addition, since DOL did not have sole responsibility for all the manpower programs, the RMA had to share his responsibilities with OEO and HEW representatives. He was in the unenviable position of having responsibilities without administrative authority to run the programs.

In March 1969, DOL reorganized its regional operations and centralized more of the authority in the hands of the RMA. While he has the basic responsibility for funding many of the manpower programs, he is open to the political and community pressures of the various agencies and organizations involved. Nevertheless, the strengthened image of the RMA cannot offset the disadvantage of being short handed, relative to the workload of his office. Nor can his new image offset frequent reorganizations and reassignments of personnel who had little prior experience with their new responsibilities.

Massachusetts Division of Employment Security

As an old-line agency operating for 30 years under essentially the same policy guides, MDES has had difficulty adapting to the rapidly changing policies and added functions of the past few years. A rigid civil service system, over which MDES has no control, developed a corps of employees with a vested interest in maintaining their jobs and the program. Relatively low salaries combined with inflexible civil service rules have obstructed the recruitment and retention of a competent young staff. The state's veterans preference law creates more problems. Any veteran able to pass the civil service exam jumps ahead of any nonveteran on a register. Administrators have learned how to function despite such rules, but at the expense of delays in upgrading desired candidates or difficulty finding personnel for the temporary positions which usually are created to administer new manpower programs.

Staff turnover has been high, especially for several years just before the 1969–70 recession. Counselors in particular left for higher paying jobs in other states or to higher paying jobs in the growing number of social agencies and community organizations.

Community leaders have criticized MDES for the middle-class white mentality of its staff, a charge not applicable to many young interviewers and counselors recently hired. None of its regular offices are in the black ghetto area, although as previously noted, this situation was not necessarily deliberate. Top MDES administrators are sensitive to the criticism that the service does not relate to the disadvantaged or to the black hardcore unemployed. However, as an organization, it probably cannot deliver some crucial services needed by the disadvantaged, which community-sponsored organizations have provided. For example, MDES has not had on its staff many neighborhood workers who could make known to the disadvantaged person on the street the services available in manpower programs and where he could get assistance. Only recently have the civil service rules permitted MDES to employ a small number of such persons provisionally, but they must take and pass the regular exam within a specified period of time.

The location of ES facilities, internal procedures, and the orientation and experience of the staff acquired over the years probably still limit the extent to which MDES can deliver manpower services to the hardcore unemployed or to the disadvantaged black. Yet MDES has improved and is continuing to do so. The average staff person is conscientious and hard working. Those ES personnel stationed in other community agencies come to relate to their new clientele and to develop a close relationship with their host organizations. The shift in orientation from an employer-serving labor exchange to an agency charged with providing employment assistance to those most in need of help is taking hold. MDES also has served as a model for other agencies with respect to data-keeping procedures. In addition, it has responded with services requested by community agencies; and by and large, these have been competently delivered.

Action for Boston Community Development

ABCD is a totally new contribution of the social welfare and anti-poverty efforts of the past decade. That the budget of ABCD's manpower division is $7.2 million in contrast to the total ABCD budget of $18 million a year indicates the importance of those functions in the overall antipoverty effort in the city, not all of which is represented by ABCD. The division operates with a staff of approximately 50 persons.

With the exception of MDES personnel, NEC staffs are selected from the local community and tend to be sensitive and responsive to the needs of the specific locality. Their continued employment in NEC depends in part upon personal relationships with the local neighborhood. With such local community involvement, it is not surprising to find a wide range in ability and competency among the staff. The majority are nonprofessionals, but with experience working in the community. The work experience at the NECs has brought forth the latent capabilities of many persons in the community. A number have proved to be competent administrators, and some have moved upward through ABCD into jobs in other agencies, in industry, and in education.

Since the three ABCD orientation centers are citywide and are not part of the APAC structure, staff appointments are made directly by the manpower division. While formal clearance with the area planning councils is not necessary, attempts are made to keep the local communities involved and informed of the persons appointed to the orientation centers.

The Regional Manpower Administration applauds the philosophical commitment of ABCD to hire indigenous, talented blacks whenever possible. However, there has been concern about some of the practical implications. ABCD appears committed to enlarge the extent of community control in its operations. The top administrators in the manpower division of ABCD, though cognizant of the trend toward community control, have indicated no concern. They share a philosophical commitment that the local communities should have greater control over the manpower programs, and they are confident that sufficient direction can be maintained.

The turnover and the mobility of the ABCD staff have been high. Promotion from within is a common practice, and a large number of the positions at the ABCD headquarters are staffed with persons who were promoted from field positions. Private employers, social agencies, and community organizations pirate many capable persons from the ABCD staff, but it should be noted that pirating also occurs among all the manpower agencies. Salaries are not particularly high, especially in the field operations of ABCD, causing a low retention rate of better personnel. The high turnover has given many persons who have stayed with ABCD opportunities for advancement and experiences which permitted top staff personnel to move into well-paid positions in private enterprise and in universities. Since many of these persons were nonprofessionals with little prior experience in the area, ABCD has been an important training ground for many blacks.

An average member of the ABCD field staff has some concern about the security of his job and the organization. He sees ES personnel doing what he considers equivalent work for higher pay and with civil service job security. Because many of the local staff are indigenous to the community and many are black, there is a certain fear and resentment against ABCD Central, located in downtown Boston. It is sometimes referred to as "Whitey's world," and for some community people, the blacks who make it to ABCD Central have sold out. Overall, however, one is impressed with the commitment of the top staff of the manpower division and their willingness to acknowledge problems. Given more funds, their programs could be even more successful; certainly they would be better able to serve more of the disadvantaged.

NAB-JOBS Program in Boston

The NAB-JOBS program has had only a limited impact on the practices of a few business firms in Boston, but from the viewpoint of serving the disadvantaged, that impact has been almost totally positive. That the numbers claimed in Boston have been few while those placements which have occurred have been high quality has been the contribution largely of the metro director. He has developed a working relationship with top administration of ABCD and with the various community organizations and is trusted by the black leadership of these organizations. He has not sought or developed great popularity with the business community. DOL staff were concerned because the high-quality policy made Boston look bad in contrast to the numerical reports of other cities, but the Regional Manpower Administration has become a convert to the policy for which ABCD and local community organizations had pushed.

The Boston NAB program has undergone several organization changes during its brief existence, the most significant of which was the establishment of a technical assistance staff. In the fall of 1969, DOL entered into a technical assistance contract with Boston's NAB, enabling the latter to employ a staff of 10 persons (many from ABCD) capable of providing technical assistance to businesses interested in the JOBS program. One significant function is providing expertise in the negotiating of contracts so that all the necessary manpower inputs are included. A technical adviser is assigned to each prospective contractor with responsibility for the specific details of the contract.

The NAB Boston staff also has a representative from the Human Resources Development Institute of the AFL-CIO. This representative has the principal responsibility for dealing with unions and companies that pledge jobs under the JOBS program and for dealing with other labor-management problems that arise in companies involved in the program. His relationship with the metro director is good, but it is difficult for one person to speak with authority about the problems of all Boston unions.

Opportunities Industrialization Centers

Originally starting in Philadelphia in 1964, more than 70 OICs have sprung up over the United States. The OIC has a philosophy of self-help, and its strength lies in close relationships with the community. In Boston, OIC has a committed staff and a dynamic, capable executive director. Operating an orientation center under a subcontract with ABCD, OIC has established courses that have been in great demand, and the program's job retention rate has been good. The turnover rate of the OIC staff is low, but there have been opportunities for upward mobility within the organization and from it into private industry.

There seem to be stable internal relations among the OIC staff. However, there has been some resentment toward ABCD and MDES. OIC, being a subcontractor of ABCD, feels closer to the community and less likely to accept what others propose. It has criticized ABCD programs as "handouts" which the community has not initiated and feels that ES is interested only in bodies and numbers, not in "soul." OIC claims that it aims at counseling "the whole man."

OIC also independently operates a part-time evening program, partly financed by the Massachusetts Department of Education, which is intended to upgrade people working on low-level jobs. In addition, OIC works directly with a number of companies and offers specialized daytime training programs geared particularly to the needs of specific firms. The tie-in with a number of local firms guarantees the trainees in these programs certain jobs when they complete the program.

Interrelationships among Agencies

The interrelationships among the agencies and organizations dealing with manpower programs in Boston are complex and difficult to disentangle. Since programs and components of programs overlap each other, the organizations with responsibility for programs developed a competitive spirit which has caused conflicts.

Duplication of effort may exist, but the extra costs if any are probably worth the additional options available to clients and the induced interagency rivalry, both of which probably improve service. Coordination of effort implies agency specialization with specific target groups . . . which would eliminate the benefits of interagency rivalry. Moreover, in light of the unpredictable short-run changes in federal priorities, specialization might leave an agency with no clients and no experience to serve alternative groups.

One strain common to manpower programs and agencies is uncertainty. The annual budget negotiations and the frequent budget extensions on a month-to-month basis result in a sense of insecurity in the staffs of the organizations, as well as in the programs themselves, and provide little time or ability to devise and test innovative ideas. The constant shifting of emphasis among the different programs has compounded the uncertainty and insecurity from which their clientele are not immune.

However, all agencies are not equally affected. The old-line agencies that predate the manpower programs and hire through the civil service are less subject to insecurity. Those organizations, however, which are totally or almost totally involved in the new manpower programs have a different attitude. While the staff may have a total commitment to the program, they have a much higher degree of uncertainty about their future. When one adds to this the difference in personalities of top leadership and the differences in commitment to doing something for the disadvantaged, reasons accumulate to explain the problems and conflicts in relationships among various community groups, public agencies, private organizations, and federal, state, and local government agencies.

Regional Manpower Administration's Relationship

The Regional Manpower Administration not only has funding responsibilities, it also has the responsibility of seeing that the organizations conducting various components of the manpower program are living up to their contracts. As a result, the Administration becomes the focus of many frustrations, some from the inadequacies and the conflicting goals of its jurisdictions, some from its own staff shortages and administrative weaknesses.

As a relatively new organization, the Administration, in its regional office, appears to know its responsibilities, strengths, and weaknesses, has tested its range of discretion, and has begun to demonstrate to manpower agencies in the region and in Boston the services it has to offer and the extent of its authority.

The single largest expenditure of funds in the manpower area in Boston is to ABCD for CEP. A new regional staff arrived with some initial suspicion reflecting national office suspicion of ABCD. Local agency heads are always wary of any change in relations with their funding source. The Administration was particularly concerned with ABCD's use of funds and the efficacy of its manpower activities. Some viewed ABCD headquarters as inefficient, overstaffed, and uncoordinated, and its control over activities such as the NECs as too loose and ineffective. There was little confidence in ABCD statistics.

These problems have since declined in seriousness, and Administration-ABCD relationships have improved notably. One key factor in these improving relations appears to have been the conclusion of the Administration's long, drawn-out reorganization. Lines of authority and communication were clarified.

The second CEP contract ran out on July 28, 1969, and was extended on a month-to-month basis through the remainder of the year. The temporary extensions resulted in considerable uncertainty in ABCD about program and about staff positions. There were complaints that long-term commitments were impossible under the current contractual arrangement with the Administration. Yet despite these concerns, ABCD as an organization continued to operate as if it were a permanent organization with continuous funding. Only by this policy, it felt, could it keep its staff and programs. To ABCD, this was a rational approach; and it operated on the assumption that it would be political suicide for the Regional Manpower Administration to curtail drastically the ABCD functions. The Administration looked at such activities as fiscal irresponsibility. But despite these apparently deep feelings, there was "arm's length" cooperation in striving for the goals of CEP.

However, the marathon contract renegotiation provided the forum for colloquy on issues and the establishment of what appears to be a markedly improved working relationship. A number of factors account for this improvement: The negotiations had access to the mediating talents of the mayor's assistant for manpower; the Administration was shown to be both in a strong position for, yet not vindictive of ABCD, despite national guidelines strengthening the ES role in CEP vis-à-vis that of the CAA. ABCD's position was not undermined; and finally in the direct MDES-ABCD negotiations, mutual acquaintance and respect increased, while MDES representatives agreed that they lacked the ability to absorb the total service delivery function.

The regional office has direct jurisdiction over MDES as an operator of manpower programs, but little authority in regard to the regular ES and unemployment insurance roles of MDES. Though some of the regional staff have been less satisfied with the services performed by ES for the disadvantaged and specifically for blacks and other minorities, significant operational conflicts between the two organizations have not arisen. Despite the size of MDES on one hand and the Administration's lack of direct authority over many of the former's function on the other, important shifts in orientation have occurred in ES.

Relations between NAB and the Regional Manpower Administration have been relatively good. Because of mutual respect and understanding, a *modus operandi* has been developed. When problems arise, they are quickly ironed out by a personal phone call between the metro director and the Administration.

The Massachusetts Division of Employment Security

Because of the service functions of the local offices of MDES, the operations of this agency are related to nearly every organization involved in the manpower programs in Boston. That involvement has provided the agency with new tools and has been responsible for changes in its emphasis. The agency has gone a long way in reorienting its operations to servicing the disadvantaged workers of the city.

While MDES and ABCD staff cooperate well at the lower level, the new CEP guidelines have added to interagency friction by raising doubts about responsibility for and authority over joint activities. The relationships between the two organizations have clearly been strained. The local MDES offices referred relatively few persons to the orientation and training centers operated by ABCD. In turn, ABCD's NECs have referred few people to the MDTA institutional training program administered by MDES because of the lack of openings.

MDES personnel participated in the drafting of a number of early NAB-JOBS contracts, but ABCD was not consulted. ABCD was critical of the process and also critical of the competence and sympathies of the MDES staff. ABCD contended that the contracts contained poor jobs at poor wages with inadequate supportive services.

Another issue arose between the two organizations over the question of certifying workers as qualified for employment and training under NAB-JOBS contracts. ABCD accused MDES of applying the criteria loosely so long as the employer was willing to hire the worker. ABCD also charged MDES with having made no attempt to evaluate the merit of the job or the wage rate so long as the wage was at or above the legal minimum.

MDES responded with criticism of incompetence and nonprofessionalism at the NECs. Each has indicated at times that the manpower programs in Boston would be improved considerably if all the manpower funds were funneled to it rather than to its adversary. Whether the apparent increased accord growing out of the second CEP refunding negotiations will have a permanent effect on these past conflicts remains to be seen.

Because the metro director of NAB adopted the philosophy that a JOBS program which stressed quality was more significant than one which stressed quantity, he too came into conflict with MDES. The latter was related to the JOBS program in four ways during the first year and a half: (1) the writing and negotiating of contracts, (2) handling job development activities within the NAB unit and being administratively responsible for recruitment, (3) providing manpower services to prospective job trainees, and (4) working within the NECs in helping ABCD staff carry out the placement function.

The metro director of NAB was in some way concerned and critical of MDES in each of these four areas. The new metro director, in his opposition to funding contracts which did not provide jobs with promise, saw MDES accepting employer proposals for contracts to train people for jobs they could easily obtain in the absence of a JOBS program. He was also critical of the alleged ease with which disadvantaged applicants were certified for employment and training under the contracts.

The Manpower Division of ABCD

As the community agency with which the government has contracted the CEPs, ABCD has the principal responsibility for delivering manpower services to the poor in the ghetto areas of Boston. As such, it has regular contact and relations with a wide range of public and private organizations which are involved in assisting persons to become more employable. Inevitably, problems and conflicts arise between ABCD and other institutions on a wide range of issues.

The general success of ABCD in its conflicts with other institutions is based principally upon its support from the community — especially from the APACs. The APAC organizations represent a majority on the board of directors of ABCD. While the various APAC organizations do not always view a problem in an identical way, they are likely to present a united front to defend ABCD and its programs. In addition, the local APACs do influence administration of the NECs, even if only tacitly. The staff members of the NECs are on ABCD's payroll, but their appointments are dependent upon clearances with the local APAC. This is a recognized political move by the community to control a significant operating arm of the manpower programs in the local communities. Despite this apparent decentralization, ABCD Central has implemented evaluation techniques that have increased its ability to influence internal administration of the NECs.

In contrast to the conflicts and problems rising between ABCD and the ES, a comparatively harmonious and cooperative arrangement has been worked out between ABCD and NAB-JOBS, although there are some recent indications that it is fraying at the edges. Relations between ABCD and NAB were somewhat strained during the first several months of the JOBS program. In part, this conflict was probably due to the apparent distrust of ABCD and its operations by the first metro director.

Another difficulty between ABCD and NAB during this early period has been attributed to NAB's overreaction to black militancy. Immediately after the assassination of Martin Luther King, Jr., a large number of black community organizations in Boston allied themselves in a "Black United Front" and held an outdoor rally. This alliance, which presented the white business and political leaders with a list of demands, was contemptuous of ABCD, regarding it as a source of patronage for white politicians. The NAB people, responding to the Black United Front's characterization, snubbed ABCD and signed contracts that permitted employers to hire through whatever sources they wished. As a result, ABCD, which saw itself as the principal deliverer of manpower services, was reduced within the NAB operation to the role of a certification agency. Even this role was shared with MDES, which also had the power to certify individuals as eligible under a JOBS contract.

An additional source of disagreement between ABCD and NAB in the early stages of the program was over the definition of "meaningful job." Apparently ABCD and some black community organizations were much more inclined than NAB to ignore jobs paying less than $2.00 per hour, whereas NAB thought that more attention should be paid to a job's promotional or training possibilities. The present metro director and his staff are in much closer agreement with ABCD about what constitutes a meaningful job, and both wages and promotional training prospects enter into consideration.

The ability of the current metro director and his staff to develop a cooperative arrangement with ABCD was partly due to their shared assessment of ES. In the judgment of the metro director, ES lacked a real understanding of the problems of disadvantaged persons, especially blacks. Once this judgment was made, an operating alliance with ABCD was natural for NAB and welcomed by ABCD. In the process, the role of ES in the JOBS program was sharply circumscribed.

Community Leaders

The views of community leaders (and therefore of the community) about manpower programs and agencies may help determine their success or failure. A major problem in this matter, however, is in determining who are the important community leaders. In an effort to obtain such a sense of community feeling, eight persons with reputations as spokesmen for groups within Boston's black community were interviewed. The interviews were open ended and involved discussions that covered the various manpower programs and agencies in the city. The black community leaders interviewed ranged from highly militant to conservative; however, they do not constitute a statistically representative sample. Each was frank and open in his discussion about manpower programs of Boston. The following is a summary of their key views:

(1) Except for some breakthroughs here and there, manpower programs have helped persons who probably could get jobs anyway. The programs have failed to reach the severely hardcore unemployed.

(2) A major problem is insufficient funds to do an adequate job in training larger numbers and for longer periods. The 15-week training period restriction is a severe limitation.

(3) The programs fail to deal with the "internal dynamics" of the company to which an applicant is sent. Little effort is made to reorient or readjust a company's personnel policies or to give sensitivity training to supervisors and other employees.

(4) Most jobs obtained through manpower programs do not provide sufficient incentives, either in money or in the respectability of gainful employment, to compete with street jobs such as hustling. After investigating training programs offering stipends as low as $45 a week for a single man, many applicants return to the street where they can make considerably more.

(5) In its recruiting, the NAB-JOBS program does not want the hardcore unemployed but uses the program for publicity purposes. The firms involved in the program are using it to obtain employees for jobs they always had trouble filling — those demanding the most menial chores. In this sense, the manpower program has become the recruiting office for such jobs.

(6) The annual funding of programs prevents long-range planning. Only some assurance of continuous funding will permit better planning.

(7) Educational components of the manpower program are seriously compromised by their marriage to the Boston school system which is considered to be at least 50 years behind the times.

(8) MDES personnel, especially counselors, are not attuned to the goals of the manpower programs. The staff is traditionally oriented and impervious to new ideas and ways of thinking.

(9) The attitude of labor unions, especially the explicit discrimination of the building trades and their apprenticeship programs, is considered a major impediment to the success of manpower programs.

While fairly critical of the overall manpower program, most community leaders did recognize that some progress was being made in a number of different areas. However, many felt that a major breakthrough was possible only if Washington poured in sufficient funds.

Community leaders seemed less knowledgeable about organizations with which they had little personal contact or involvement. In particular, public agencies which lack ways to use leaders in advisory roles or on boards of directors suffer. The misinterpretation of goals and policies can damage undeservedly the reputations and hence effectiveness of such organizations.

Cooperative Area Manpower Planning System (CAMPS)

The CAMPS organization for the Boston area underwent a major reorganization during fiscal year 1969. The original structure of the Boston area CAMPS included representatives of organizations whose responsibilities covered the Boston SMSA. The SMSA includes nearly 80 cities and towns spread in a rough semicircle approximately 30 miles in diameter around Boston. The manpower problems and interests of the city of Boston and those of most of the other communities in the SMSA are different. Those concerned about Boston's problems are not particularly concerned about the problems of other cities and towns, nor are the latter concerned about Boston's problems. Consequently, CAMPS of Boston's SMSA was reorganized into a federation of seven subcommittees corresponding to geographical and program areas sharing common problems. Each subcommittee agreed to meet separately and to submit its own CAMPS plan.

The Boston CAMPS committee has met regularly and has concerned itself with examining major manpower programs in Boston. Agency representatives attending the meetings have found them to be a useful place to exchange information and ideas and to meet on a quasisocial basis their counterparts in other organizations associated with manpower programs. Significantly, the one successful effort to influence a program was possible because a federal directive gave CAMPS the authority to approve the

MDTA institutional plan. Withholding approval eventually led to the establishment of another Skills Center, this one near low-income areas occupied by minority groups.

Despite the efforts of the last CAMPS chairman, who represented the mayor of Boston, CAMPS has yet to develop into a viable organization for making policy decisions on manpower . . . and it is not likely to become one unless granted more authority. Some of the participatory agencies, such as BSD, the Boston office of the Department of Public Welfare, and MDES, are not likely to voluntarily surrender their ability to make their own final decisions. Each agency has a political base either in the city of Boston or in the state, and could use this base to attain its own goals.

So long as CAMPS is viewed principally as a place to exchange information, local agencies have no need to be concerned about attendance or who has the right to participate. However, when Boston's CAMPS seriously attempted to develop a comprehensive manpower plan for fiscal year 1970, it realized the importance of having a definite membership and having rules regulating attendance and voting. To develop a meaningful manpower plan for the city could require agreements on a number of major changes in the operations of some manpower programs.

For these reasons, efforts have been made to strengthen the Boston CAMPS subcommittee. As a first step, a committee was appointed to recommend which organizations should be considered permanent members, how decisions should be made, and who should have the right to vote. It is possible that some agencies may refuse to participate in CAMPS if it means presenting their programs to CAMPS for a vote. Even a list of voting members may crystallize an open break. Despite conflict among the agencies involved, they have tended not to challenge each other's plans. Efforts to make the Boston CAMPS organization viable with decision-making power and authority could intensify interagency conflicts.

THE IMPACT ON THE CITY

The existence of competing programs and agencies has generated a significant amount of new competence in the manpower field. The various organizations, both public and private, that are sponsoring or administering manpower programs have had to employ a large number of people and acquaint them in the various aspects of manpower problems. Numerous job opportunities for indigenous persons were opened as a result of all the activities of manpower agencies. It is estimated that these agencies employed about 1,200 persons. These competing programs and agencies have also resulted in greater public awareness and concern over manpower problems.

The shortage of trained personnel or experienced people in the field has led to a great deal of interagency staff mobility. This has permitted a considerable amount of upward mobility, especially among nonprofessionals such as neighborhood workers, follow-up workers, and vocational counselors who had been hired from the community. Despite the disruption of excessive mobility, the movement of people among the new agencies has contributed to a better mutual understanding of their capabilities and has increased interagency cooperation, partly because of the personal relationships among the individuals involved.

Another impact of manpower programs on Boston has been the creation of a number of new neighborhood facilities, such as the NECs and the orientation centers, and community organizations, such as OIC. These new entities have given the residents of local communities greater opportunities to enroll in various programs. They serve geographic areas of the city, especially ghetto areas, that the older organizations had not served well. The development of self-help organizations with the goal of servicing specific groups, such as the blacks and the Spanish-surnamed, has given minorities more political leverage.

Except for MDES, the policy and organizational changes of the past few years have had a marginal impact upon traditional agencies involved in older manpower programs. MDES, however, was pushed or pulled into making basic changes in its methods for dealing with the disadvantaged. For various reasons, some outside its control as an organization, MDES did not offer its services in areas of the city where most of the hardcore unemployed reside. Nevertheless, MDES has been made aware of those problems and has made a meaningful response.

The programs of the '60s have heightened the interest of the city government in the funds, facilities, and programs affecting Boston's manpower. The mayor's former manpower specialist was chairman of Boston's CAMPS and was a major force in efforts to strengthen the Boston subcommittee. There is no doubt that the city administration has become more sensitive to the needs of hardcore unemployed persons who previously had little or no political influence.

Disadvantaged persons in Boston are better served now than before . . . if for no other reason than that there are more agencies prepared to help them. More social services are available to the disadvantaged, especially blacks and now the Spanish-surnamed. However, Boston does not have a coordinated, systematic municipal manpower plan, despite subcontractual ties and a growing tendency to refer applicants to a variety of social services and to other programs.

In the final analysis, it is the private employer who has the job opportunities. It is the employer who either does or does not employ the disadvantaged and thereby either makes manpower programs look good or bad. In Boston, the number of employers involved and the extent of their commitments probably have not been sufficient to have had a major impact on the functioning of the labor market and the share of primary jobs going to the disadvantaged.

SUMMARY

There is little doubt that Boston is different today because of the manpower programs of the '60s and early '70s. While the degree of differences is difficult to specify, it is rather obvious that the overall impact has been modest compared to the need. In addition, the impact has not been uniform in respect to target population or institution.

Local groups concerned about urban social problems existed in Boston prior to the onset of manpower programs. Some of these groups were affected, but not greatly, by adding manpower to their interests and concerns. Some, such as ABCD, acquired a new role as a result of the manpower programs and grew significantly; others were not affected and did not grow. At a minimum, the Boston business community has been made much more aware of the problems of the hardcore unemployed and underemployed and of the efforts of government programs to alleviate the situation. With notable exceptions, however, the reaction of business and industry in the city has been mild. The manpower programs have been a factor in sparking the city government into showing a deep interest in the problems of unemployment, poverty, and skills training, but city action has directly affected only modest numbers of disadvantaged thus far. Manpower programs have also made more of the public aware of the existence of poverty and the hardcore unemployed in the city. However, mere awareness or mere concern has little or no effect on the objective factors of the situation.

An estimated $10 to $12 million has been spent or committed for spending in Boston over the past few years by government manpower programs. The overall impact of these millions of dollars has been relatively small — if measured by the numbers of persons who have obtained jobs as a result of the manpower program. The best estimates indicate that about 5,600 disadvantaged persons were placed in jobs following participation in manpower programs (from their inception through fiscal year 1969). It is exceedingly difficult to determine the proportion of ES's HRD placements who meet the strict criteria for designating the disadvantaged or hardcore unemployed. The majority of placements by the NECs probably did meet the criteria for disadvantaged, and it is estimated that these offices made approximately 9,500 direct placements in the period 1966 through 1969. In broad terms, total placements of the disadvantaged per year averaged no more than 4,000 persons, with little or no statistics on how many of these are currently unemployed, underemployed, or no longer in the labor market.

Despite the approximately 4,000 disadvantaged persons placed on jobs annually in Boston, MDES has estimated that the universe of need in Boston in 1970 to 1971 was more than 100,000 persons. While one can question the concept and the figures of the universe of need, there is little doubt that the placement impact of the manpower programs has been relatively small in view of the overall need.

It is possible to attribute the relatively small impact to a number of factors. One such factor is that the proportion of disadvantaged has been increasing relatively rapidly by the in-migration of blacks and of Puerto Ricans and other of the Spanish-surnamed. In addition, many youths leave school either as dropouts or graduates, inadequately prepared to hold a job in a competitive society.

The "quality" approach taken by some manpower programs also may have contributed to the relatively small impact upon the city or its universe of need. Until 1969 to 1970 the labor market was relatively tight, and there were numerous unskilled openings. These jobs remained empty while the NAB-JOBS program stressed contracts with "meaningful" jobs that paid well and had advancement possibilities. Also concerned with "meaningful" jobs, NECs and the orientation centers of ABCD have tried to limit placements on menial jobs or on jobs paying less than $2.00 an hour. This concern for quality employment may pay off in the long run, but it can create difficulties in the short run.

Emphasis on jobs with upward mobility, without defining the term, has undoubtedly limited job opportunities for some of the disadvantaged. Instead of some vague goal of advancement, the goal should be a job offering relatively good wages and reasonable security in a firm or agency with modern personnel practices. Mobility should be defined in terms of work experience and self-confidence that permit movement among different employers in pursuit of better opportunities. The concept of a career ladder smacks excessively of a civil service bureaucracy or of unrealizable expectations.

In view of the shifting emphasis in the manpower programs and of the limited expenditures relative to the overall needs, it is exceedingly difficult, and perhaps patently unfair, to fault the manpower programs for not "solving" the unemployment and underemployment problems of the disadvantaged. Regardless of the effectiveness of training programs, success is measured by a job placement which depends upon the needs of employers. If employers have no vacancies or do not see their way clear to employing the disadvantaged, it is impossible for the manpower programs to be successful. Many of the manpower agencies had difficulties placing many of their trainees even when the Boston labor market was relatively tight. The loosening of the labor market in 1969 to 1970 and the overall economic recession that hit the nation at about that time undoubtedly make it impossible for any manpower program to "succeed" as measured by job placements. This in no way implies that the manpower programs are not performing a service. In their small way, the programs are making a growing number of disadvantaged more employable, and hopefully, those who have acquired some training and skills will obtain relatively good jobs when the employment opportunities become available.

Part 2
The Denver Experience

Reed C. Richardson

Strength through Diversity: Economic, Social, and Political Environment of Denver's Manpower Programs
5

Denver attained big city status only after World War II, largely as a result of the war and its aftermath. Although it ranks low in the seriousness of its manpower and poverty problems, it has accumulated its share of the complex, inner city, urban problems.

Known as the "mile high city," Denver is located more than 5,200 feet above sea level, east of the Continental Divide, and almost midway between the Great Plains and the Mountain West. Beginning as a mining town, it grew to become a center of supply and finance for the rich ore lodes of the Rocky Mountains on its west. Soon it added an agricultural base, when the plains on its east succumbed to the plow, and later diversified into small manufacturing.

By 1940, though small by standards of most of the nation, Denver had become the economic focal point of an area which includes all or part of seven states. Largely because of the climate and its close proximity to the West Coast, yet shielded from any possible foreign invasion by a natural mountain barrier, Denver became the location for intensive military training and supply activities during the war. The Veterans Administration Hospital in Denver also housed the greatest numbers of wounded and injured men of the military.

Denver profited from the general westward drift of population after the war, but the greatest impetus for its postwar growth has been its role in the nation's space and missile programs.

In 1970, approximately 1,250,000 people, 57 percent of Colorado's population, lived within the five-county metropolitan complex which comprises the Denver standard metropolitan statistical area (SMSA), compared with 320,000 or 40 percent of Coloradoans who lived in the Denver metropolitan area in 1940 and the 930,000 or 53 percent in 1960. If the

95

present relative population growth continues, the Denver metropolitan area is expected to hold two-thirds of the state's population by the year 2000. Yet true to national patterns, the population of suburban counties is increasing faster than that of Denver County. Whereas in 1940, 72 percent of the five-county metropolitan area (Denver, Adams, Boulder, Arapahoe, and Jefferson) lived in Denver County, only 53 percent lived there in 1960 and 41 percent in 1970.

Manufacturing, particularly of durable goods, was the fastest growing sector of Denver's economy from 1965 to 1969, though manufacturing is now outnumbered as a source of employment by (1) wholesale and retail trade and (2) government and services, in that order. Each of the latter continues to increase substantially as does total nonagricultural employment; but manufacturing employment appears to be leveling off.

Denver's nine institutions of higher learning, its public, private, and military medical research and treatment facilities, and its administration, research, finance, marketing, and public relations employment, as well as federal, state, and local government, accounted for almost one of every five civilian employees in 1969.

The diversity of employment and the small size of individual firms have resulted in (1) a highly stable economy which neither drops into the depths of recessions nor rises to the peaks during the boom periods, and (2) an average income level which is above the national level. Unemployment is typically below national averages . . . yet labor shortages have been rare. The income pattern is characterized by relatively few families at the extremes, compared to similar metropolitan areas. The characteristics of diversity, stability, and concentration of other than mass production industries as an economic base are expected to become more pronounced in the coming years.

ETHNIC AND EDUCATIONAL STRUCTURE OF THE POPULATION

Typical of western cities, Denver has as its largest unassimilated minority group those classified as persons with Spanish surnames. (In Denver, there are few Puerto Ricans or Latin Americans — mostly Mexican-Americans ["Chicanos"].) Other groups considered as minorities are blacks, American Indians, and Orientals, with others (which constitute a majority) lumped together as "whites." Although the Spanish-surnamed are the largest minority group, they rank behind blacks in most characteristics. Many of the Spanish-surnamed were once migratory field workers in the agricultural regions surrounding Denver. When they were displaced by rural technological advances, these families settled in the Denver metropolitan area. Their average educational attainment of 8.9 years of school in 1960 is far below the average 11.9 years for blacks and 12.2 years for the total population.

Most blacks in Colorado are residents of the Denver metropolitan area, but the city has escaped some of the influx of poorly educated, unskilled blacks of rural background because it is not in the mainstream of northward migration of southern blacks. (Denver's reputation as a relatively difficult area in which to find a job if one is undereducated or unskilled may have discouraged some migration.) Blacks in Denver were formerly pullman car porters and service trade employees. Colorado does not have a history of black farm workers . . . the "stoop" labor was mostly performed by the Spanish-surnamed. The community has never had large industries with low-paid labor. Colorado's blacks average slightly less education than the Colorado population as a whole.

The education comparisons are particularly significant since: (1) Colorado ranks second among the states and territories of the United States in average educational attainment of residents 15 years of age and older, (2) only the District of Columbia exceeds Colorado's record of almost 11 percent of the state's population having college degrees, and (3) although Colorado has only 1 percent of the nation's population, it has 1.5 percent of all bachelors' degrees granted, 1.3 percent of all doctorates, and 1.8 percent of the nation's scientists.

If we extend present trends to the beginning of the 1980s, it is estimated that between 8 and 10 percent of the population in the city of Denver will be persons with Spanish surnames, and that an additional 11 to 12 percent of the city's population will be blacks, representing little change in the proportions for the former but a near doubling for the latter. Denver's ethnic minorities work in all kinds of private industry and in large numbers for federal, state, and municipal government. They are also found living in every census tract in the city and in all kinds of homes. Public accommodations, public and parochial schools, and all private universities and colleges, plus the two state institutions of higher learning, are open to minority groups. But while Denver's minority groups seem relatively well off, inequalities remain, as the concentrated incidence of unemployment, underemployment, and lack of income detailed below shows. Rarely do blacks and Spanish-surnamed hold high-level managerial and supervisory positions. While minority people live in every census tract, they are still disproportionately concentrated in depressed and poor housing areas of the city. More than 70 percent of the total Spanish-surnamed population in the city and county of Denver lived in 21 census tracts, according to the 1960 census, with 85 percent of the blacks in nine contiguous census tracts.

Unemployment and Poverty in Denver

Data on unemployment and poverty in Denver are limited to 28 census tracts designated in 1960 by the U.S. Bureau of the Census as the Denver poverty area. At that time, 71 percent of the nonwhite population of Denver lived in this area, along with 66 percent of the Spanish-surnamed and 18 percent of the "white-other" population. Because of the significant shift of the nonwhite population to the adjacent Park Hill area outside the designated poverty tracts, only 36.8 percent of the nonwhite population lived in the area designated "poverty" in 1967.

The unemployment rate among the noninstitutional population 16 years of age and older in the Denver poverty area reflects in part the nature of the area's economic problems. The overall unemployment rate of the poverty area in 1967 was 11.5 percent of the labor force, but this included an unemployment rate of 14.5 percent for nonwhites, 13.6 percent for Spanish-surnamed, and 8.4 percent for whites. At the time, the overall unemployment rate for the United States was 3.8 percent, with 3.9 percent for the nation's biggest SMSAs and only 3.1 percent in the Denver SMSA.

Unemployment rates, however, present only part of the picture of economic stress in the poverty area. Subemployment within the Denver poverty area, according to the U.S. Department of Labor (DOL) definitions, reached a rate of 23.6 percent in 1967, or about one of every four of the noninstitutional population (16 years of age and older). For nonwhites, the subemployment rate was 30 percent; for Spanish-surnamed individuals, it was 27 percent; and for whites, the total rate was 18 percent.[1]

The median family income of Denver County was 26 percent above that of the target area and 30 percent higher than that of the SMSA; in both cases, a difference of more than 25 percent. Even this picture has a favorable bias, however, since none of these comparisons takes into account family size, which is likely to be higher in the target areas.

The Political Environment of Denver's Manpower Programs

Denver, a city once dominated by mining interests and later by industrial interests, is now a city with no identifiable power structure. There is no dominant industry, church, or ethnic group. There is no strong labor movement and no real "first families." The mayor's office is the only unifying force, and the tradition of nonpartisan elections has given political machines a personal rather than party coloration, limiting their survival. Since 1902, Denver has been simultaneously a city and a county with a common set of officers to administer the affairs of both. The school districts are also coterminous with the city — all of which limits the number of power bases and points of patronage disposal available.

With the exception of the city council, judges, the civil service commission, the district attorney, the auditor, the zoning board, and a few others, the mayor alone appoints all department and staff agency heads.

---

[1] R. A. Zubrow, *et al.*, *Poverty and Jobs in Denver: A Study of Employment, Unemployment and Job Vacancies in the Denver Labor Market* (Economic Development Administration, U.S. Department of Commerce, June 1969).

Though all employees are protected by a strong merit system, the mayor still has considerable patronage at his disposal.

One penalty of the coterminous city and county unit is lack of any political unification between city and suburb. The city of Denver can expand only by annexation at the expense of surrounding suburban counties. It also controls the quantity and prices of water reaching the suburbs — to the irritation of the suburbanites. The three suburban counties are one congressional district. Suburban politicians get elected by "tweaking Denver's nose." Most of the population and industry growth in recent years has been in the suburban ring, and the city and county of Denver suffer the familiar pains of watching the higher income residents flee to the suburbs and the tax base decline.

Denver favors metropolitan government but has faced strong suburban resistance. A "Committee of 100" appointed by the governor strongly recommended metropolitan government, but the legislature failed to put the issue on the ballot (due to opposition by suburban groups and by public officials of local governments who would have been phased out). There is no prospect of a metropolitan government's succeeding in the foreseeable future.

Denver has seen a strong black movement in the recent past, but one without riots. It is also experiencing a lesser push from its "brown" community, the Spanish-surnamed. Although the advent of the manpower and antipoverty programs has provided some dollars for which black and Spanish-surnamed organizations can compete, gaining political experience in the process, the "politics of poverty" is of no direct significance in the Denver political scene. It is also doubtful that enough Denver voters are aware of the existence of manpower programs to make such programs of any political significance.

Yet despite its relatively small size, Denver is not unique in its problems; but the key to understanding this city is its diversity . . . of its economy, in its political structure, and among its racial and ethnic groups. This same pattern is apparent throughout its manpower programs and agencies.

Delivery Systems for Manpower Services

6

Denver's manpower programs have been characterized by their independence and autonomy. Only the employment service (ES) and the Concentrated Employment Program (CEP) have any claim to comprehensiveness in the delivery of manpower services . . . and even they have little interrelationship with each other and with other manpower agencies. All other programs are run with almost complete autonomy.

THE EMPLOYMENT SERVICE AND THE DISADVANTAGED

Until the advent of the manpower programs, the primary responsibilities of ES in Colorado were to provide a work test for the administration of unemployment insurance and to furnish the very best applicant available to fill each employer's job order. The chief executives of the Colorado Department of Employment and the state ES still consider service to employers their primary obligation, and they are frank to say that they consider the emphasis on the disadvantaged to be misguided. It is their conviction that maximizing the employer's satisfaction will bring in more job orders and, in the long run, will serve the disadvantaged (as well as the advantaged) better than concentrating on applicant needs. Emphasizing the disadvantaged, they argue, will just send the employer elsewhere for his recruiting.

These officials believe that they are complying with federal directives on behalf of the disadvantaged to the best of their abilities, but they do this without enthusiasm. This attitude is well known and accounts for ES's reputation among community action-oriented organizations that ES is more interested in servicing the already qualified than in taking on the much harder job of trying to place the disadvantaged. Everything that is

100

said about ES in Denver manpower programs must be assessed in this perspective.

However, some of the less emotional among the organizations serving the poor agree that ES has been cooperative, despite its lack of enthusiasm, and admit appreciation for receiving frank expression of position and intent from the ES leadership. In addition, the attitude at the top does not necessarily represent the entire organization. The full context of ES activities at all levels and for all programs must be examined. There is mounting evidence that, beginning at the local levels with those directly involved in manpower programs, a change in attitude is taking place. Commitment toward "screening in" rather than "screening out" the disadvantaged is gradually making itself felt, beginning with ES personnel stationed in the several Youth Opportunity Centers (YOC), in CEP, and also in other antipoverty agencies, and spreading upward more recently through the Work Incentive (WIN) program teams. The Colorado ES can hardly be characterized as a "do-gooder" organization dedicated to the welfare of the disadvantaged and the oppressed, but some parts of the working levels of the organization are moving slowly in that direction.

Placement *and* service to the individual, such as counseling, testing, training, giving medical and legal assistance, special schooling, rehabilitating, motivating, creating good work habits, and job developing, as well as making job referrals, are increasingly viewed as appropriate tools for ES. Whereas the placement record was formerly the main determinant of the budget, much of the budget is now justified upon employability, the development of which is defined as identifying and assisting individuals not readily employable by providing the kinds of assistance necessary for them to become productive members of the work force and of society.

Relative priorities are indicated by distribution of staff in the Denver office into four categories: (1) employability development, 32 percent, (2) employer relations and placement, 40 percent, (3) manpower and employment information, 2 percent, and (4) administrative technical support, 26 percent. In addition, the local ES conducts continuous refresher courses for its employees in dealing with the problems of the disadvantaged. The results show in the attitudes and statements of those ES staff members working with the WIN teams, the Manpower Development and Training Act (MDTA) staff, CEP, and Job Opportunities in the Business Sector (JOBS). Old habits cannot be eradicated overnight, but the message is beginning to work its way up from the front-line organization of ES to the higher echelons, at least in the Denver office. The YOC centers, three of which are operated from the state ES office, are located in the right areas for serving the disadvantaged, and receive favorable comments from neighborhood groups.

The Human Resources Development Programs

Efforts and success in the Human Resources Development (HRD) program are one measure of ES's effectiveness and commitment in serving the disadvantaged. A sampling of 249 HRD participants who were placed in jobs during the period from September 1969 to February 1970 through the three placement areas — YOC-HRD, the special HRD unit in the Denver local ES office, and ES's mainline placement processing of HRD individuals — illustrates the employment results for those who primarily are receiving counseling and placement without enrolling in training or other programs.

Ethnically, the HRD participants in Denver were 13 percent black, 33 percent Spanish-surnamed, 27 percent white, and 27 percent American Indian. (The last resulted from the efforts of an especially effective Indian HRD staff member who was a nonpareil in counseling.) The average age of HRD recipients in Denver was 21.6 years; almost nine of 10 were male, and they averaged 10.9 years of education. Inasmuch as no reliable figures are available for the ethnic composition of Denver's disadvantaged, it is impossible to tell whether these proportions in HRD are representative. Furthermore, since HRD deals primarily with an overflow of disadvantaged from other programs, determining ethnic representativeness of HRD services is of little value.

Comparing employment and earnings before and after HRD services, we find that the average hourly wage rate increased $0.25, or 14.7 percent. Blacks and Spanish-surnamed experienced $0.24 and $0.22 an hour average increases, respectively, with American Indians gaining $0.41 an hour, compared to $0.12 for whites. The American Indians also constituted one in four placements . . . another tribute to the Indians' counselor. Since the gains were between the last job before and the first job after placement services were received, there was no substantial lapse of time during which improvements in labor market conditions could have been responsible for the wage gains.

WIN as a Placement Mechanism

Placement of WIN enrollees is another test of ES effectiveness. Only 239 of the 623 who terminated from the WIN program through January 1970 were placed in jobs, a placement rate of 38 percent. However, one of every three of the placements lasted less than 90 days. Of the 179 placed for 90 days or longer, 86 were placed by ES, and 93 applicants found their own jobs. The same relationship holds true for the 239 total placements.

Preenrollment data on 149 of the terminees placed showed that only seven (all females) were without previous job experience. Apparently welfare status had been interspersed with employment. Whether they would have again gone from welfare into a job without the WIN program would be difficult to determine. Without this knowledge, we cannot assess the full impact that WIN efforts have had to improve employability.

Though public employment comprises 19 percent of all those who work for wages in the Denver metropolitan area, 41 percent of the WIN terminees, with employment lasting 90 days or more, were placed with public agencies. Of the WIN placements made by ES, 67 percent were in public service, compared to 16 percent who found their own jobs.

Before judging the appropriateness of these placement rates, one must take into consideration the nature of the enrollees. Of the 623 terminating the program, 384 did so for reasons other than job placement. However, health, pregnancy, and other factors not within the control of the WIN program reduced the number available for placement to 365, increasing the rate of placement in jobs of 90 days or more to 49 percent of available terminees, and also increasing the rate of placement in jobs of any duration to 65 percent of available terminees. In addition, a $0.25 average hourly wage increase occurred between the "before" and "after" wage rates for those WIN enrollees employed during both periods.

The Denver Concentrated Employment Program

Denver was designated in March 1968 as a CEP II city when the CEP program was expanded beyond the 22 projects originally funded. Turmoil immediatley arose over the issue of prime sponsorship and the probable choice among four indigenous organizations as possible subcontractors for component parts of the program. The community action agency (CAA), called Denver Opportunity, should have been the prime sponsor of the program in accordance with national guidelines. However, Denver Opportunity had no prior experience with manpower programs and little related program experience. The Neighborhood Youth Corps (NYC) contracts were administered by the city and county of Denver, and the existence of units of the black-oriented Opportunities Industrialization Center (OIC), the Urban League, and the Spanish-surnamed organizations, La Rasa and Operation SER, largely served to prevent an active manpower role for Denver Opportunity. Even so, Denver Opportunity attempted preparation of a CEP proposal, resulting in a great deal of bickering with the various indigenous groups and particularly with the Colorado Department of Employment which, according to the national guidelines, was to provide most of the manpower services.

When it became apparent that an acceptable proposal was not emerging, the regional manpower administrator (RMA) told the mayor and Colorado Department of Employment that the only way Denver could have a CEP program was for the city to assume the role of prime sponsor, building on the already successful NYC experience.

The mayor retained two consultants to write a proposal, with the help of ES and the regional office staff. The single greatest problem faced in drafting the proposal was to decide how to handle the bids if La Rasa, OIC, and others ran component parts of the program. Therefore, a decision was made to reject all subcontract proposals and have the prime sponsor run the program. The indigenous organizations reacted bitterly, having expected that CEP would be an umbrella organization that would delegate actual program components to them. The major reason given for excluding various groups was the lack of time imposed by a three-week deadline for proposal preparation. Some apparently thought from this explanation that they were to be brought into the program at a later date. Failure to do so created further resentment. However, while the contrary decision created serious antagonisms, it proved to be wise.

Prior to its submission to the RMA, the Denver CEP proposal was presented to the local Cooperative Area Manpower Planning System (CAMPS) committee. After the proposal was briefly discussed at a committee meeting, a motion to temporarily reject it was passed, with representatives from OIC, La Rasa, Operation SER, the Urban League, and the welfare department opposing approval, and only the three representatives of the Colorado Department of Employment voting that the proposal be submitted for funding. Ignoring the CAMPS action, the representatives submitted the proposal which was funded on June 27, 1968, by the Regional Manpower Administration, obligating the federal government to $2,247,000 for a 13-month period ending August 7, 1969. Except for $209,500 of MDTA money, all of the funds were in a single contract with the city and county of Denver.

The Denver CEP proposal, following the guidelines set by DOL, included the following components: a two-week orientation program; Operation Mainstream to provide work experience through an effort to physically restore the city's blighted areas; a Work Training Experience (WTE) program paid by the NYC funds but open to adults for on-the-job training (OJT) and education, using federal, state, and local government agencies and nonprofit organizations as training locations; an MDTA institutional program for individual referrals; and the New Careers program. Using existing national guidelines, CEP developed its proposal to minimize the administrative budget in order to use the maximum for wages, stipends, and services.

Two units, both within the city and county government and both under the mayor's office, were assigned major responsibility for administering the CEP program. An entirely new unit was created and housed apart from any existing government facilities to provide the central administration of CEP. The CEP Central facility housed the director and his top administrative staff, the orientation unit, and the administrators of all job placement, coaching, and counseling. The Operation Mainstream component also operated out of CEP Central. Outreach and intake were subcontracted to Denver Opportunity because this agency operated five CAAs in the target area. Only one member of the three-man team at each outreach station was a Denver Opportunity employee, while one was an ES placement man and the other a CEP Central staff member. The WTE program, the New Careers program, and an expanded NYC were originally assigned to the unit of city and county government that had previously been established to administer the out-of-school NYC program. WTE and New Careers were later brought back under CEP control. These two administrative units were entirely separate and, for all practical purposes, uncoordinated.

Operation Mainstream was retained at CEP Central so that the enrollees could take full advantage of the orientation and counseling services available there. The plan was to enroll only extremely hardcore unemployed males who wanted to work a 36-hour week with an additional four hours for counseling. The MDTA-OJT component was also kept at CEP Central, while the MDTA institutional component was retained by the Colorado Department of Employment which had the necessary legal authority to handle the program.

A person could come into CEP from one of the five outreach stations or by referral from city agencies, ES, Operation SER, La Rasa, or other indigenous organizations, or as a walk-in to CEP Central. The first assignment would be a two-week orientation program during which he would be paid $50 per week. Theoretically, by the second week the enrollee would be assessed, and decisions would then be made as to which component to assign him.

The Denver CEP was hampered from its planning stages by problems, delays, and setbacks. None of the problems were insurmountable, but the constant pressures can be directly identified with the early lack of success. At the outset, CEP was intimidated by the short length of time allowed for the planning and editing of its proposal. It was also hampered by the continuing jealousy of the various other manpower organizations and by the strife between its director and his deputy. The fact that the deputy was a black and the director a Spanish-surnamed individual tended to freeze opinions among staff, enrollees, and the community. The firing of the black only five months after the Denver CEP was organized so disturbed the morale of other employees and the workability of the CEP program that in mid-December it had to close its intake of enrollees while officials "hashed out" the problems before the office could resume its responsibilities in January. The total effect was that the Denver CEP did not really begin its activities until more than six months after it was created.

Administrative problems continued to hamper the efficient operation of CEP, and it was September 1969 before they were resolved. Then because of a shortage of jobs or work experience and training slots in which to place CEP enrollees after orientation, it became necessary in October to again shut down intake and orientation to "clear the air." One cost of the leadership problems has been a conviction by blacks that CEP is not their organization. The less than successful performances of several of the components and the general lack of impact of the total organization must be viewed in this context.

However, the Denver CEP also had the advantage, after some staff shakeup, of competent and dedicated administrators. Relations with ES were sound and improving. A *modus vivendi* was emerging with the various indigenous organizations. On the other hand, the economy was no longer growing as rapidly, and though unemployment was not yet rising, neither were employers under great pressure for manpower. The greatest weakness was in the available components. There was very little in what the Denver CEP had available to improve employability and increase the availability of jobs. New Careers and OJT were dropped from the second phase contract because of their disappointing progress. Relations with the National Alliance of Businessmen (NAB) were good, but few employers were participating and few jobs were available. The Denver CEP stood isolated, with limited linkages to other agencies and few channels of access for its enrollees into the mainstream of the Denver economy.

Given time in the fall of 1969, through the cessation of activities, Denver CEP administrators engaged in some soul searching and appraisal of the first phase activities and experiences as a basis for a much more constructive and meaningful 1970 program. With a CEP budget in 1970 of more than $2 million, an experienced staff, and benefiting from hindsight on more than a year's experience, CEP administrators looked forward to 1970 with greater anticipation of success.

A number of constructive changes were planned and implemented to ensure improved administration and operation of the program:

(1) Emphasis in 1970 was on a comprehensive program to a limited number of people (750 in 1970) in contrast to the 1969 program which attempted to be all things to all people. For example, in the 1969 program, a person needing a hernia operation would be taken care of by CEP, but not under the 1970 program. The CEP objectives became more selective and were ranked according to performance. The objectives were as follows:

(a) Enroll and retain only persons who can benefit from the CEP service system.

(b) Assist the enrollees in setting high but achievable goals.

(c) Provide individual packages of services.

(d) Obtain enrollee concurrence in the employability development plan.

(e) Place the enrollee in employment consistent with the plan.

(f) Provide an uninterrupted flow of services.

(2) CEP representatives were withdrawn from outreach centers. CEP no longer uses outreach centers for placement — only as a source of enrollees. This and more limited objectives with respect to clientele (mentioned above) allows CEP to do a more concentrated and complete job by using the same staff as before, but concentrating on the nonjob-ready individuals only; those who are job ready are referred to HRD or ES.

To replace the outreach centers as the source of CEP intake, a single outreach center was established. All CEP intake is through this office whether the persons are referrals from OIC, La Rasa, Operation SER, the state parole board, ES, neighborhood health centers, the five Denver Opportunity centers, or walk-in traffic. A five-man staff made up of an ES supervisor and four CEP paraprofessional employees operate the CEP outreach center.

(3) In conjunction with NAB and ES, CEP instituted a new and much improved job order procedure which established closer cooperation among the three organizations and could be integrated into the Job Bank which was then in the process of being established.

(4) A technique was worked out by which CEP administrators could more precisely determine what should be happening at every point in the flow of services, both in terms of time and numbers of clients. This technique resulted from bringing together a knowledge of characteristics of the clientele, the metropolitan area labor market, funding, and intuition. A loading chart was developed which showed, in terms of number of people and a time frame, what happens to individuals from point of input to point of output.

From this general loading chart was formulated a more detailed breakdown into 13 different routes with appropriate time frames and numbers of people from orientation through first job entry, job placement, and second job entry to second job placement. With this method, a determination could be made month by month of the effect that enrolling a certain number of individuals would have on each step in the service flow of the CEP program. This month-by-month determination made it possible to ascertain in advance if the program was operating properly and the number of individuals who should be at each step of the 13 routes from orientation to placement at any given point in time. If the actual results do not agree with the predicted result, CEP administrators know exactly where to look for an answer.

Job Development and Placement

To this point, attention has been directed to the general administrative and intake functions of CEP. The ultimate success of CEP must be measured in terms of its placement and job development activities since the end objective of all manpower programs is employment at decent levels of income.

Six job source categories are used by the seven CEP teams in their placement activities: (1) WTE conversions from work sites to permanent positions, (2) CEP-developed jobs, (3) ES Job Bank listings, (4) NAB contract jobs, (5) NAB noncontract jobs, and (6) enrollee self-developed jobs which can be attributed to the training by CEP.

The conversion of WTE work sites and the use of CEP-developed jobs provide almost half the jobs, the best retention rates, and among the highest starting wages. A spin-off from the CEP training is indicated by the fact that more than one of every five jobs were developed by the enrollee himself, and these jobs had the highest starting pay. But since the usage of this category by the CEP teams is not manageable, only two of every three trainees retain their jobs beyond 30 days. The ES Job Bank has not been used with any measure of success, either as a job source or in terms of wage levels or retentions. NAB, contract and noncontract, accounts for more than 25 percent of the jobs, but relative to the sources other than the ES Job Bank, the wages and retention rates have been low.

Operation Mainstream

The Operation Mainstream component of CEP was the first experience in Denver with specialized concern for the very hardcore unemployed. The original plan was to employ the enrollees at cleaning up the Platte River and in boarding up abandoned homes and stores in depressed neighborhoods. The expected level of capability was indicated in the structure of the program: (1) close supervision consisting of small teams of 10 to 12 men, each with an on-the-site team leader in daily communication with the Operation Mainstream supervisors, (2) relatively high support levels with, for instance, four hours of counseling per week programmed for each employee, and (3) relatively long periods of involvement, the contract calling for 46 slots with a total of only 100 enrollees during the 11-month period for an expected duration of five months per man.

A 32-year-old Spanish-surnamed social worker, college trained but with no degree, was employed in August 1968 as the Operation Mainstream supervisor, and the success of the program is mainly attributable to him. His qualifications for the job consisted largely of his experience in dealing with the employability problems of the parents of children in the Headstart program and his own personal background.

An analysis of Operation Mainstream activities through 1970 indicates that 112 participants of the program had been terminated, a third of them by placements in regular jobs. Approximately half of those available for work upon completion of their training were placed. All of the enrollees who completed the course were male, and more than four of every five were younger than 35. Four of five were without a high school diploma, and none had education beyond high school. In their last full-time job before they enrolled in the program, only one of four Operation Mainstream participants had earned more than $2.00 an hour, mostly in irregular employment. Two of three had yearly incomes of less than $2,000 in the year preceding their enrollment with Operation Mainstream.

A further breakdown of the statistics shows that family size averaged about 2.5, which when coupled with the family income, would indicate that most enrollees were below the poverty threshold. Seven of ten completers were Spanish-surnamed, as were eight of ten placed, reflecting once again the energetic and dedicated efforts of the dirctor of the program rather than proportions in the population.

Not only were placement rates low, but only the small number of whites and blacks made significant gains in wage rates (see Table 6-1). Since the average elapsed time between pre- and postprogram employment was nearly a year, something like $0.10 per hour wage gain might have been expected, even without the influence of the program.

Denver's Operation Mainstream program is not without blemishes. There are indications that average job attendance has not been as high as claimed (88 percent on a typical day). Such work assignments as helping move families for "Metro Fair Housing," a Denver make-work project, not only provided limited work experience but seriously exposed enrollees to temptations to pilfer and to drink on the job. The limited success of Opera-

TABLE 6-1

Average Wage Rates in Pre- and Postprogram Employment
for Operation Mainstream Placements
(By ethnic origin)

Category	Average Wage per Hour			
	All Placements	Blacks	Spanish-Surnamed	White/Other
Preprogram wage	$2.14	$2.28	$2.05	$2.76
Postprogram wage	$2.17	$2.80	$2.06	$2.40
Wage difference	$0.03	$0.52	$0.01	$0.36

tion Mainstream was achieved despite the high incidence of alcoholism among the enrollees. (It has been suggested that the employability problems of the Spanish-surnamed alcoholic, because of his cultural and religious identification, may be solved more readily than those of the black drug addict. The existing central records unit of the Denver CEP is not able to provide statistical breakdowns on race and ethnicity to analyze this important possibility.)

WORK TRAINING EXPERIENCE

The Denver CEP's WTE program was designed as an adult NYC, using NYC funds and supposedly providing a combination of counseling, education, training, and work experience. It turned out to be a holding operation — a place to put people after they had completed the orientation portion of the program and until jobs were found for them.

During the first 15 months of the WTE program, 764 people were enrolled in 211 slots. At the end of that period, 279 persons had gone to jobs elsewhere, but 190 were still enrolled, including 43 in a holding status (i.e., in hospitals, in jail, or otherwise unavailable). As many as 290 had been enrolled at one time. There had been 110 dropouts during the training stage, while the remaining 116 had been transferred to other CEP components.

The host employers, 65 different federal, state, and city agencies together with private, nonprofit organizations, were engaged primarily in office and clerical activities; thus the work experience was most useful to women. Though 60 percent of the enrollees were men, only custodial-type activities were available to them. The federal agencies, in general, provided the most useful work stations, with city agencies next. Others tended to treat the enrollees as free labor, leading the CEP administrators to cease using hospitals and private, nonprofit organizations and to bring about transfer of WTE responsibility from NYC to CEP Central.

The original contract stipulated a 40-hour week, with 60 percent of the time spent in supervised work, 5 percent in counseling, 15 percent in remedial education, 15 percent in supplementary vocational training, and 5 percent in self-improvement activities. But until the administrative change, 90 percent of the OJT experience and 10 percent "on-demand" counseling appeared to be more typical. There was no group counseling until the change in administrative structure. The quality of the counseling performed was also questionable. Counselors noted the impossibility of providing adequate, individualized service, with caseloads averaging 50 to 60 enrollees per counselor; in some instances, the caseloads were more than 70. The 211 slots were divided among four counselors, but participant levels commonly exceeded the allotted slots by 20 to 80 enrollees per counselor. Caseloads varied widely among counselors, with no apparent relationship between caseloads and the professional abilities of the counselors or to enrollee characteristics. One WTE counselor who aggressively argued for a smaller caseload was assigned 30 to 40 enrollees thereafter, while another, passively accepting responsibility, was found to be carrying typically 60 or more. No special training had been given supervisors, counselors, or anyone involved in training in the program.

Analysis of WTE under the direct administration of CEP shows that (1) men still constitute about two of every three participants, (2) in excess of 80 percent of the enrollees were 35 years of age or younger, (3) about 70 percent were without a high school diploma, (4) four of five had not earned more than $2.00 an hour in the last preprogram employment, and (5) placements, though proportional to ethnic group representation among enrollees, showed a high proportion for Spanish-surnamed (53.4 percent) and blacks (34.5 percent).

When wage rates before entering the WTE program are compared with wage rates received after the program, the average wage rate improvement following WTE enrollment was $0.42, with each ethnic group sharing equally in the gains, but with females lower both before and after (see Table 6-2). A pre- and postprogram elapsed time of approximately a year or less suggests a normal (no program) wage gain expectation of $0.10 per hour.

Placements as a percentage of terminations reflect greater success for WTE than for Operation Mainstream. The gross placement rate, placements to total terminations, was 40.3 percent, while the net placement rate, placements to controllable terminations, was 59.4 percent.

An obvious implication of the WTE experience is that the quality of the job sites vary directly with the organizational responsibility for providing a client service, and inversely, with the extent to which the enrollee is a source of free labor; and given the attendant circumstances, it produces a marginal physical product approximately equal to the real wage borne by the estab-

TABLE 6-2

Average Wage Rates in Pre- and Postprogram
Employment for WTE Placements
(By race and sex)

| Category | Average Wage per Hour | | | | | |
	All Placements	Blacks	Spanish-Surnamed	White/Other	Male	Female
Preprogram wage	$1.81	$1.94	$1.80	$1.77	$1.95	$1.60
Postprogram wage	$2.23	$2.25	$2.21	$2.23	$2.38	$1.99
Wage difference	$0.42	$0.31	$0.41	$0.46	$0.43	$0.39

lishment. The immediate contention may well be that those job sites which will be secured will offer generally improved services when there are tangible returns to the firm for enrollee performance and tangible costs when there is enrollee dereliction. In general, it seems that in programs doing public service for the sake of such service, there is a tendency to be content with the image of doing the service — unless institutionalized policing occurs.

New Careers

The New Careers program was the Denver CEP's least successful component (for reasons which are probably not due to correctable factors). The disappointments were based in misassessments of the ability of the community to define and invest in jobs which corresponded to the aspiration of New Careers advocates.

New Careers began with high hopes, reflected in an original funding for 120 slots assigned to the Police Academy, the welfare department, and three hospitals. Optimism flagged as the Police Academy withdrew entirely, and the welfare department reduced its commitment from 40 to 20 job opportunities. Even more damaging for the hope of realizing "new careers" was the awareness that the hospital slots, in particular, fell far short of a concept of paraprofessional development. A more appropriate classification of the jobs seemed to be work experience as hospital orderlies. Enrollee dissatisfaction with the characteristics of hospital slots was high and resulted in few permanent hires. On the other hand, the less traditionally dead-end placements with the welfare department resulted in much greater success. Apparently in Denver, hospitals were no more willing than police departments to consider the disadvantaged as eligible, or qualified, for development as New Careers-trained employees.

A total of 78 persons enrolled in the New Careers program between July 1968 and the demise of the program in the fall of 1969. A survey of program results conducted in March 1970 indicates that 42 of those enrolled in the program were placed in permanent career employment. Of the career ladder placements, 17 were with public schools, 14 with welfare, six with the county health department, and only five with a hospital.

All were engaged in educational activity during their enrollments. Of the 76 enrollees, 44 participated in the general education development (GED) course in which 11 were successful, and four were still enrolled in September 1969. Ten were enrolled at the University of Colorado, nine of whom successfully completed at least one course for one semester. Fifty had been enrolled at one of the three community college campuses, with 22 completing at least one course for one quarter. Those who completed some phase of an educational activity can probably be counted as an achievement, though the fact that they could enroll, did so, and were successful in college courses gives an indication of the selectivity.

A post mortem of the New Careers program indicates the following concerning the enrollees in the program: Of the 78 New Careers enrollees, about half were male; only 36 percent of total placements were male; two of three were 35 years of age or younger; 35.9 percent were black, 57.7 percent were Spanish-surnamed, and 6.4 percent were white-other; three of five had less than a high school education; the overwhelming majority were below the poverty threshold in their earnings on the last job held prior to entering New Careers; and relative to their proportion to all enrollees, blacks fared best, constituting 35.9 percent of enrollees to 42.9 percent of placements, while Spanish-surnamed constituted 57.7 percent of enrollees but only 50 percent of placements.

Table 6-3 provides available information concerning improvement in wage rates for enrollees in the New Careers program who were placed. The average wage rate improvement for all placements was 29 percent, or $0.51 per hour. Blacks and Spanish-surnamed fared much better than white-other, resulting in a much greater wage rate equality in the postprogram employment. Female placements increased their average wage rates by $0.62, compared with $0.27 for male placements, but were still 12 percent behind male hourly wage rates. The no program wage gain expectation over the year of less elapsed time might have been $0.10 per hour.

Placements in the New Careers program ran at 53.8 percent of total terminations and at 70 percent of controllable terminations. However, a word of caution must be made concerning the use of these figures. It is too soon to determine whether this fairly high placement rate in fact reflects also the development of career jobs. There is some indication, especially in the medical placements, that quality career jobs in terms of their permanence and meaningfulness have not developed as hoped; and to the extent that this is true, the high placement rate is not reflective of achievement of the goals of the program.

TABLE 6-3

Average Wage Rates in Pre- and Postprogram Employment
for New Careers Placement
(By race and sex)

Category	All Placements	Blacks	Spanish-Surnamed	White/Other	Male	Female
	Average Wage per Hour					
Preprogram wage	$1.76	$1.74	$1.73	$1.99	$2.15	$1.54
Postprogram wage	$2.27	$2.20	$2.29	$2.25	$2.42	$2.16
Wage difference	$0.51	$0.46	$0.56	$0.26	$0.27	$0.62

Project Value

Questions concerning the final outcome of New Careers can be sharply contrasted with the sustained optimism over Project Value. The apparent differences in program achievement are not due to systematic differences in the quality, orientation, or capabilities of the enrollees. Rather, the differences appear to be (1) the care taken in the development of Project Value positions to assure employability in civil service-type employment, and (2) what consistently reappears as a necessary condition for success: an institutionalized commitment on the part of the employer to do whatever is necessary to make the program work. For this there is no level of dedication or effort on the part of CEP which can substitute.

Project Value is similar to New Careers but without the onus the name "New Careers" carries in Denver. The major purpose of Project Value, however, is to place individuals for training in military installations where the training may lead to career ladder jobs. In the Denver area, Project Value has operated through Lowry Air Force Base, Fitzsimmons Hospital, and the Air Force finance center. A similar project is being carried on with the Denver Post Office.

Of 83 enrollees involved in the four projects, 44 found jobs and nine remained in training positions leading to permanent placement, with the whereabouts of the remaining 30 unknown. Compilation of reasons for termination from the Project Value program show a gross placement rate of 55 percent and a net rate (placements to controllable terminations) of 65.8 percent.

Enrollees were predominantly in the younger age groups, 93 percent being younger than 35 and none older than 44 years of age; three of five were female; 61 percent had less than a high school education; approximately 90 percent were living in poverty prior to the program; and 90 percent were minority group members — 49 percent Spanish-surnamed and 41 percent black — but 55 percent of the placements were Spanish-surnamed compared to 40 percent for blacks. The average wage rate difference (Table 6-4) for the 44 Project Value enrollees placed was $0.59. The same considerations for prevailing wage trends hold true for this as for other programs.

Neighborhood Youth Corps

Combining the programs of the three agencies conducting NYC programs — in school, out of school, and summer — we find that total funding for fiscal years 1966 to 1970 amounted to $4.6 million and covered in excess of 7,000 enrollees. Inasmuch as there was no way of determining the length of time each enrollee spent in the program, no meaningful figure can be computed which would indicate the average funded cost per en-

TABLE 6-4

Average Wage Rates in Pre- and Postprogram Employment for
Project Value Placements
(By race and sex)

Category	All Placements	Blacks	Spanish-Surnamed	White/Other	Male	Female
	Average Wage per Hour					
Preprogram wage	$1.66	$1.59	$1.63	$1.77	$2.02	$1.48
Postprogram wage	$2.25	$2.17	$2.29	$2.47	$2.66	$2.05
Wage difference	$0.59	$0.58	$0.66	$0.70	$0.64	$0.57

rollee. The same problem would be faced in attempting to arrive at the average expenditure for each enrollee.

A profile of the NYC programs for 1966 to 1970 shows that while the in-school program was dominated by male enrollees, both the out-of-school and summer programs showed a decided trend in favor of female enrollees. The median age of the in-school and summer enrollees was approximately 17, while the out-of-school median age was one year older. Both the in-school and summer programs showed a definite increase in the proportion of black participants, although the predominant group continued to be white. Unfortunately, the statistics do not provide an ethnic breakdown within the white category; but from observation, the major portion would be Spanish-surnamed. This would indicate a heavy participation in the NYC program by minority group youngsters. The NYC enrollees were predominantly those with nine to 11 years of education. The median family income for in-school enrollees averaged $2,400, compared to about $2,000 for out-of-school enrollees and $2,700 for summer enrollees. From 35 to 48 percent of the enrollees in all three programs came from homes on public assistance.

The declared purpose of the NYC program is to aid students to remain in school and to develop a favorable attitude toward work, as well as to induce those who have left school to either return to school or to prepare themselves more adequately for employment. The work stations in Denver have been limited to governmental and to private, nonprofit institutions. The Children's Education Fund (CEF), a private organization which operated in-school and out-of-school programs until 1968, used the U.S. Department of Health, Education and Welfare (HEW), the Internal Revenue Service, and the United States Civil Service Commission in the federal sector, and the state archives, revenue office, civil service commission, and fish and game department in the state sector. Most of these jobs were of a clerical type and involved out-of-school trainees. The largest group of enrollees, however, was placed in city and county parks and recreation department activities and in public works. In-school youth were placed in city and county recreation jobs since these jobs offered more flexibility in scheduling because they used the youth in the evenings. CEF also tried to place youth as near their homes as possible.

CEF made a distinction between in-school and out-of-school trainees and placed the latter in a stricter job environment, such as libraries, printing establishments, rehabilitation centers, offices, hospitals, etc. Mercy Hospital was an especially desirable spot for the out-of-school enrollees because the hospital staff would take a 9th grader with no experience, find out what he could do, and if possible, place him in regular employment.

CEF used a variety of sources for referrals, such as public housing representatives, recreation directors, probationary and parole officers, rehabilitation centers, reformatories, and public assistance programs. It reported no problems in filling its projects and especially praised the YOC centers as a recruitment source. After its own slots were filled, CEF usually referred the surplus enrollees to either the school district or to the city and county NYC programs. Community acceptance was excellent, as witnessed by the fact that CEF had good relations with other youth agencies and was influential in dealing with the courts on behalf of a youngster in trouble.

Denver's Public School District No. 1 confined its program to in-school enrollees. Excellent support was reported for its program from such groups as the Denver Opportunity's CAA center, the city school administration, other community groups, and the general populace, not only with referrals but in rehabilitating youth who got into trouble. The school district program used 65 work stations. Examples of these are the botanical gardens, the Boy Scouts of America, the Boys Club of Denver, several community centers, a number of locations under the Public Housing Authority, the various neighborhood action centers, the state public health and public welfare departments, 16 recreation centers, and some other nonprofit groups such as Selective Service and the YMCA.

The Denver city and county NYC program was entirely an out-of-school program. Its high turnover rate may relate to the type of youngster who enrolls with the city and county compared to the population available to CEF and the city schools. The administrator of the program believes his clients are an even less disciplined group than those of the other NYC programs. Some are referred by the YOC centers and by probation and parole centers, while others are walk-ins.

The 67 work stations originally were in four general areas: (1) components of the city and county of Denver, such as the assessment division, the county court, the Public Housing Authority, the parks and recreation department, the public library, and the zoo; (2) federal agencies, such as the Armed Forces examination and entrance station, the Federal Aviation Administration, the Armed Forces recruiting stations, the Veterans Administration, and HEW; (3) state groups, such as the University of Colorado, the state archives and the planning office, and the YOC centers; and (4) other groups, such as the Allied Jewish Community Council, the chamber of commerce, Denver Opportunity, the Metro Youth Education Center, Operation SER, CAA centers, and the federal credit union.

The city and county program has had excellent support from the school district. Not only has the public supported the program strongly, but the city itself has opened avenues of employment not previously available to NYC enrollees. A memorandum was issued, making it possible for NYC trainees to be considered for regular employment in beginning-level career service in certain areas without having to take merit examinations.

An overall assessment of the Denver NYC program in the absence of any follow-up information on individual enrollees would be that the programs seem to be well run with a competent staff. The past willingness to settle for occupying time and providing income appears to be giving way to a greater concern for constructive work experience. The parks and recreation department jobs, as well as menial work around schools, are useful income sources, but they offer little preparation for meaningful employment. The trend has been to shift to work sites in the state planning office, the Denver public library, YOC centers, the Armed Forces examination and entrance station, community centers, IRS, HEW, the VA Hospital, the assessor's and the clerk and recorder's offices, the county court, and Denver General Hospital, to name a few. Occupational training situations include drafting, clerical, teachers' and medical aides, machine and teletype operators, painting and plumbing aides, recreation leader, shipping and receiving, carpentry, meat cutting, auto mechanic, and cashier. These not only provide meaningful work experiences but also the possibility that the employee can work into a more satisfying job with more pay.

Denver NYC administrators, however, have doubts about the increasing emphasis of the new NYC-2 guidelines concerning more time allocated to formal education (which often is beyond the capability or interests of many of the enrollees) at the expense of what the Denver NYC feels is becoming, in practice, a more productive emphasis . . . training, work experience, and counseling as a means by which the young enrollee can become more job ready. The Denver NYC feels that for many of these young people, the impetus to return to school or to complete their GED comes after they become involved in a job and not before. Excluding the private sector as a work experience source for enrollees seriously limits the job development and placement activities of NYC, especially when many private industry employers are willing and able to participate.

The administrators of the program have also noted a changing attitude among the enrollees who are more interested in job readiness and more motivated than before. As a part of the Denver program, the NYC has been trying to enrich the experiences of the enrollees beyond the job itself by providing them with such things as tax information and involving them in cultural activities (such as concerts) and also in sporting events.

If the objective of the NYC program has been increased incomes for the disadvantaged, success has been automatic. Denver NYC administrators claim additional contributions such as the following:

(1) NYC enrollees being placed in meaningful work environments come to better grips with themselves in relationship to the world in general. They feel less alienated and more as though they belong to the society, especially if they are able to afford an apartment of their own or a car.

(2) The program helps the enrollee to relate to adults. He finds that people in agencies where training takes place are not so strange, no different from himself.

(3) The program provides an exposure to the way things really are, compared to what the enrollee thought they were.

(4) For the first time, many of the enrollees find that they can develop something that has marketability. The world is not so mysterious and awesome. They just need to get out into the world.

(5) The enrollee finds, through experience in the program, that he can rise above normal family problems.

The Impact of the ES and CEP Programs

The NYC program, though subject to high enrollee turnover (primarily a reflection of the age group) has evolved from a simple holding operation providing income and some useful activities into a program with much greater emphasis upon meaningful work experience as a preparation for regular work. ES, under the impact of its own component programs (HRD and WIN) and the pressure of other manpower groups, has moved slowly toward a commitment to a "screening-in" program but still has considerable room for improvement. Until ES is fully committed to screening in, its own programs and those which it services cannot achieve their full potential. The changeover requires political as well as philosophical adjustments.

The optimum mix of job sources is that which results in the greatest number of well-paying jobs and a substantial level of retention. It is not unreasonable to expect from the overall performance of the Denver CEP that retention would average about 75 percent and the average starting wage about $2.20. The success with WTE conversions and CEP-developed jobs indicates values in continued use of these sources.

Several conclusions concerning individuals involved in these programs seem clear cut: Older people were the exception. Male participants outnumbered females in all but Project Value (40 percent male), ranging from 51 percent in New Careers to 100 percent in Operation Mainstream. Low earnings prior to entry into a CEP program characterized all the various components. A range from 58 percent of enrollees in New Careers to 82 percent in Operation Mainstream had less than a high school education. Minority groups were dominant among the enrollees, ranging from 88 percent in WTE to 95 percent in Project Value. As would be expected from relative proportions in the general minority population, Spanish-surnamed constituted the largest of the minority groups, especially for Operation Mainstream where they comprised 79 percent of all enrollees placed.

Considerable variation was found among the programs relative to their placement rates. Calculating placements as a percentage of controllable terminations, we find that New Careers led the group with 70 percent, followed by Project Value with 64 percent, WTE with 59 percent, and Operation Mainstream with 47 percent. Wage rate improvements between the pre- and postprogram rates varied from only $0.03 in Operation Mainstream to $0.59 in Project Value. However, the differences among wage rate changes tended to narrow the rate differences rather than create greater disparity in postprogram wage rates. The average wage rate in the postprogram jobs ranged from $2.17 in Operation Mainstream to $2.27 in the New Careers program. Some narrowing of the differential was observed also between male and female, but the difference still remained substantial.

In terms of individual welfare, the placements out of controllable terminations and the wage rate improvements for those placed point to a moderate degree of success, especially in view of worsening labor market conditions. In terms of total impact on the Denver labor market, it is doubtful that any net improvement in the job situation resulted since the placements were probably at the expense of other workers who would have obtained the jobs in the normal course of events.

The most serious obstacle to an effective manpower program in Denver continues to be molding the various parts of a manpower program — intake, assessment, training, job development and placement — into a single, well-coordinated, smoothly functioning machine . . . when the various parts are under separate management and financing, are often in conflict with each other, and have different motivations and goals. These factors will remain an obstacle until such time as the various divergent groups are either brought under one effective coordinating or managing authority or establish mutual objectives for a comprehensive Denver manpower program and then give more than lip service to it.

Skills and Jobs for Denver's Disadvantaged

7

A continuing dichotomy within manpower policy has centered around the extent to which the unemployment and low incomes of the disadvantaged could be attributed to their own lack of employability and the extent to which institutional arrangements were denying them employment opportunity. To the degree that the former is true, it was the individuals who needed changing. If the institutions were at fault, they needed changing — a much more difficult assignment politically. Remedial fundamental education and training programs have sought to improve the basic employability of their enrollees. In doing so, they have also not been without their institutional impacts on the community.

Denver's school system places great emphasis upon preparing its students for college but does not provide equal facilities for those who desire vocational and commercial training. For many years, the city has maintained skill-training facilities outside the more formal education system, but these facilities have been capable of handling only a fraction of the total need. Thus the major portion of the public education system has been aimed at a level somewhat higher than that characteristic of the majority of the disadvantaged. MDTA, WIN, OIC, and Operation SER in Denver have sought to make up for these deficiencies of the education and training system as well as the deficiencies in the skills of the eligible individuals.

Of the CEP program, only New Careers has sought basic institutional change; the others have primarily sought income transfers, with incidental useful activities attached. NAB-JOBS, though ostensibly a training program, fits better into the category of institutional change because its main impact, where successful, has been to influence the employer to change his recruitment, selection, and other personnel policies.

DENVER'S TRAINING FACILITIES

Three public training facilities have been available to the disadvantaged and have been used by both the regular school system and by manpower programs. Despite the availability of these systems in Denver, there is a clear need to (1) broaden the education system to meet the varying needs of all its population, (2) locate educational facilities more conveniently for the recipients, and (3) take a hard look at the nature and quality of the teaching methods to determine whether they are meeting the real needs of those who should have more educational background. These points are especially pertinent to the needs of the disadvantaged who are not being well served by the present system.

Although the three facilities discussed below are open to the disadvantaged for training in many categories, the real answer to the problems in Denver must find its way into the elementary and secondary schools.

The Emily Griffith Opportunity School

The Emily Griffith school is a source of continuous training for Denver's labor market and has been used extensively by business and industry to train employees. Its basic orientation is not to the disadvantaged but to successful workers who need additional skills for advancement or to keep up with the pace of technology. Disadvantaged students have not been merged with the regular students and have been made aware of their special status.

Competition with other facilities has caused the school to examine its own program and to provide more flexible and continuous enrollment of MDTA trainees. The main advantage of this school is its location near the center of town where busing for the disadvantaged is not necessary, while other facilities are on the outskirts of Denver.

The Denver Community College

Denver's community college has three campuses, one of which houses the MDTA Skills Center. The college has been more flexible than the Emily Griffith school because students under MDTA training can be placed in ongoing classes with the regular student body; i.e., they are not separated and labeled as "disadvantaged" and they can gain some social and cultural adjustment by associating with nondisadvantaged people. As a result, most of the MDTA training has been shifted there.

The MDTA Skills Center consists of a separate group of administrators within the college to keep track of the enrollees who are differentiated in no way, nor do they take separate classes. MDTA students earn college credits; and a few have chosen to work toward an associate degree. Each MDTA student works at his own level and pace. Registration is open ended, making it possible for the student to join a class at any time and not just at the beginning of a set term, and cutting down on the waiting time between enrollment in MDTA and the start of a program at the college.

For all students, the college stresses open-entry, modular curricula and individualized instruction.

Although the community college is attempting to meet part of the three needs discussed above and admits students irrespective of their past educational background (or lack of it), the college is not without its problems . . . it has been criticized for permissiveness and lack of discipline. More traditionally oriented vocational educators ask how the enrollees can hope to hold a job unless they learn to submit to industrial discipline.

The Manpower Development and Training Act

With the enactment of MDTA in 1962, the potential was created to broaden the training facilities available to Denver's disadvantaged. By December 1962, the first MDTA program was under way in Denver. Through 1970, approximately 3,000 Denver residents had been referred to MDTA institutional training, with funding in excess of $6 million. Statistics concerning these trainees — who they were, what happened to them — and the general operation of MDTA are not easily accessible because no one place has the information. Indeed some data on how many there were are completely missing. Though the numbers (of trainees) available unfortunately do not always agree, the data from the different sources give some idea of the nature, effectiveness, and problems of the Denver program.

A profile of MDTA trainees over the years shows a nearly even number of male and female students. Approximately 75 percent were heads of families; the 10th grade was the average educational attainment, with an average age of 26.6 years. The disadvantaged minorities constituted 39 percent of the enrollees, with blacks comprising 15 percent, Spanish-surnamed 19 percent, and the remaining 5 percent being American Indian and Oriental. Because of the concentrations of unemployment among these groups, need for improvement was recognized, and increased efforts on behalf of minorities raised their proportion among MDTA trainees to 53 percent by the end of 1970. However, this still fell short of the other manpower programs and suggests a continuing white, job-ready bias of the MDTA enrollment system.

For those it served, the Denver MDTA had a relatively good program record. For the state of Colorado, between December 1962 and the end of fiscal year 1968, the placement average for graduates who could be located was 77 percent, compared to the national average of 75 percent. For the same period, Denver had 1,252 known graduates, of whom 891 could be located and from whom information was derived. Of these, 78 percent indicated that they were employed and 66 percent were in training-related. occupations; 103 were unemployed, with an additional 91 having left the labor force.

In 1969 and 1970, the placement success held up despite a slackening of the job market in Denver. A follow-up study found the MDTA enrollees to be employed two-thirds of the available time following training, compared to 59 percent for the three years prior to their enrollment and 63 percent for the previous year before training. Average hourly wages improved $0.40 over those of the last 36 months preceding enrollment and $0.47 over the last preenrollment year. Combining the wage improvements with the improvements in employment stability, we find that the average Denver MDTA enrollee in the follow-up sample who worked after training would have increased his annual income $1,020 over that of the year before training.

Those responsible for administration of the Denver MDTA program both in ES and the Board of Community Colleges and Occupational Training appear well qualified and adaptable in their thinking. Evidence of this is seen in their willingness to test multi-occupation projects and individual referrals as superior to the earlier class type of referral, and to shift from the Emily Griffith school to the community college when they felt that the former was following an approach too rigid for the needs of the disadvantaged. The Board has also been willing to place MDTA projects in private schools.

The program has been improving the employment experience and prospects of a predominantly white group whose obstacles to successful employment were undoubtedly real but are not likely to be so serious as those of the blacks, the Spanish-surnamed, and the American Indians. Although whites predominate among Denver's poor, the follow-up study indicates that enrollment in the slackening labor markets of 1969–70 had shifted sharply in favor of the minority groups.

THE WORK INCENTIVE PROGRAM

Primary responsibility for the WIN program in Denver rests with the Colorado Department of Employment, with the city and county welfare department providing physical examinations, casework services for WIN enrollees (in relation to family planning and budgeting), child care, child support, medical planning and services, housing, casework services (in relation to the recipients' becoming self-supporting), and other services which are a part of the provisions of the existing state welfare plan.

The WIN staff of ES has total responsibility for enrollment, assessment, assignment, orientation, basic education and skills training, work experience, placement, follow-up, and termination. Included as part of these components are counseling and testing, enrollee supervision, job development and placement, supportive and ancillary services, and an employability plan as part of the counseling process.

As elsewhere in the nation, the Denver WIN program has suffered from the absence of a critical category of services originally intended in the program concept. Enrollees were to have been placed as job ready, made job ready through training and school, or have had special work projects arranged for them. Since the special works projects (category 3) were never funded, ES has been forced to assign to other categories those who would have been better served by a work project, resulting in difficulties in keeping these individuals in the program because, more often than not, they have found themselves in components beyond their capacities. The WIN staff has had to terminate the enrollees and return them to welfare or try another component where the enrollees might fare no better.

Between September 1968 and April 30, 1970, the metropolitan WIN program had enrolled 1,592 individuals. A survey of the ethnic composition of these referrals during the first nine months shows a heavy weighting to minority groups, with 22 percent being blacks, 55 percent Spanish-surnamed, and 33 percent whites, with only a sprinkling of American Indians. Of the total, 1,499 had been enrolled in the city of Denver; 810 of the 1,499 had been terminated, and 689 were still "on board."

Seven of the 810 terminees were younger than 35 years of age, 73 percent had less than a high school education, about half were female, 99 percent showed a work history of some sort but also showed substantial periods of unemployment, family size exceeded the U.S. average, and 75 percent were employed in their last preprogram employment at less than $2.01 an hour. On the average, those who had completed or left the program had spent a total of about 29 weeks in the program and its components, with 12 percent involved in the basic education component and 34 percent in institutional vocational training; one-third experienced prevocational training; only one was assigned to OJT; and less than 6 percent were involved in sub- and paraprofessional training at entry jobs in public service fields.

The WIN program in Denver appears to be well operated by a group of dedicated individuals. The flexibility in the program allows them to pursue an employability plan which looks at the rehabilitation of the whole person; and they have high hopes that in the long run, they will successfully get at the problems of the hardcore disadvantaged welfare clients. Despite the evidence of staff capability, many problems, some historical and some current, impede or have impeded the progress of WIN in Denver.

Realization of these problems has (1) motivated WIN to develop new and better record-keeping methods, which should make analysis of program results easier and much more meaningful, (2) initiated programs to develop smoother communications between welfare recipients and the WIN staff, the latter having been looked upon as strangers initially, (3) improved the capabilities of the WIN staff, most of whom started with relatively little experience, (4) moved to prevent the institutional rigidities and red tape of ES from slowing up the handling of clients where the timeliness is often the difference between success and failure, (5) tried to resolve basic philosophical conflicts between welfare and WIN, and (6) sought to reduce the caseload of WIN teams which has been 175 to 200 enrollees to a team, compared to 65 enrollees for a team in the CEP program.

The Denver WIN program director appears open minded, flexible, and eager to improvise. He tries new approaches and, insofar as possible, prevents the institutional rigidities of ES from imposing serious obstacles to a successful program. Whether or not this is achieved, only more experience with the program and the relationships of the WIN staff (both state and local) with their ES administrators, welfare, and educators will tell. The state WIN staff also appears problem oriented and, within their authority, willing to make changes as experience indicates.

But with all of these administrative efforts, the basic problem remains: Relatively few WIN enrollees are employed after training, largely because they are not realistically in the labor force.

Operation SER

Operation SER originally evolved from the experiences of two organizations, the League of United Latin American Citizens and the American GI Forum. In the spring of 1965, job placement centers were operated for the Spanish-surnamed in Houston and Corpus Christi, Texas, under the banner of "Jobs for Progress," and were staffed exclusively with Spanish-surnamed volunteers. They claimed to have done more for the Spanish-surnamed in their short existence than permanent public agencies had been able to accomplish over the years. The two merged to form "Jobs for Progress, Incorporated," declaring as its objectives the elimination of poverty in the Southwest — with special attention to the culturally different — and was named Operation SER which was jointly funded for job development and referral, including a regional skills bank, by the U.S. Office of Economic Opportunity (OEO) and DOL, in June 1966. A small staff was established initially with headquarters in Albuquerque, and the skills bank started placing people in nontraditional jobs.

Sufficient groundwork had been laid by the spring of 1967 through community surveys and development to establish state offices (in Arizona, California, Colorado, New Mexico, and Texas), and the first five local Operation SER projects began during the summer of 1967, one of which was the Denver project. Both the Colorado state office of Operation SER and the local Denver office have operated from the same facility.

A fourth function was added to Denver's Operation SER responsibilities with the approval of an MDTA institutional program comprising 300 slots under an allocation of $550,000 for fiscal year 1969. This MDTA assignment was to conduct orientation and prevocational training (in temporary quarters until the construction of a new building for Operation SER was completed at the end of 1968). Because it is located within the Spanish-surnamed community, the added advantage (in communications with the target group) of easy access to classes is apparent.

The follow-up study of Operation SER enrollees reveals that 53 percent were in the program from three to eight months, 97 percent were in GED and basic education, 74 percent were between 21 and 34 years of age, 91 percent were Spanish-surnamed, only 11 percent were high school graduates, one of three was single, and there was about even division between males and females. Of the Operation SER participants, 81 percent were heads of households, 62 percent had one to three dependents, and two of five were on welfare. Based on a comparison of the pre- to the posttraining hourly wage, Operation SER graduates showed positive improvement for those employed and about a 75 percent placement rate. However, stability of employment in the posttraining period was poor. Those who found jobs after participation worked only one-third of the available time, with 81 percent of those placed unemployed 50 percent or more of the posttraining employment period. The average for the small sample therefore was a worsening in employment stability. As a result, though average hourly wage rates improved substantially, there was no significant improvement in average incomes. On the surface, Operation SER is impressive . . . it has a nice building, an adequate staff, and national recognition . . . but there are no records upon which anyone can make an evaluation or judgment.

Opportunities Industrialization Center

The Denver OIC is loosely affiliated with the national OIC organization begun in Philadelphia under the leadership of the Reverends Leon H. Sullivan and Thomas J. Ritter. Typical of the national OIC programs, it was left to the initiative of each community to marshal its own resources for an OIC program and then to associate with the national organization. Financing of the initial planning and action stages of the Denver OIC in 1967 came through a grant of approximately $20,000 from Denver Opportunity and through private donations. The first director was a good public relations man but a poor administrator who was asked for his resignation when he used the planning grant for payment of people and services involved in the program.

Between January and July 15, 1968, when the present director assumed office, OIC was successively directed by leadership from the national OIC, by a director who stayed one month, and by an acting director. In the meantime, with the aid of the national office, the program was being reorganized. In addition to the original grant, OIC has been the recipient of a $22,000 grant from the state. Aside from these funds, OIC has been entirely dependent upon private contributions. It receives some technical assistance from the national OIC and is subject to regular evaluation of its program.

Denver's OIC does not seek to serve blacks exclusively, but because of its location and perhaps its national affiliation, most clients are blacks. For example, from May 20 through October 2, 1968, the counseling department reported a total of 674 referrals, of whom 500 were black, 95 Spanish-surnamed, and 79 white.

Program components include recruitment, intake, orientation, basic education or prevocational training, vocational training, supportive services (including agency referrals, guidance, and counseling), and job placement. A major objective is motivation and a sense of self-worth.

OIC has projected for the future ambitious plans which must remain dependent upon funding. For example, a planned commercial education department, if realized, would result in more than 1,000 students being accommodated. The instructors and staff appear sufficiently well qualified technically and possess a high degree of dedication to serving the disadvantaged. They appear to have done a great deal with a minimum of support, though they have no data with which an outsider can check their performances. The empathy of the organizational staff with its clientele is one decided advantage of the program.

OIC complains that referrals of NAB-JOBS openings first to CEP and the Denver Opportunity centers imposes a hardship on OIC and other private agencies seeking to serve the disadvantaged. OIC would like to see more direct contact and a faster referral system which would not show favoritism. Also, it feels it is the only organization prepared to serve the blacks because CEP and the other manpower programs, for the most part, lie outside the black community, while OIC facilities are ideally located in the middle of the black population in Denver.

DENVER'S TRAINING PROGRAMS IN SUMMARY

Denver has the usual variety of training programs which are funneled through the Emily Griffith school, the community college, and a number of private schools. The schools have generally offered an adequate quality of instruction and training but with strengths and weaknesses uniquely related to the particular type of school. The Emily Griffith and private schools have enjoyed a locational advantage over the community college which is some distance from the group to be served. The community college offers the advantage of a less structured approach, with open registration and learning geared to the progress of each individual. The private schools, though sometimes not up to the quality of Emily Griffith and the community college, are nevertheless better structured to bring the individual enrollee through training to job proficiency within a set framework of time. The community college, through its assimilation and the absence of separate identification of manpower program enrollees, serves an important function in helping participants become socially adjusted. Aside from these institutions involved in training the disadvantaged, Denver fails to provide a balance between the needs of those students who will seek less than a college level type of employment compared with those who will go on to college.

With respect to the training program sponsors, it is questionable whether MDTA in Denver has been sufficiently oriented toward the disadvantaged and the minorities, although the last year shows great improvement. WIN appears to offer promise and has made a good start. However, training is only the first step toward employability — the real test of success is in placement results. Other training groups such as Operation SER and OIC have probably had only minimal impact. In practice, these programs have been inwardly oriented, aimed at specific ethnic groups, and divisive and duplicative rather than blending into a coordinated effort to solve Denver's manpower problems. Offering both the advantage of ethnic group identification and blending into a coordinated manpower effort seem to be much better accomplished by the inclusion of ethnic counselors and job developers on staffs such as CEP.

No program or set of programs, however, appears to be surmounting the handicap of separateness and the lack of coordination among various program efforts on behalf of a common target group. While there is a certain amount of communication from one program to another in Denver, there is little evidence of a real effort to make the disadvantaged individual the chief focus of all efforts, with all agencies and organizations in the city working toward a common goal. Each agency uses services of the others to some extent, but still acts as an independent program with its own needs to serve, its own budget to protect, and its own image to protect — even at the expense of the common objectives. Factors such as these result in overlapping services and the playing off of one program against another by the disadvantaged and others (such as small businessmen) who see promise of financial gain.

THE DENVER JOBS PROGRAM

Denver has a unique history in the development of its NAB-JOBS program. The Denver Metropolitan Chamber of Commerce had created and had begun to implement a program almost identical in concept with NAB-JOBS before Lyndon Johnson asked for a new partnership between government and private industry to train and hire the hardcore unemployed, and thus created NAB during his administration.

The initial beginnings of the Denver experience started about a year before the national JOBS program was announced. In June 1967, the mayor of Denver held meetings — with labor leaders, with leading businessmen, and with educational administrators — to explore the extent of the unrest and scope of problems facing the city's ghetto residents. The primary reason for the meetings was to institute action to avoid the kinds of riots other cities had experienced. Following this initial exploration of the problems of the severely disadvantaged, the mayor approached the Denver Metropolitan Chamber of Commerce and asked it to develop a positive employment program (since unemployment and underemployment had clearly emerged as major factors generating unrest in other cities).

The chamber of commerce had already organized into action-oriented, functional subcommittees, and this specific task was assigned to a 15-member "Committee for Metropolitan Political Affairs" who, in turn, asked the president of the local telephone company to be chairman to develop a still-unspecified program aimed basically at widening employment opportunities for disadvantaged persons. At least 10 of the 15 committee members were at the vice presidential level of their firms. The chairman felt that the committee must have top leaders from the business community if it was to get the response of full commitment needed to find means of employing the disadvantaged. He chose one of his own vice presidents who had previously been president of the chamber of commerce as a working director of the committee.

The committee's first effort was aimed at obtaining an accurate, in-depth picture of the employment problems of Denver's minority population. Most staff work in this regard was done by the research department of the telephone company which produced a good statistical profile of Denver. The committee was astonished at the brobdingnagian chasm which separated the disadvantaged from the economic mainstream in Denver and attempted to involve minority businessmen in its efforts. However, it found that there were no businessmen from ethnic minorities in the area. There were barber shop proprietors and owners of small shops, but virtually no blacks or browns who owned businesses which employed others.

Not wishing to raise the hopes of the minorities, the committee, late in 1967, prepared a presentation for Denver's white businessmen, asking for commitment to "hire and train" the city's disadvantaged. When, through a series of sensitivity meetings, the committee felt that the commitment was sufficiently assured, it approached the minority leaders to reveal its carefully structured efforts and plans . . . but met an unexpectedly negative reaction! The blacks especially were disturbed because they had not been consulted and had been left out during the planning process. Eventually, after serious discussions and efforts to obtain the confidence of the minority leaders, the critical issues began to be resolved. For example, it was jointly decided that employers should forego any formal testing until after the disadvantaged employee had established himself as part of the work force. Police records were not to be a deterrent to employment, and there was general agreement on across-the-board lowering of hiring standards.

Before a press conference could be held to "kick off" the planned effort, the NAB program was launched nationally; and the chairman of the businessmen's committee was asked to be the Denver metro chairman. He accepted because the programs were so similar, and tapped his subordinate as full-time metro director. The businessmen's presentation was modified to reflect the joint NAB-Denver chamber of commerce program. The original concept of program self-support was scrapped. Quotas which had been studiously avoided in the original chamber of commerce plan were established.

Initial pledges were secured by bringing businessmen to the briefing center at the chamber of commerce in groups of 15. After the briefing and initial sensitivity session, a pledge request was made, written information — including a pledge packet — was distributed, and the men were sent back to their companies to confirm a final number of pledges. Although the program was able to fill its quota of pledges, less than 1 percent of Denver's 7,000 to 8,000 businesses responded to any extent; and the pledges from the city's large companies were relatively small.

In February 1969, the second pledge campaign was begun. NAB requested and received about 20 executives on loan from local firms. Their effort was aimed at direct business contacts to obtain both summer youth and permanent pledges. The result was pledges for 700 permanent jobs and 200 summer jobs. Because of the relatively poor response on the summer jobs, a special campaign was organized to boost these pledges. The second round was done by phone, staffed by volunteer women from the city's social and political service organizations. As a result of this last effort, 1,447 summer jobs were obtained, bringing this total to 1,647.

For the total period, June 1967 to August 1, 1969, permanent jobs totaling 2,500 were pledged, 1,038 persons were hired, 647 were reported as still employed, and 1,108 summer youth hires had been made.

In the first 18 months of the program, the Denver NAB-JOBS organization had two metro chairmen, three metro directors, two steering committees, and two job managers — a tremendous turnover in administration and staff, making it very difficult to maintain any sort of consistent effort and continuity. Except for the original metro director, there had been no full-time personnel — except two staff people provided by the chamber of commerce. Another metro chairman took office through the spring of 1971, intending to be relieved of that position after he had completed two years. The result was the first sign of stability in the organization. Initially, little contact occurred between the NAB organization and CEP and other manpower agencies outside ES.

CEP was funded in 1970 for an employment relations group consisting of several employer relations specialists. The major function of this team was to convert employer pledges into job orders. Starting from the printouts of pledges developed by the Denver NAB, team members worked back to the employers to determine why so many pledges had never been converted into job orders or jobs. Wherever possible, they attempted to interest the businessmen in contract support and referred them to the Colorado ES unit responsible for writing the JOBS contracts. As an early result of this effort, the staff recommended the elimination of the annual all-out pledge campaigns. These campaigns, they reported, result in a gigantic backlog of pledges that could not be followed up adequately. Pressure under which the pledges were made resulted in commitments which the employers had no intention of fulfilling, making it difficult for the program to retain credibility in the community. Instead, the CEP team advocated a continuous and persistent follow-up program whereby leads furnished to the employer relations group could be converted into job orders of real substance. The CEP staff considered the chamber of commerce effort primarily one of public relations and were convinced that they could do a better job of employer contact, seeking simultaneous pledges and job orders.

Local chamber of commerce officials and the business community remained jealous of the fact that the Denver NAB-JOBS program was basically an extension of a local idea and program already developed, even though not fully implemented before the NAB program was announced. After accepting the NAB-JOBS program, the local NAB officials refused to allow the national NAB executive director to visit Denver to help launch the program. In fact, throughout its history, the Denver NAB has been cool in its relationship with Washington and the national NAB office.

Most of the limited number of Denver employers who involved themselves in the NAB-JOBS effort even slightly prided themselves on their commitment to private enterprise and their resentment at government interference, despite the relative importance of defense contracts in the area. This attitude was reflected in the extremely limited use of the DOL contracts in the first two years. A total of 108 jobs was negotiated in the first round of contracts. Contracts varied from the largest with a missile maker for 44 female clerical trainees to a contract with an electrical contractor for two male electrical helper trainees. Only eight contracts were entered into initially, with five being for less than 10 jobs and three contracts ranging from 20 to 44 jobs. Ten contracts were concluded in the second round, two with firms already having contracts and one with a consortium representing automobile dealers.

With experience, ES increased its commitment to the Denver NAB-JOBS program, both in the intensity of effort and the number of staff people involved. The ES team reported that the bulk of the contracts it had written had been the direct result of its own initial contracts with employers rather than a follow-up on NAB pledges or through contracts from any other group. The attitude of the ES staff was to dismiss the effectiveness of NAB and to play down the efforts of CEP as a promoter of job orders, though the ES team accepted CEP as a filler of job orders. Even there, the NAB team of ES credited ES's HRD activities for most of the referral and placements under NAB-JOBS. ES also took great pride in the quality of its job orders and placements and in their retention rate, but it provided no hard data to support its claim.

Looking at the pattern of the ES placements, we find that ES apparently retained the same traditional preconception of the kinds of jobs disadvantaged people could fill. Predominantly, these were laborer's jobs in furniture manufacturing and upholstering establishments, meatcutters, skinners, packers, and shoe repairmen.

Only one of the NAB contractors appeared to have a deep commitment to hiring and retaining the disadvantaged, though others did well with what they were doing. Most of the participants saw their activity as a civic duty. However, a few were brash enough to state that the employment obstacles for the disadvantaged were too serious for solution, but they had no objection to some additional cash flow if it was available for hiring those they would have hired anyway. Some of the more enlightened companies appeared to be doing their duty, though with considerable "skimming." Others were hiring the disadvantaged in small numbers with a severely limited commitment of their own resources.

Random interviews with employers who did not have NAB-JOBS contracts disclosed that very few were aware of the program, and where awareness existed, it was limited to just a few in each company. The tendency was for the individual to have his knowledge limited to newspaper reports, making presumptions concerning the program generally negative. Information had come to their attention only when a controversy about manpower programs had arisen.

Some had made pledges but had not taken them seriously or fulfilled them. Some had made pledges and accepted applicants, but after a bad experience with one or two, had disavowed further involvement. By and large, these firms appeared to consider the objective of the program good but not really very practicable. When race was mentioned in a negative manner with reference to manpower programs, it was always in the context of blacks causing trouble as contrasted with Spanish-surnamed.

From the beginning of the program until January 1971, it was claimed that 2,881 individuals had been hired under the NAB-JOBS program in Denver, terminations had numbered 1,332, and 1,549 individuals were ostensibly "on board." The Denver economy had not suffered as seriously as that of other cities from the economic downturn throughout the nation. Unemployment remained at about 3.5 percent for the entire city, with estimates of 7 to 12 percent in those areas where disadvantaged persons were concentrated. Because of the general strength of the Denver economy, the NAB-JOBS program had retained its goal of 2,600 individuals hired and "on board" by July 1, 1971, though it was clear that this objective would not be reached.

Before the advent of NAB-JOBS, the largest MDTA-OJT contractor in Denver had been the Spanish-surnamed action group, La Rasa, which obtained a 1,000 slot DOL contract. Though its program was generally well run, particularly in coupled institutional-OJT effort, La Rasa was accused of subsidizing second-rate employees. For example, it had contracts with mattress and furniture manufacturers which had turnover rates of up to 100 percent per year and paid minimum wages. Nevertheless, when NAB-JOBS came on the scene, $3,000 a head looked better than $25 per week for 26 weeks. These employers sought and received NAB-JOBS contracts, and La Rasa found itself with no more takers for OJT.

CEP, the agency in Denver probably most directly aware of the needs and attitudes of the disadvantaged, operated a two-track job referral system in relation to these NAB-JOBS orders. When a job came through from one of the mattress or furniture firms or others characterized by low skill and high turnover, CEP would either choose not to refer anyone or tended to refer those persons it considered to be transient or less motivated. It reserved the better jobs and those which had been developed as the result of CEP efforts to CEP's own enrollees.

Those involved in the Denver NAB-JOBS program seemed to know little about the characteristics of the enrollees, the turnover rates, the reasons for termination, or the reasons for success. ES in its contract-writing process tended to predetermine what kinds of employers would hire the disadvantaged by choosing the employers it offered contracts. CEP continued to develop its own ties with employers, with the conviction that only it had the skill and knowledge to convince employers that to hire the disadvantaged was a socially desirable action. The NAB organization continued to flounder, trying to use task forces and other on-loan assistance to accomplish things that could only be effectively done through a higher level of commitment from the management and directorship of the chamber of commerce that in fact existed.

The impact of NAB-JOBS is harder to judge than that of the training programs. One firm made an outstanding commitment and contribution. Several did very well by the few disadvantaged they were willing to accept. Many others probably changed their personnel practices to a significant degree. The total involvement in Denver was very small, but it was all a positive improvement.

The use of DOL's NAB-JOBS contracts rose during 1970 and 1971. Some combination of the increased need for cash flow on the part of the employers and the more aggressive efforts of CEP and ES seemed to be the reason. Two messages appear to have surfaced from the Denver experience: (1) Few employers could be won to a wholehearted commitment to help the disadvantaged, but a respectable number of employers could be convinced to change their recruitment, selection, and hiring practices modestly, and (2) in the long run, the employer-contracting task could only be carried on by a public agency.

Impact of Denver's Manpower Programs

8

Denver's manpower problems differ little from any other large city in the Southwest . . . a centrifugal migration to the suburbs of both people and jobs, leaving a central city vacuum to be filled by immigration of blacks and Spanish-surnamed who lack education and job skills. Beginning with MDTA in 1962, NYC in 1965, and CEP, WIN, and the NAB-JOBS program in 1968, along with some special programs such as Operation SER, La Rasa, and the Labor Education Advancement Program, the city exhibits the usual complement of program activities.

A key feature of the Denver manpower programs has been the lack of an integrated network or system of manpower services. Rather, there has been a variety of separate and largely unrelated programs with only minimal impact on each other. Even those run by the same agency have evidenced a remarkable separatism. Neither the city of Denver, which is the designated sponsor of the NYC program and CEP, nor the Colorado Department of Employment, which is playing a key role in all the programs, nor CEP, which was to serve as an umbrella organization for manpower programs, has in any real sense served to tie the programs together or to transfer favorable experience from one program to another.

The lack of a central system for administration, information, and evaluation has appreciably hampered the achievable success of the Denver manpower programs. This had resulted in the following problems:

(1) Overlapping and competition among disparate self-serving programs for enrollees and jobs

(2) Duplication of services to potential enrollees

(3) Enrollees playing one program against another

(4) Generally poor methods of data keeping which impair effective and objective evaluation of individual and, more importantly, overall program services

(5) Confusion in identifying manpower goals and failure to establish implementing machinery which will bring the total resources of the community to bear most effectively on manpower problems

(6) Failure to project an image of community cooperation in attacking community manpower programs, which would enhance participant and public support of the efforts of the various manpower groups which might have developed had there been a united front among manpower programs

While the lack of a central system for administration, information, and evaluation has hampered efforts in Denver, the manpower programs are not without their successes or a positive impact on Denver. A complete judgment can only be arrived at through a more detailed examination of the impact, both qualitatively and quantitatively, of these programs upon Denver, its institutional and manpower services, and its disadvantaged peoples.

TOTAL IMPACT

If we acknowledge the impossibility of isolating all other forces which might affect the impact attributed to manpower programs upon Denver, it still seems valid, without attributing degree of impact, to make the following observations based on generally conservative estimates:

(1) In excess of 20,000 citizens of Denver were served by manpower programs between 1962 and 1970.

(2) In excess of 7,000 citizens of Denver were placed in jobs through manpower programs between 1962 and 1970.

(3) In excess of $35 million in federal funds were allocated to the Denver area for manpower programs between 1962 and 1970.

(4) The manpower programs themselves account for more than 400 staff jobs to meet their administrative needs.

The attitudinal impact of the manpower programs upon Denver is not measurable but is undoubtedly important. While attitudes have not been affected as much as they might under a more unified and goal-oriented manpower system, the various ways in which the manpower programs have affected attitudes cannot lightly be dismissed. More than 20,000 individuals have come in contact, for better or worse, with manpower program efforts in their behalf; businessmen, educational institutions, elected officials, and unions are now more involved and more knowledgeable concerning manpower problems than before; traditional conveyers of services to the unemployed, such as ES, have been made aware that their obligations go deeper than the screening-out process allowed them to go in the past; and the public has been made more aware that the problems of the disadvantaged in their midst cannot be ignored or wished away. All in all, the social consciousness, which grew at an accelerated rate under the impact of the civil rights movement, was broadened and increased in magnitude as manpower programs dramatized the plight of a permanent and growing disadvantaged population. For the Denver area, this growing social consciousness must be considered, qualitatively at least, a positive and favorable effect of Denver's manpower programs, not so much in terms of what it has caused to happen but in terms of the ground it lays for future program development.

Impact on Existing Institutions

Five institutional groups with relevance to programs of the disadvantaged predate the emergence of manpower programs and are vital to the success of such programs. The impact of manpower programs upon these groups — education, political groups, business, unions, ES — is therefore relevant in any assessment of the effect manpower programs have had on the Denver area.

Education

The manpower programs have made no noticeable dent in the Denver education system in general but have impacted upon the two institutions most directly involved. The Emily Griffith Opportunity School has been forced to reassess its stance vis-à-vis the disadvantaged, though the change has been relatively minor. The community college increases the capability of Denver to meet manpower training needs, to provide flexibility of programming, and to bring about social and cultural adjustment of the disadvantaged with the nondisadvantaged. It suffers from location, permissiveness, lack of discipline, and program control, but is one of the outstanding institutions in the nation for bridging the gap between the disadvantaged and the mainstream. Its manpower program involvement has undoubtedly been a major factor in establishing its philosophy.

Political Groups

The state of Colorado has not as yet really committed itself to action in the manpower field. This is largely attributable to a fractured administrative arrangement in the state, the reluctance of the governor to take on the political battles involved in moving into the manpower area, and the fact that most of the advice he is getting is to "go slow" in this area. The governor has taken a "hands off" attitude relative to manpower programs in the city and county of Denver. Colorado's "wait and see" approach may be typical of many states presently, although it is unclear what they will do as CAMPS guidelines become more specific in moving toward manpower planning councils and in terms of the kind of federal legislation that might finally emerge.

At the city level, it appears that officials in the mayor's office are increasingly aware of the city's problems and are willing to take on almost any federal program that will give them the capacity to deal with the social problems of the city. However, they are focusing their priorities on the programs in which they have actual control of the program dollars — assuming with apparent correctness that they are not going to have much success in interfacing with the programs where these are largely state controlled. As a consequence, the city has made little attempt to tie in with the state programs such as vocational rehabilitation and vocational education, has shown only marginal interest in the WIN program, has viewed CAMPS as a paper tiger, and believes strongly that it matters little whether or not the state is involved in the area manpower program.

The mayor has established a coordinating office for city social programs (the Urban Resources Development Agency) which may eventually become a program planning agency for the city with responsibility for interfacing the specialized federal aid programs with the city's ongoing activities. So far, results have been minimal. Even if, through political clout, a unification of manpower policy for the city of Denver could be achieved, it still would leave unresolved the even more difficult task of bringing together the divergent political interests of the other metropolitan area counties in order to bring the manpower programs together at the most effective level — the labor market area. There is little likelihood of achieving this unification of manpower programs through the logical mechanism, metropolitan government.

Business

Business occupies a key position in the success of any manpower program since the end objective of the program is employability and business is the major purveyor of jobs. Favorable reaction of Denver businessmen to manpower programs and the needs of the disadvantaged has been agonizingly slow in developing, miniscule in size, and somewhat mixed in results, but promising. Companies that were surveyed reflected varying degrees of commitment, ranging from deep concern to willingness to do civic duty, to a source of cash flow available to hire those they would have hired anyway. Some were doing well with what they were doing, some seemed to be doing their duty but with considerable "skimming," some made pledges to employ the disadvantaged but did not take their pledges seriously, and others were hiring the disadvantaged in small numbers but with a severely limited commitment of their own resources.

Unions

Until 1969, union involvement in Denver area manpower programs was conspicuously absent. The Labor Education Advancement Program (LEAP) of the building trades was the significant exception. Most unions were so established in their middle-class philosophy that they were hardly aware of the problems of the disadvantaged and the goals of the manpower programs. Nudged by the AFL-CIO, Denver unions established a Human Resources Development Institute in 1969 to bring organized labor into partnership with other groups seeking to aid the disadvantaged. During the initial phases of the program, apathy continued to reflect union attitudes toward manpower programs. Gradually through the efforts of the Institute's director, apathy began to be replaced by awareness, then understanding, then interest, and finally by action of Denver unions.

Chief among the obstacles which had to be overcome was a breaking down of the old ethnic prejudices of the unions, especially craft groups. "Buddy" programs have been initiated to help the disadvantaged adjust to the job and skill environment, to effect cooperation between unions and employers in placing and training the disadvantaged, and to bring about broader coalitions of unions, employers, and minority representatives to deal with employment problems of not just the disadvantaged but the minority disadvantaged. Illustrative of the latter is the Denver coalition representing the construction trades, building contractors, and a minority coalition. Evolving from this coalition is the Metropolitan Denver Minorities Construction Agreement of 1970, the purpose of which is to increase minority employment in the construction industry and admission into unions. In the coalition are three contractor representatives with responsibility for jobs, three union representatives with responsibility for training, and six minority group representatives responsible for recruiting and counseling. Goals of the organizations are (1) to recruit 400 minority employees in the first 18 months and 300 a year thereafter for five years, and (2) in each union to bring minority membership to the same proportion of total membership as in the general population (17 percent). Concrete results of significance are still in the future, but changes in attitudes, though gradual, are readily identifiable.

Employment Service

Despite the intransigence at top levels, those closest to the action in Denver ES offices have clearly changed their attitudes and commitments. The attitude change is taking place more rapidly in programs such as WIN, less rapidly in programs such as MDTA. The progress will continue to be slow so long as the former administrator occupies a position where he can influence state policy and continues to feel that the focus on manpower is in fact rapidly sending ES "to hell in a handbasket" and that the best policy for Colorado should be little more than watchful waiting.

ENROLLEE IMPACT

The ultimate test of a manpower program must be its impact upon the employment and earning experiences of the target groups for which it is designed. Given the emphasis of national manpower policy upon the problems of disadvantaged minority groups, Table 8-1 must reflect credit upon Denver's manpower programs. Every program for which information is available shows a very strong emphasis upon minority group placement.

TABLE 8-1

Percentage Distribution of Placements
(By program and ethnic group)

Program	Black	White/ Other	Spanish- Surnamed	American Indian	Other
WIN	24.0%	16.0%	50.0%	9.0%	
New Careers	43.0	7.0	50.0		
WTE	35.0	1.0	53.0	11.0%	
Operation Mainstream	10.0	10.0	80.0		
Project Value	40.0	5.0	55.0		
Operation SER		3.0	93.0		6.0%
LEAP	74.0%	12.0%	14.0%		

It is important to note the pull of ethnic counselors or groups upon individuals of their own ethnic group, as shown by Operation Mainstream and Operation SER.

Of the more than 20,000 individuals served by the Denver manpower programs, approximately 58 percent were male. Some programs such as Operation Mainstream and LEAP were the exclusive province of males. Other programs, such as WIN, while serving more females than males, had been expected to involve much higher proportions of females than actually occurred. Denver's manpower programs have been predominantly the province of the young, the mean age of the enrollees being 27. Only a few programs have served enrollees older than 45 years of age — WIN, MDTA, WTE, New Careers — but in no case in excess of 11 percent. Since pre-enrollment wages averaged only $1.89 an hour, while the average enrollee worked only 43 percent of the time during the preceding 12 months and had 2.6 dependents, the average enrollee was clearly below the poverty line. While some programs such as MDTA showed a substantial proportion of their enrollees with 12 years of schooling or more, this was somewhat atypical of enrollees in all manpower programs in Denver and reflects the MDTA continuing preference for the job-ready individual. For all enrollees, the educational pattern of an average of 9.7 years of schooling was consistent with other enrollee characteristics.

The end objective of manpower programs is employability — a job generating a decent level of living. Considerable variation was found among the programs for which data were available relative to their placements, but the overall picture, if assessed against a tightening labor market and a difficult-to-place clientele, indicates moderate success. The placement rate as a proportion of those available for work after training for those programs for which data were available is as follows:

Program	Placement Rate
MDTA	73.0% (all terminations)
New Careers	70.0
JOBS	68.0
WIN	65.0
Project Value	64.0
WTE	59.0
Title V	49.0
Operation Mainstream	47.0%

Note that New Careers, which was discontinued because of program problems, had the highest placement rate, while Operation Mainstream, dealing with some of the most difficult to place, had the lowest.

Overall program results indicate some improvement in wage rates from an average of $1.89 an hour in the preprogram period to an average postprogram wage rate of $2.07, or an increase in average wages of $0.18 an hour. At the same time, employment stability increased from 43 to 57 percent in the same period. Since the period was one of slack labor markets, there is no reason to have expected an improvement in employment stability in absence of program participation. However, wage rates in the whole economy were drifting upward and may have accounted for one-half of the average wage gain.

If we combine employment stability with average wage rates for the two periods, this would indicate an increase in annual income from $1,634 in the preprogram period to $2,640 in the postprogram period. Individuals in different manpower programs, of course, experienced varied outcomes in terms of wage and earnings changes. There were also differences by sex and ethnic groups.

Preprogram wage rates as shown in Table 8-2 do not show great differentials for enrollees in various programs except for Operation Mainstream. Postprogram wage rates reflect an overall improvement for all programs over the preprogram rates, with considerable leveling between programs except WIN and HRD. This seems to indicate, despite variations in preprogram employability and in program services both within and between programs, that the strictures of the labor market upon employment opportunities to formerly disadvantaged people prevent differences in programs and program services from manifesting themselves in the postprogram wage rates. The poorer postprogram wage rates of WIN and HRD cannot be accurately compared to the other program results because WIN results are heavily biased by the inclusion of a substantial group of youth (18- and 19-

TABLE 8-2

Average Wage Rate Changes in Pre- and Postprograms
(By manpower program)

Program	Preprogram Wage Rates	Postprogram Wage Rates	Change in Average Rates
MDTA	$1.72	$2.19	$0.47
WIN	1.74	2.00	0.26
New Careers	1.76	2.27	0.51
WTE	1.81	2.23	0.42
Operation Mainstream	2.14	2.17	0.03
Project Value	1.66	2.25	0.59
HRD	1.70	1.95	0.25
Operation SER	$1.76	$2.25	$0.49

year-olds) placed through the YOC-HRD program. The leveling off of postprogram wage rates between programs — including WIN and HRD at the lower end of the spectrum — may also indicate that further expectations for wage improvements of those placed are poor and that the major value of the involvement in manpower programs for enrollees placed in jobs has been achieved.

Wage gains did not differ significantly by ethnic grouping, even though whites enjoyed the highest wages both before and after enrollment. Employment for women, while improving relative to men, was still considerably less. Female enrollees increased their average wage rates by $0.73, more than twice as much as the $0.34 by which the average wage rate for men increased. Yet the average postprogram wage rate for men was still at $2.28 an hour, significantly above the average wage rate of $1.83 an hour for women.

In summary, improvements in average rates between pre- and postprogram employment, when combined with stability of employment, showed a definite increase in annual earnings, but still left most of the individuals at relatively low levels of income. Though the differentials in average rates between whites and minority groups and between males and females were narrowed, the evidence is that discrimination on ethnic and sex lines is still a basic fact. While enrollees on the average experienced improvement in wages and income, the narrow range of the gains and the posttraining wages suggests a limitation in the kind of jobs available and the possible wage and income gains.

SUMMARY AND RECOMMENDATIONS

Manpower programs have not been without impact upon Denver. Money has flowed into the city that would not have been available without such programs; institutions and people have become more cognizant of the social and economic implications of poverty; genuine efforts have been made by various groups involved in Denver's manpower programs to do something about the problems of the disadvantaged. Furthermore, there is evidence that many individuals have been placed in jobs and that for those placed, there has not only been a wage rate improvement but also greater stability of employment.

On the other hand, much of Denver's manpower efforts have been dissipated through duplication of services, through the inability of the various manpower groups to put aside personal differences and mount a coordinated onslaught on manpower problems, through the confusion and difficulty in trying to apply conflicting and sometimes unrealistic national guidelines to the local situation, and through the limitations that the labor market has imposed upon job development and long-term income improvement.

If Denver's manpower programs are to have sufficient impact to keep pace with and perhaps exceed the rate at which the problems of employment of the disadvantaged are increasing, a number of changes must be effected.

1. Manpower programs, though funded nationally, must be regionalized or localized in the sense that they need to be formulated to fit problems of each individual area. Much waste and confusion are caused by trying to impose uniform, nationally conceived programs on areas each of which has its own unique characteristics and program needs.

2. There is a need for the state of Colorado to assume a much more positive and direct role in determining program and fund distribution to various areas of the state.

3. There is need for central labor-marketwide manpower administration. Only the total area, where the major forces determining the employment of people are in interplay, is workable as the base for effective administration and coordination of manpower efforts. Anything short of that leaves uncontrolled forces that may affect the results within the area being administered. Despite the difficulties of central administration and coordination within an area in which there may be competing local political units, an effective manpower program can only be mounted if, through a workable coalition of municipal governments or the formation of a metropolitan government, a central system of manpower administration is established contiguous to the labor market area. This would help solve a serious administrative problem now hampering the success of manpower programs in the Denver area; namely, molding the various parts of a manpower program — intake, assessment, training, job development, and placement — into a coordinated, smoothly functioning operation.

4. Along with the need for a system of central administration, there is also a need for a central information system based on the labor market area. This provides a much more meaningful basis for the service efforts of manpower programs since it relates to the appropriate area — the labor market — in which jobs must be found and income generated by (a) providing more concise and accurate information of the nature and number of job openings and thus affording more accurate direction to training efforts, (b) providing a more efficient and faster system of matching men to jobs, (c) eliminating competition and duplication of efforts among manpower agencies using a variety of information sources, and (d) establishing a basis for more uniform and comparable data collection.

5. Since the major market forces determining both the nature and size of the manpower problem are a function of the labor market, evaluation is most meaningful if conducted on the basis of the labor market area as a whole. To achieve the maximum effectiveness, an evaluation unit should have complete access to data concerning manpower programs in the area, the methods of record keeping should be standardized for the labor market as a whole to bring about comparability for evaluation purposes, and the evaluation unit should be independent of but have access to the operational aspects of manpower programs in the Denver area. Agencies currently spend an undue amount of time educating a stream of evaluators, one after another, whose origin, responsibilities, and relations to each other and the programs are uncertain. Resident, professional, labor-marketwide, multi-program evaluation could provide objective, continued understanding and permanent resource for manpower planning.

Part 3
The San Francisco-Oakland Bay Area Experience

Lloyd Gallardo

The San Francisco-Oakland Bay Area

9

The key political issues which set the environment for manpower and antipoverty programs in the San Francisco-Oakland Bay area are those of region and race. The standard metropolitan statistical area (SMSA) encompasses a geographical spectrum of more than 3,000 square miles (including the inland waterways), divided among the five counties of Alameda, Contra Costa, Marin, San Francisco, and San Mateo. Yet half of its population of more than three million is crowded into 250 square miles — the SMSA's urban core — along the shores of San Francisco Bay in Alameda, Contra Costa, and San Francisco counties.

That core on the west side of the bay has consisted of the city and county of San Francisco — the two have identical boundaries and share a single government — the state's second most populous city. San Francisco is the administrative center of the bay area as well as the headquarters for many finance, transportation, manufacturing, and government establishments.

On the east side of the bay there are the "flatland communities," as the area between the bay and the foothills to the east is called, extending from Hayward in the south to San Pablo in the north. Located here is the traditional industrial heart of the San Francisco metropolitan area, the three adjacent cities of Oakland, Berkeley, and Emeryville. Within the urbanized core are found the area's three central cities, Oakland, Richmond, and San Francisco, each with the same general economies and varied problems that beset central cities across the nation.

Region and Race: The Problems Compounded

Politically, the bay area is highly complex . . . highlighted by the fact that it embraces 15 cities abutting on each other . . . and has had difficulty operating to solve regional problems. One recent illustration was the long delays and intercity squabbles over financing experienced by the bay area rapid transit system which was supposed to supply the area with an efficient, rapid transportation network.

Although the bay area's sizable population of minority groups has obvious difficulties in using existing transportation systems (irrespective of where they may live) and although the cost of intercity transportation is prohibitively high for the bay area's poor, the transportation issue has a direct effect on manpower efforts only in Hunters Point, the deteriorating World War II concentration of shipbuilders on the waterfront southeast of the city. Transportation "down the peninsula" is not only expensive but also inconvenient for Hunters Point residents, and access to the growing industrial complex southwest of Oakland on the East Bay side is nearly impossible. Yet there is nothing in the transit system's plan that would relieve the isolation of Hunters Point. Other disadvantaged populations are handicapped by the restricted mobility posed by water barriers and limited transportation, but not to the degree that makes the lack obvious. For most, the deficiencies of their own neighborhoods and communities are greater irritants.

Another illustration of the regional problems has been the inability to jointly plan land use to safeguard the bay from filling up with debris and being encroached upon by landfills for new industrial and residential properties. Central city deterioration, including dilapidated housing, is a fact of life in all metropolitan areas in the United States. The national norm holds true for the San Francisco-Oakland Bay area. The clumsiness of federal efforts at urban renewal has produced some harsh political confrontations, particularly in San Francisco.

The same political separatism is reflected in the area's manpower and poverty programs. Thus it contains five community action agencies (CAA), two Skills Centers, four model cities programs, three Concentrated Employment Program (CEP) offices, and three Work Incentive (WIN) programs.

The Convergence of Regional and Racial Problems

Many of the bay area's manpower and poverty problems are direct consequences of World War II developments which attracted thousands of rural workers to urban war industries and then left them stranded. Though Oakland before the war had the largest concentration of blacks on the West Coast, they numbered only 8,500 in 1940, or 2.8 percent of the population. By 1960, 23 percent of Oakland's population, 83,600 of 367,500 persons, were black. By 1970, the number had reached 125,000 and the proportion 35 percent.

Most of the city's blacks lived in West Oakland in 1950. During that decade, however, they moved increasingly into the neighboring sections of North and East Oakland and to the adjoining cities of Berkeley and Emeryville. There they occupied the homes vacated by whites fleeing to the suburbs to the extent that Oakland's white population decreased by 17.7 percent in 10 years.

The increases in the black populations of the coterminous city and county of San Francisco and Contra Costa County were even sharper: in the former, from 4,800 in 1940 to 74,000 in 1960; in the latter, from less than 600 to 25,300. These figures had risen to 96,000 and 42,000, respectively, by 1970. The Bay View-Hunters Point and Western Addition sections of San Francisco became black ghettos. In Contra Costa County, most of the blacks settled in or around Richmond, with North Richmond 99 percent black.

Spaniards were the first European settlers in the bay area, but from the 1850s on they were never a large proportion of the population. It was not until the 1950s that dropouts from the southwestern migrant stream and immigrants from Latin American countries caused the numbers to grow significantly. However, by 1960 Spanish-surnamed individuals constituted the second largest minority population in the SMSA with 177,200 persons. Most of the 92,700 Spanish-surnamed in the East Bay were Mexican or Mexican-American, with geographical concentrations in Richmond and the Fruitvale district of Oakland. The majority of the 51,600 residents in San Francisco, with concentration in the Mission district, were immigrants or descendants of immigrants from 21 different Central and South American countries.

Added to these two largest minority groups are other ethnic minorities, more than 100,000 of them in 1960, the four largest of whom were the Chinese, Filipinos, Japanese, and American Indians. From these there emerged during the 1960s a manpower problem unique to the area as 10,000 Chinese immigrants in five years flocked to the area from Hong Kong, Singapore, and Taiwan, most of them without functional English.

A multiplication of racial and ethnic populations is not inherently a problem situation. It was postwar changes in the labor market structure which, contrasted to the skills and education of these residents, caused trouble.

LABOR MARKET TRENDS

The influx of blacks — as well as whites — during World War II was a response to the unprecedented expansion of industry, especially shipbuilding, and military installations in the area. Richmond alone, a small city of 23,000, suddenly acquired 90,000 new workers along with their families. That many of these migrants were from rural backgrounds, with little in the way of industrial skills and formal education, did not hamper their employment. Jobs, especially in the shipyards, were restructured to accommodate them.

With the termination of the war, however, that employment ended. Industry changes and relocation decisions over the next two decades further adversely affected the opportunities of these wartime migrants and those also lacking urban skills and formal education who followed them during the 1950s. Jobs in the blue-collar industries were decreasing in the central cities where housing was relatively cheap and available to minority migrants. The employment expansion that was occurring in the central cities was beyond them in skills and education requirements.

If three-year averages centering on 1959 and 1967 are compared, employment in manufacturing fell in San Francisco by 8,800, while wholesale and retail trade jobs decreased by 3,900. In contrast, white-collar industries (government, services, and finance, insurance, and real estate) increased by 51,700 employees. Oakland's experience was similar, with white-collar professional, managerial, and clerical-sales jobs providing most of the net growth between 1958 and 1966, while manufacturing employment dropped from 40,400 to 31,300. Yet employment for the total metropolitan area grew in every category, including an increase of more than 9,000 jobs in manufacturing. Industry was relocating outside the central cities and hence beyond the reach of much of the minority population.

Increasing central city demands for skills and education, in short supply among the minority residents there, were being filled by commuters from the suburbs. About 40 percent of San Francisco's workers in 1969 were commuters, mainly managers, professionals, skilled craftsmen, sales personnel, etc. There were few laborers or low-skilled workers among them.

The consequence of these developments for the ethnic minorities was revealed by special surveys conducted in November 1966 and cited in part 1 of this book for Boston. In January 1967 the unemployment rate for the United States was 3.7 percent; for the SMSA, 4.3 percent. Yet during the month of the survey, the rate reached 11 percent in the Fillmore-Mission district of San Francisco and 13 percent in the flatlands of Oakland. The subemployment rates were 25 and 30 percent, respectively. In the Fillmore-Mission district, 51 percent of the residents were nonwhite, while 60 percent of the residents of Oakland's flatlands were black and 8 percent Spanish-surnamed.

POLITICAL GROUPINGS AND POWER

One finds the classical American pluralism in bay area politics, with the business community dominant but challenged by a strong union movement. Indicative of the power of organized labor in the area is that the movement on each side of the bay has successfully brought off a general strike — a rare event in the annals of American labor history. Another manifestation is that the San Francisco Central Labor Council successfully backed one of its own for mayor.

Given the growth in their numbers (relatively and absolutely) during and since World War II, their confinement to ghetto neighborhoods, and their relatively disadvantaged economic status, the minority populations expectedly sought political power to command a larger share of the community's attention and resources, particularly for better housing, education, and employment, and for civil rights. Nor is it surprising that blacks, given their numerical superiority among the minorities and the national trend among them toward greater militancy, became the most aggressive of the groups.

Moreover, the blacks achieved some success. By the mid-1960s, they held a number of prominent public positions — albeit still few, relative to their numbers — including seats in San Francisco on the California State Assembly, the county board of supervisors, and the municipal court; in Alameda County, on the county superior court; in Berkeley, on the city council and on the board of education; and in Richmond, the mayoralty. Furthermore, as a result of pressure from the black community, San Francisco inaugurated a human rights commission which sought to break down discriminatory hiring practices; and Berkeley, for a short time, had an ordinance forbidding discrimination in housing.

In even more dramatic demonstrations of ethnic solidarity, the San Francisco chapters of NAACP publicized the failure of Candlestick Park to hire black girls as ushers, and boycotted a local cab company for its discriminatory hiring practices. To the same end, the United San Francisco Freedom Movement — a coalition of NAACP, the Congress of Racial Equality (CORE), and an ad hoc committee to end discrimination (itself a loose collection of 12 student groups) — conducted sit-ins at the Sheraton-Palace Hotel, the Cadillac agency, and the Bank of America. Even more significant was the long struggle conducted by the leaders of CORE and Freedom House, a neighborhood center, in the Western Addition of San Francisco to influence redevelopment in that section of the city so that its residents would not be dislocated. The most articulate and politically minded black leaders of the bay area during the mid-1960s were developed during that struggle.

When the war on poverty came to the bay area, it was assumed in all of the communities affected that it would be a largely black program. From the beginning, blacks occupied most of the top positions in the CAAs. Yet everywhere the local governments sought to retain ultimate control. Also everywhere black leaders, under the banner of "maximum feasible participation of the poor," sought to wrest control from the local governments and to use the resources from the war on poverty to further the organization of the black community for more effective political action.

The fight to free the CAAs from control by the local governments met with some success in all of the communities. Yet autonomy, rather than resulting in more effective organization of the black communities, was a signal for internecine warfare among various black factions. Whether or not the cause of black power was served in the long run is probably still open to question. Certainly it damaged the prestige of middle-class black spokesmen as it popularized the "black power" concept and brought prominence to more militant young men from the ghetto.

However the war on poverty affected black power, it is undoubtedly true that blacks were more influential in bay area politics in 1971 than they were in 1964. Evidence of this is that Berkeley in 1970 elected three blacks to the city council and one to Congress, and Richmond now has its second black mayor.

The other ethnic groups, though slower to stir, have not been totally inactive. However, the Spanish-surnamed have seemed more concerned with establishing their separate identities within the context of the war on poverty than with winning political power vis-à-vis the larger community. Thus the Spanish-surnamed community in Oakland won for itself a separate skills training program at the San Hidalgo Institute and representation, purely on an ethnic basis, on the Oakland Economic Development Council, the city's CAA.

A struggle with the mayor in San Francisco for dominance of the poverty program resulted in control by the neighborhoods so that each of the major minority groups ran its own program, the blacks in the Western Addition and the Bayview-Hunters Point area, the Spanish-surnamed in the Mission district, and the Chinese in the Chinatown-North Beach area. Even here, however, the occasion arose for the Spanish-surnamed to assert themselves and win a separate model cities program for the Mission district. Originally, only the predominantly black Hunters Point area was scheduled for a model cities grant. Pressure from the Mission Coalition, an organization of organizations, won a reversal of previous decisions made jointly by members of the black community, the city of San Francisco, and the U.S. Department of Housing and Urban Development (HUD). San Francisco's planning grant was split between the two districts.

THE UNIVERSE OF NEED

Supposedly the war on poverty offered more to the minority populations than enhancement of their political powers. It aimed at reducing, or even eradicating, the poverty that afflicted them. Manpower programs for the disadvantaged, an integral part of the war on poverty, had a narrower aim: They sought to increase the employability of the poor and find jobs for them.

In chapters 10 through 12 of this book, the evolution of these programs in the bay area is traced, with an attempt to assess their impacts. Before that story can be told, however, it seems prudent, especially in light of the narrower objective of the manpower programs, to get some notion of the size of the problem. Not all minority people are poor and not all poor people are members of the ethnic minorities, nor are all of the poor potentially employable.

A survey was designed and conducted for HUD by the Survey Research Center of the University of California at Berkeley, but using a lower income figure than the Social Security criterion used by the U.S. Department of Labor (DOL). The survey reported 46,720 poor persons in Oakland households in 1966, including 32,160 who were members of the racial and ethnic minorities, this from a household (not total) population of 365,500. The Cooperative Area Manpower Planning System (CAMPS) estimate of the number of Oakland residents eligible for manpower programs was 9,740, of whom 2,240 or 23 percent were not employed. Applying the same ratio as prevailed between the HUD survey and the CAMPS estimate to the entire study area, we find that the number eligible for manpower programs was estimated to be 35,100 persons, of whom 8,072 were unemployed.

These then are the universe that the programs described in the next three chapters were designed to rehabilitate to successful employment.

Development of Bay Area Manpower Institutions

10

Though the bay area involves an overlapping of labor markets, contrasts between the East and West Bay economies and political jurisdictions resulted in different histories in the development of manpower programs. Because the East Bay's poverty problems were more readily apparent and because of Oakland's designation as a "hot city" where riots were expected but never came, Oakland became the recipient of probably the largest input of federal manpower, antipoverty, and economic development funds per capita of any city in the nation. San Francisco, in contrast, did not view itself nor was it viewed as in trouble until after the Hunters Point riots of 1966. The pattern of federal expenditures and efforts reflects that belated recognition.

Before the advent of the manpower programs, little was available by way of employment preparation and assistance for the minority poor. The public schools were of limited help. The secondary schools stressed academic rather than vocational education, training for white- rather than blue-collar jobs, and among the latter, apprentice-related instruction for union-controlled crafts. Access to the apprenticeship programs, except for plastering, cement finishing, and carpentry, was blocked by entrance requirements — high school graduation plus oral and written examinations on which minority youths consistently scored lower than their white counterparts.

Three institutional factors set the bay area manpower institutions apart from the other cities: (1) the strong and sympathetic role of the California State Employment Service (CSES), (2) the strength of the unions which opposed training in apprenticeable crafts and contributed to the initially predominant female enrollments in training programs, and (3) the relative militancy of bay area minority groups.

154

MANPOWER PROGRAMS IN OAKLAND

When manpower programs for the disadvantaged developed in the bay area, Oakland took the lead, and appropriately so. Its high unemployment rate caused it to be designated a redevelopment area, first under the Area Redevelopment Act and later under the Economic Development Act. On the demand side, it appeared to be a more favorable market for those with limited skills and education than San Francisco. It was, and still is, a major industrial center and the principal forwarding port of war matériel bound for the Pacific and the Far East. Compared to other bay area cities, it had received, during the influx of the 1940s and 1950s, more than its proportionate share of minorities with neither urban skills nor educations. So apparent were its poverty problems that after the Watts riot in Los Angeles, it was designated as the city where the next riot was to be expected. Furthermore, Oakland was alert to the significance of the increasing federal funding sources and began qualifying itself for every possible form of aid. By 1966, it was involved in 140 ongoing, federally financed programs with annual funding of $87 million in aid available to economically depressed areas.

Oakland's war on poverty may be said to have begun in 1957 with the formation of the Associated Agencies, an organization composed of the senior executives of five local public agencies, with the city manager as chairman, for the purpose of improving the delivery of social services to the poor. In December 1961, the Associated Agencies was awarded a $2 million grant by the Ford Foundation to design and implement programs for the minorities who had migrated to the city during the previous two decades. The resulting interagency project did not, however, take on a manpower flavor until 1964 when the adult minority employment project was launched. The latter consisted of outreach stations and job development efforts; and although it placed less than 12 percent of its more than 6,500 applicants between September 1964 and January 1966 in jobs lasting three or more days, it brought the services of CSES to the target population and an awareness to CSES of the problems of the disadvantaged minorities.

Oakland's next major venture into manpower programs for the disadvantaged came with the establishment of the East Bay Skills Center early in 1966. The prime movers were CSES and the Economic Development Administration (EDA). The latter decided to make Oakland a demonstration of its ability to solve urban unemployment and poverty through economic development and promised large sums of money in support of the Center. The promise was not kept, but it did serve as a significant impetus to the Center's establishment. Also in 1966, before the announcement of the national CEP, the mayor established a manpower commission for the city — made up of representatives from various government, labor, business, and community organizations, and funded by EDA — to coordinate the activities of all organizations involved in combating unemployment among the disadvantaged.

When the federal government launched its war on poverty, the citizen advisory committee of the Associated Agencies became the nucleus of the city's CAA, the Oakland Economic Development Council (OEDC). The staff of the interagency project was reconstituted as the Oakland Department of Human Resources to serve as staff for OEDC. Though OEDC had the power to initiate and approve proposals for funding, the city council retained the right to approve the release of funds, and hence held ultimate veto over the decisions of OEDC.

Though the CAA program, the federally sponsored and inspired local war on poverty, began in Oakland as an arm of the city government, it nevertheless contained from the beginning the seeds of rebellion. Much of the minority community looked upon the program as property belonging to them. Furthermore, in confirmation of their belief, a disproportionately large number of them were selected to represent their community on OEDC and to serve on the staff. It had to be only a matter of time before those selected would have their loyalty to their community tested over differences with City Hall. That came during OEDC's second year of existence. The issue was a proposal for a police review board, first submitted in December 1965.

OEDC overwhelmingly endorsed the proposal and, more importantly, persistently pushed it in the face of strong opposition from the chief of police and the city council. Its support of the proposal had two roots: First, there was apparently substantial sympathy for it within the minority community, especially among the poorer elements, and secondly — and this became more important as time passed — OEDC felt compelled to prove its independence from the city council in determining poverty policy.

The police review board issue was really the first opportunity for OEDC to prove its independence. The city council was adamantly opposed, yet CAA was under heavy pressure from its own target area advisory committees (TAACs), upon which the poor were represented. Caught between the proverbial "rock and a hard place," OEDC in 1967 voted to sever its ties with the city and to become an independent, nonprofit corporation.

During the dispute the mayor adopted a mediator's role, attempting to persuade each side to moderate its position. Nevertheless, he had been increasingly dissatisfied with OEDC since the year before when it had sought funding from the Ford Foundation, bypassing the city council in the process. The mayor not only considered that act a breach of faith, he had decreasing faith in the service and community organization approach of OEDC. He was now more manpower oriented, and established a manpower commission as a step toward developing such a program.

When Oakland was selected in 1967 as one of the cities to receive a CEP grant, the mayor understandably felt that his commission, already charged with responsibilities similar to those contemplated by CEP, should be designated the prime sponsor, rather than the less manpower-oriented OEDC. Although he failed to achieve his prime target, after much hard bargaining, he induced the federal administrators to provide the East Bay Skills Center with $1 million and to turn the job development function of CEP over to the commission. That further strained relations between City Hall and OEDC, the latter becoming CEP sponsor over the mayor's objections, believing that its grant had been reduced by the sum that was given to the Skills Center. OEDC became independent of the city the next year as the Oakland Economic Development Council, Incorporated (OEDCI).

It is not easy to describe the role of OEDCI as sponsor of CEP. In one sense, CEP was thoroughly integrated, administratively and programmatically, into the structure of OEDCI. Not only was it housed in the CAA's physical facilities but also there was no bloc of offices or an office, aside from the central records unit, within those facilities that could be identified as a CEP installation. Its administrative officers, aside from two middle management types, were OEDCI staff who allotted a portion of their time to CEP. The OEDCI director was usually identified as the CEP director, though he tended to delegate the administrative responsibilities to someone else.

Yet CEP was only one of OEDCI's many interests, not the main one. It provided less than half — though more than any other single source — of the $8.5 million funneled through CAA during fiscal year 1969. OEDCI was becoming increasingly community action oriented; and, after its separation from the city, it seemed most interested in ensuring a larger political voice for the ethnic minorities, especially the blacks. Consequently, it performed its CEP functions in a rather perfunctory fashion, subcontracting all but the Neighborhood Youth Corps (NYC) to other agencies and investing its major manpower energies in controlling the subcontractors.

Two examples of the importance attached to this question occurred in relations with the Opportunities Industrialization Center (OIC) and the New Careers development agency. OIC obtained a contract from CEP in 1967 to provide prevocational orientation and basic education, and unsuccessfully sought a monopoly over those functions. The Spanish-surnamed Unity Council, having no love for OEDCI, fearful of black domination and with ingrained ambitions, won the right to give its own basic education. Fearing further ethnic splintering, and hoping to woo the Spanish-surnamed back, OIC instituted in January 1969 an interethnic program that provided a basic education course for monolingual, Chinese-speaking persons and prevocational training for American Indians. However, this ran counter to the desires of the more militant groups within OEDCI and the TAACs which wanted an all-black OIC.

However, the OIC director had a more basic problem with the black militants than his interethnic program. He was imbued with the philosophy of the OIC movement and had in fact been sent from national headquarters in Philadelphia to head the Oakland installation. That philosophy was anything but militant. OIC viewed itself as a grass roots, self-help organization that had learned how to persuade employers to give it assistance and to hire its graduates. When it was approached for job orders, it emphasized the quality of its applicants and the care with which it had prepared and selected them. It invited employers to participate in panel discussions during prevocational training sessions and to give advice on the operation of OIC. Care was taken to refer only the best available trainee to any particular job opening.

It sought as enrollees persons who had the desire to improve or change their lot. The director argued against paying enrollees to attend training. The first test of an enrollee's desire to improve was his willingness to participate without any promise of an immediate reward. Paying allowances invited individuals to enroll solely for the money. Not only did they use up available slots unproductively, they also became sources of disruption in the classroom. To many a militant, the OIC approach seemed an "Uncle Tom" tokenism.

When OIC became a subcontractor to OEDCI, it subjected itself to the rule that 51 percent of a delegate agency's executive board consist of representatives from the TAACs. Late in 1968, OEDCI began pressing OIC to conform to this rule. The OIC director delayed on the plea that he was unable to obtain a quorum at board meetings to transact business. When he finally consented to a membership meeting to hold elections in May 1969, all of the incumbents were defeated, and a militant faction was swept into office demanding his resignation.

When the Oakland CEP was funded, the New Careers development agency, which claimed to be a national organization (though having no facilities and few activities outside Oakland), became the subcontractor for the New Careers program. The development agency in turn came under pressure from OEDCI to increase the TAAC representation on its executive board. The issue was complicated by interethnic rivalry. Four of the five TAACs were black dominated. The fifth was the Spanish-surnamed advisory committee, created expressly to assure a voice for the Spanish-surnamed. To them, dominance by TAACs was tantamount to black control.

The governance of the New Careers development agency became an issue between the two communities because the director of the national organization was Spanish-surnamed and that of the local organization, a black. When finally OEDCI, over the protest of the Spanish-surnamed Unity Council, ordered the change demanded by the TAACs, the feared black control became a fact. Afraid of being submerged in an organization dominated by blacks, the Spanish-surnamed community sought to protect its interests and to reserve positions of leadership for itself by fighting for and winning a Spanish-surnamed advisory committee, basic education, and prevocational orientation through a Spanish-dominated organization, *Educacío para Adelantar*, instead of OIC, and skills training at the San Hidalgo Institute rather than the East Bay Skills Center.

OEDCI was unhappy with these arrangements, branding them as ethnic separatism, and eventually moved to abolish the Spanish-surnamed advisory committee. This developed apparently as the result of a communication from the regional Office of Economic Opportunity (OEO) directing OEDCI to reapportion its council seats according to available demographic information to assure "one man, one vote." In response to that directive, a subcommittee of the executive committee recommended that the Spanish-surnamed advisory committee be dissolved, or in lieu of this, that its relative voting strength be reduced. The latter alternative was adopted by the executive committee, but only after the president cast his vote to break a tie.

Except for minor changes, the CEP design remained much the same until it was drastically revamped at the insistence of DOL in 1971. The major change was to increase the responsibilities of CSES (by then renamed the Department of Human Resources Development or DHRD) until it became in essence the prime cosponsor. DHRD assumed total responsibility for job development, coaching, follow-up, record keeping, and the coordination of supportive services, in addition to the functions that it had been performing since the beginning of the program. Other important changes included the elimination of OIC as a subcontractor, enlargement of the New Careers program, the location of orientation and basic education at the East Bay Skills Center, and the creation of a separate and identifiable CEP staff within OEDCI.

It is difficult to evaluate the contribution of the Oakland CEP. Certainly the 1971 reorganization indicated DOL dissatisfaction with the program operated by the politically minded OEDCI. No significant program innovations were developed in the Oakland CEP. One major claim was that it processed 4,409 enrollees until the end of 1970, of whom 1,181 were placed in jobs. At a total expenditure of approximately $13 million, this averages about $2,900 per enrollee, or $11,000 per placement.

MANPOWER PROGRAMS IN SAN FRANCISCO

In contrast to Oakland, San Francisco before 1966 seemed almost apathetic about manpower programs for the disadvantaged. In fact though possessing twice the population of Oakland and partly because of the lack of aggressiveness in pursuing funds, it received smaller NYC and Manpower Development and Training Act (MDTA) allotments. The latter funds had actually been reduced to help finance the East Bay Skills Center.

This attitude changed with the Hunters Point riot of September 1966. Among the grievances of the residents of the area was the lack of jobs.

When the mayor became aware of how intensely the grievance was held, he took the initiative in bestirring the city. He called upon the entire community to join a program to find jobs for San Francisco's poor, and furthermore dispatched a telegram to the President of the United States demanding federal assistance, including the restoration of the city's full MDTA allotments.

The mayor's plea to the community brought a pledge, subsequently unfulfilled, of 2,000 jobs from the San Francisco Chamber of Commerce. His appeal to the President brought more tangible results. The city's MDTA allotment was increased by $400,000, and a federal task force, composed of the regional directors of various agencies of the national government, was established to help the mayor initiate programs for San Francisco's poor. A consequence of that aid was a federal employment program to hire, outside civil service regulations, 900 disadvantaged persons in agencies of the national government.

A few months later San Francisco was selected for a CEP. According to the program's guidelines, the presumed sponsor was the San Francisco CAA, the Economic Opportunity Council (EOC), but it had been left in shambles by the struggle for control between the minority community and City Hall, and among the various factions within the minority community. It had just been swept by a wave of resignations, including its chairman, three of its five area directors, and all of the union delegates to the council. Though a new chairman had been installed a week earlier, most of the vacancies remained unfilled. In addition, a federal audit had charged it with misuse of funds and inefficient administration.

There was general agreement among city officials, community leaders, and representatives of the federal government that EOC was hardly in the position to assume responsibility for a $5 million CEP. Consequently, DOL suggested that a manpower commission, composed of representatives from labor, business, and the poverty community, be instituted. This plan was accepted by all of the interested parties except OEO, which insisted that major responsibility for administration be vested in EOC.

The commission's functions were to be limited to drafting the proposal, establishing policy, and monitoring and evaluating the program. This, however, was unacceptable to the San Francisco Central Labor Council. It refused to endorse any plan that included a role for or representation from EOC. It suggested as an alternative a tripartite board composed of representatives from organized labor, the federated employers of the bay area, and the general public. That plan was unacceptable to the new chairman of EOC, a retired judge, and the San Francisco Chamber of Commerce, all of whom would have been excluded from participation. Unable to produce an alternative — it even approached CSES only to be turned down — DOL reluctantly awarded the program to EOC, making it the major sponsor of manpower programs in the city.

The initial CEP package approved for funding contained a subcontract with the chamber of commerce to develop 1,200 jobs, continuation of the federal employment program, utilization of CSES to provide all manpower services, provision for a large child-care program, allocation of most of the city's non-CEP-MDTA slots to CEP enrollees, two nonallowance language centers for persons unable to speak English, and NYC, New Careers, health care, and legal aid components.

As might be expected, CEP's first year produced successes, failures, and lessons. Among the most notable of the lessons occurred in the conflict between the chamber of commerce, charged with job development, and CSES, responsible for placement. The former claimed to have developed 1,042 job openings during the year, of which CSES could fill only 179. The chamber of commerce accused the placement agency of sending it candidates who were not job ready, whereas CSES charged the chamber of commerce with developing job openings that either were not suitable for disadvantaged workers or with employers who would not accept the disadvantaged. Neither of them seemed to appreciate the inherent conflict between the two functions.

To persuade employers to accept disadvantaged workers, the job development agency tends to understate the shortcomings of the available worker-clients and to be selective among those it refers to employers. Otherwise its chances of developing further job openings may be jeopardized. The placement agency on the other hand is under pressure to place its applicants, and it is the harder to place who tend to accumulate in the active files. The chamber of commerce as job development agency was caught in much the same position that CSES had been when it was accused of failure to serve the disadvantaged. But now it had made a different commitment and sought to avoid "skimming" and to concentrate on the hardcore unemployed. There is, of course, a potential bridge between the two points of view. By counseling, orientation, basic education, work experience, skills training, etc., the hardcore unemployed can theoretically be converted into job-qualified workers before referral. No one really believed, however, that the San Francisco CEP or any other possessed that capability.

Job development in the public sector was much more successful as an aftermath of the Hunters Point riot in 1966 when 1,000 disadvantaged workers were placed in federal civil service jobs in 700-hour and not to exceed one-year appointments. No records were kept except for the 500 placed with the San Francisco Post Office. Since they had to qualify for a regular civil service appointment when the time ran out, they were tutored two hours a day on their own time. Before commencement of classes, 273 were tested and 13 passed. After training, 413 took the test and 263 qualified for permanent appointments. Over three years' time, 519 were enrolled and more than half achieved permanent appointments. The post office later reported the turnover and performance of the disadvantaged to be superior to their regular employees. Its success in developing public sector jobs later led CEP to negotiate similar agreements with city agencies, including the fire department and the municipal transportation agency.

The great failure of the year, perhaps better described as a fiasco, was the child-care component, administered, along with legal and medical services, by the only CEP components directly under the aegis of EOC. All others were subcontracted. Plans called for an expenditure of $500,000 to finance five centers, staffed by a combination of professional and subprofessional personnel. The component was to provide employment in an expanding field for CEP enrollees, become self-supporting within a year, and fill an unmet community need.

The program was plagued with difficulties throughout the year. The first six months were consumed in planning. The search for facilities was slowed by the difficulty of finding structures in poor neighborhoods that met fire and safety regulations. Administration inefficiencies led to such bizarre consequences as the daily delivery at one center of catered lunches for two weeks in advance of enrolling any children, and the payment of a staff for five months to man another center that never opened for the lack of any eligible children in the neighborhood. When finally four centers did open, the cost per child per annum proved to be $2,100 compared to $1,200 in licensed day-care centers elsewhere in the city. Despite these experiences, the centers were continued into the second year, but primarily with funds provided by the city and the U.S. Department of Health, Education and Welfare (HEW).

The San Francisco CEP was not notable in its overall performance. Its enrollment lagged behind other CEPs, and at the end of the first program year more than $900,000 of authorized funds were unspent. In part this was due to the San Francisco CEP's unwritten rule that enrollees would not be accepted unless postorientation outlets for them existed, and the failure of various components to develop such slots. Thus, neither the New Careers program nor the child-care centers got started until six months of the program year had elapsed, and the job openings developed by the chamber of commerce were ruled to be unsuitable for CEP enrollees. Furthermore, CEP was unable to get slots committed to it from the MDTA–on-the-job training (OJT) contractors in the city. The language centers contained unfilled openings, but their failure to pay allowances made them unattractive to enrollees. The only postorientation slots developed, other than those written into CEP itself (i.e., paraprofessionals in CSES and job coaches in Youth for Service), were those in the MDTA institutional and federal employment programs.

To remedy this situation, CEP, toward the end of the program year, instituted two new components, an intensive training unit and an adult work experience program. The first was designed to take those people among the CEP eligibles who could be brought up to job readiness for clerical occupations with just six weeks of training. It was essentially a brush-up operation. The second provided work experience and basic education for male heads of households.

In part the poor performance of CEP was due to the administrative weakness of EOC itself, for which it was placed on probation by DOL. Furthermore, its contract was extended for four months to the end of the year to give it an opportunity to redeem itself.

The administrative reforms instituted by EOC during the probationary period must have been sufficiently promising because DOL again funded the program. Nevertheless, complaints of inefficiency continued throughout the period of this study. Among them were those of tardiness in paying allowances to enrollees, failure to meet promptly the reporting requirements of DOL, inadequate communications among subcontractors, slowness in getting new components started, and rapid turnover of staff.

Whether the San Francisco CEP was worth the $13 million that it spent over the three-year period under review is difficult to judge. It enrolled approximately 6,800 persons, at a cost of $1,900, of whom 6,200 terminated. If the data available for the period October 15, 1969, to October 31, 1971, are used as a basis for estimation, 29 percent of the terminations would have been those who completed the program, 31 percent dropouts, and 40 percent in that unrevealing category of "other." Such figures, however, do not really provide much of a basis for evaluation because they do not show the lasting effects, if any, CEP had on the lives of the enrollees.

Probably more relevant to evaluation are the program innovations wrought by CEP. It added four child-care and three language centers to the resources available to the poor. Its federal employment program paved the way for the national post office worker trainee program. Its successful job development effort with city agencies, outside the expensive New Careers program, predated the Public Service Careers program. Finally, its contract with the chamber of commerce for job development in the private sector preceded and exhibited some of the weaknesses that later appeared in the National Alliance of Businessmen-Job Opportunities in the Business Sector (NAB-JOBS) program.

Manpower Programs in the Richmond Area

Neighborhood House of North Richmond, more than any other agency private or public, pioneered manpower services for the disadvantaged population of the Richmond area. It was established in the early 1950s by the Friends Services Committee of the Society of American Friends to serve the needs of the black population that had become economically stranded when the shipyards of World War II were closed and the housing projects for the shipyard workers demolished. It later became an independent corporation and a regular recipient of funds from the United Bay Area Crusade. As its name and location imply, it concentrated its efforts on the population in the unincorporated district of North Richmond.

It became a manpower agency in 1960 when it launched a job-upgrading project to prepare school dropouts and other unemployed youth for employment. In 1962, the project was assigned a full-time counselor by CSES; and in June 1963, it was funded as an experimental and demonstration project by DOL.

Once it became the recipient of federal funds, Neighborhood House used the job-upgrading project as a vehicle to operate a number of other employment-related programs. Between 1964 and 1967, it entered into contractual agreements with business firms to perform certain services. Among them was one with the Standard Oil Company of California to do weeding and gardening work at the local refinery. Another, called "Supreme Services," provided janitors.

Among the most publicized was the day camp program. When it attempted to respond to a DOL request in 1966 to submit a proposal for the summer employment of 100 youths, Neighborhood House encountered objections from organized labor over the use of low-paid youth (at $1.50 per hour) at public facilities. Subsequently it established day camps for 500 children, with the youths employed as counselors.

Still other programs included Project Growth, a summer program in 1965 of remedial education for youth, and an MDTA-OJT program that enrolled 285 persons between December 1964 and March 1967. When the Richmond CEP was funded in 1968, Neighborhood House became the subcontractor for the New Careers component.

Unlike elsewhere in the bay area, the Richmond CEP was sponsored by the city, rather than CAA, through the model cities program, for two very good reasons:

(1) Richmond and its adjacent poverty pockets occupy but a small corner of a very large county (Contra Costa) that contains two other heavily populated areas. The incidence of poverty in the other two population centers was not sufficient to attract sizable federal funds. CAA was countywide and conceivably would not have been responsive to the specific needs of Richmond. On the other hand, the model cities program and CEP served virtually the same geographical area and population.

(2) CAA, rocked from its beginning by internal dissension, periodic resignations, and conflicts with the Contra Costa County Board of Supervisors, did not appear to be a viable administrative body. The model cities board, on the other hand, being a city agency directly responsible to the city manager, gave promise of administrative stability. Furthermore, its ties with City Hall were not expected to be disturbing to the city's large black population

because the blacks for some time had assumed a share of political power ... the city has twice had black mayors.

Probably because of the sponsor, the Richmond CEP has been relatively free of the stormy controversies that plagued the others. The program was originally designed to provide jobs or skills training for 500 persons. Its major components included orientation, basic education, skills training, adult work experience, New Careers, and job development. Similar to the other CEPs, CSES was responsible for recruitment, intake, screening, counseling, referral to program components, and job placements. During the 1969–70 contract (the second year), it had responsibility also for job development.

The program experienced its greatest difficulty with the job development component. Though the CEP's original contract committed it only to place 500 enrollees in jobs and/or training, the staff felt a commitment to place them on jobs. Enrollees were not to be admitted and skills training courses not established unless job openings had been developed in advance. Thus the type of applicant enrolled and the kind of training established were to be determined by the nature of the available job.

The system was supposed to work in this manner: The job development unit received pledges from Montgomery Ward to hire household appliance repairmen. Consequently, CEP negotiated the appropriate skills training course at Contra Costa College, and the intake unit of CSES selected CEP eligibles who it believed could succeed in such a course. For such a system to work, it was necessary that the job development unit get operating in advance of the other components, which it did. It had accumulated 213 job pledges before CEP was ready to accept its first enrollee and had every reason to believe that others would soon follow. After all, the city's leading employers, through the Council of Richmond Industries, had participated in drawing up the CEP proposal and had given it their unqualified endorsement. Yet only 11 enrollees were actually placed in the original set of pledges, the others having evaporated into thin air, thus making subsequent promises difficult to come by. In the end, the principle of not starting a course until a job opening had been lined up had to be compromised. Evidence that there might be a demand became sufficient. For instance, a class of welders was begun on the news that a plant to be built in nearby Pittsburg (California) would need them.

The poor performance in job development eventually caused the mayor to intercede. He held a luncheon to solicit pledges; but though 200 firms were invited to send representatives, only 60 did. Even more disappointing, only two or three pledges were obtained that day. Even six months later, only 10 of the attending firms had hired any CEP enrollees. Hope rose momentarily when late in the program year the city's most prestigious employer, a large oil refinery, pledged itself to hire 10 enrollees per month.

It was thought that other employers might thereby be encouraged to commit themselves; yet that expectation did not materialize. By the end of the first year of operation, CEP had placed only 152 enrollees.

The failure of the employers to cooperate more fully with CEP should not be construed as apathy toward the disadvantaged. Before the arrival of CEP, several of the large employers already had programs for employing the disadvantaged and hence had developed other sources of recruitment — e.g., the Urban League, the Alliance of Churches, the East Bay Skills Center, the OIC, and Neighborhood House — that they were reluctant to abandon.

Frustration over the failure of job development led to the same kind of friction between the job development unit and CSES as occurred between the chamber of commerce and CSES in the San Francisco CEP. As in the latter controversy, there existed an inherent conflict between the job development and placement functions. The job developer, anxious to latch onto openings (especially when they are coming slowly), is apt to accept pledges, even when their suitability is questionable. Furthermore, he is anxious that the employer not be dissatisfied with the referral because that affects his ability to get further pledges. At the same time he may tend to oversell the employer on the quality of applicants to cinch the pledge. Moreover, when an employer is dissatisfied, the job developer is apt to blame the placement people for sending unprepared or unemployable applicants or the job coaches for inadequate follow-up.

From the point of view of the placement people, however, the disadvantaged consists of persons who are normally hard to place and who are often not hired. A few weeks or even months of orientation, basic education, and even skills training are not enough to wipe out disfunctional lifestyles and turn them into model employees with all the characteristics normally demanded in the labor market. Unless the employer is aware that he is buying an "inferior" product and is prepared to live with it, at least for an adequate trial period, there is no point in referring enrollees to him. Moreover, the coaches are from the target population and are in a process of personal transformation similar to that of the other enrollees. Too much job performance cannot be expected of them.

Job development during the second fiscal year, 1969–70, was subcontracted to CSES. Although there were some excellent placements at impressively high wages with oil companies and through a building trades apprenticeship program, the absolute number, only 96, was less than during the previous year. As a result, CEP sought to regain control of the job development function for fiscal year 1970–71. A compromise was worked out that permitted CEP to hire the staff and pay it from external (state) sources. The job developers, however, were to work under a supervisor — a position not filled when this study was concluded — from DHRD (the successor to CSES).

When job development in the private sector proved to be disappointing, the Richmond CEP turned to New Careers under subcontract to Neighborhood House. More slots were added to the originally planned 52; thus 119 persons were placed during the first year of operation. Another 107 were added during the second year, and 85 were planned for the third.

Other interesting components of the Richmond CEP were the basic education, beautification, and preapprenticeship programs. The basic education component is of interest because it was operated by CEP itself. Originally it had been delegated to the Richmond Unified School District under the usual format. However, a school board election in 1969 displaced an overwhelmingly liberal with a completely conservative membership. CEP's basic education program became an unwanted stepchild. Unable to find another subcontractor, CEP was faced with the alternatives of conducting the program itself or doing without it. It chose the former.

The beautification program, locally often called "Operation Mainstream" because it was originally to be funded by that source, was designed as a holding operation for enrollees caught between program components. It provided them with an income and work experience while they awaited their next CEP assignment.

The preapprenticeship program was a one-shot affair, initiated in March 1970 to provide 28 weeks of work experience and basic education for 20 young men who hoped to enter the building trades. Because of cooperation from organized labor, nearly all of the enrollees were accepted into apprenticeship programs.

THE ROLE OF THE CALIFORNIA STATE EMPLOYMENT SERVICE

From the beginning, CSES was clearly the dominant agency in bay area manpower programs. In marked contrast to Boston and Denver, it early foresaw and endorsed the emphasis on programs for the disadvantaged. Yet it has not noticeably neglected its standard functions of unemployment insurance administration and placement of walk-in applicants. It has adopted new programs with some enthusiasm and has pioneered others that later were funded nationally.

The conversion of CSES from a traditional employment service to its present stance may be said to have begun in 1962 when its director issued a letter to every CSES employee throughout the state announcing a shift in policy and declaring that the agency was now abandoning its passive role toward discrimination in employment and was instituting a policy of actively and aggressively seeking the integration of the work force. There followed a number of implementing steps, including a minorities program in each local office to place minority applicants and the development of ethnic statistics relative to unemployment insurance claims, job applicants, referrals, placements, MDTA enrollments, etc. Instructions to local offices urged the managers and staff to become responsive to the growing militancy in the black community and to offer assistance and cooperation to civil rights organizations.

In keeping with this new policy, CSES in the bay area quickly became involved in outreach activities that anticipated the Youth and Adult Opportunity Centers (YOC and AOC) that later became national policy. The earliest of these was the job-upgrading project started by Neighborhood House of North Richmond in 1960. CSES assigned a full-time counselor to it in 1962. A year later it became involved in a Hunters Point-Bayview youth opportunity project, conducted by the San Francisco Committee on Youth to give intensive and coordinated services to unemployed youths in the Hunters Point area. CSES, which was one among 10 participating agencies, provided the manpower services; i.e., the job testing, counseling, development, and placement functions, and the development of and referral to training opportunities. Beginning in 1964, it provided similar manpower services in the four neighborhood centers in Oakland. Eventually all of the above outreach installations became regular YOCs or AOCs. Furthermore, by the end of 1966, CSES had opened similar centers in every war on poverty target neighborhood in the bay area.

CSES undoubtedly learned much from this early experience about serving the disadvantaged, especially how difficult and frustrating the job can be. For example, during 1963, in cooperation with NAACP, it compiled an inventory of the job skills possessed by black workers. The objective was to demonstrate to employers that there was an ample supply of qualified black candidates for job openings. Instead CSES found that of the 2,000 people who registered with it during the project, only 127 were sufficiently qualified even to be referred to employers. Thus the illusion of easily found skills among the minorities was quickly dispelled.

Of the 2,115 youths who registered with CSES at the Hunters Point YOC between August 1963 and January 1966, some 500 were placed on jobs, many of them temporary or part time, 465 were enrolled in MDTA institutional training, and 25 were sent to the Job Corps. Of the 28,971 applications at the Oakland Neighborhood Center offices between September 1964 and March 1968, there were 11,604 placed in jobs, but only 5,718 of them were permanent (three days or more). In addition, 2,195 were referred to training. In short CSES was able to place less than half of its disadvantaged clients in job or training slots. Even this, however, exaggerates the service that it was able to render because many of the jobs were temporary or part time and no account is taken in these figures of the attrition rates in either job or training placements.

The ultimate manifestation of CSES's frustration over its new mission was the conversion in 1966 of the Western Addition AOC into a workshop to help unemployed men find their own jobs. The workshop emphasized group sessions in which the participants would criticize each other's job search efforts. The frustration that lay behind the workshop concept has been well articulated by its inventory and its director.

> The public Employment Service is being asked to . . . perform functions and reach goals which cannot be fulfilled — not because the Employment Service is . . . incompetent — but because it is intrinsically impotent. Despite its traditional posture as a job-getting agency, and its more recent role as a Community Manpower Center, it . . . neither controls nor significantly influences . . . the direction of the economy, the availability or the distribution of jobs. . . . The service is used entirely at the discretion of the employer and is totally dependent on his acceptance. The service has no legal mandate to force employers to list job openings with it, no power to force an employer to hire a referred applicant . . . no power to intrude upon the inviolability of union hiring hall contracts, to influence civil service hiring procedures or specifications. . . . It cannot affect the way existing jobs are filled. Most important — the Employment Service cannot create new jobs. . . . The job market has already been carved up — all claims have been staked out and all the deals consummated. The pre-empted Employment Service has no claim to partnership — it simply isn't where the job-exchange action is.[1]

Irrespective of its frustration, CSES had by its activities in the AOCs and YOCs been gradually transformed from an agency that served primarily private business and temporarily unemployed workers to one that catered to the needs of those persons most requiring help. It had become a Human Resources Development (HRD) agency even before that concept emerged nationally in 1968.

OTHER PROGRAMS AND AGENCIES

The emphasis in the foregoing pages has been on the emergence of the CEPs, their components, and their subcontractors, and hence failed to say much about the programs and agencies outside these structures. CEP was a system for delivering a variety of services to disadvantaged people to help them become employed and self-supporting. It was supposed to have the capacity to induce even a reluctant person to participate (outreach), to offer rehabilitative services tailor made to his individualized needs — e.g., basic education for the undereducated, prevocational orientation and work experience for those possessing only a limited acquaintance with the world of work, skills training for those without salable skills, and supportive services for those with personal problems that inhibited their employability — and to find him a job (job development). Furthermore, the system paid the person while it was helping him. CEP was the community's overall effort to solve the manpower problems of its disadvantaged population. The

---

[1] Miriam Johnson, *The Workshop: A Program of the San Francisco Adult Project Office* (California State Employment Service, September 1967), p. 72.

programs that operated outside this system were either external resources that potentially could be tapped by a CEP to complement its own services or specialized efforts for limited types of clients who were not served by a CEP. Not fitting either of these categories were the state's multiservice centers.

Representing external resources potentially available to the CEPs were the NYC out-of-school, NAB-JOBS, and MDTA-OJT programs. They added to the alternatives to which CSES might refer eligible applicants. However, CSES rarely referred persons who had been enrolled in a CEP educational, training, or work experience component. CSES had little success in referring candidates to NAB-JOBS and MDTA-OJT. The organizations administering these programs preferred to do their own recruiting and tended to view their missions as that of placing job-qualified, or at least job-motivated, ethnic minorities and did not like the kind of applicants sent to them by CSES. School youth and welfare recipients were served by specialized programs, the former by NYC and the latter by the WIN program which was administered by CSES.

The state's multiservice centers (of which there were two in the bay area, one in San Francisco and the other in Richmond) were established in 1966 to bring together under one roof all services of the state — e.g., employment and placement, vocational rehabilitation, welfare, legal assistance, housing, etc. — that were useful to the residents of poor neighborhoods. Their chief contribution to the manpower effort of the communities in which they were located seems to have been to add to the number of outreach centers.

THE DHRD EXPERIENCE[2]

The policy begun by CSES in 1962 to serve the interests of the minority labor force in a positive way culminated in 1968 in the enactment by the state legislature of the Human Resources Development Act, creating the California DHRD. The new agency, activated in October 1969, absorbed the California Department of Employment (including CSES), the state OEO, the multiservice center program, and the Commission on Aging — in other words, most of the services concerned with the rehabilitation of the disadvantaged.

The new agency was organized into four divisions: (1) tax collections and insurance, (2) job training, development, and placement, (3) farm labor services, and (4) management. The second division, as its name implies, was most directly involved with the delivery of manpower services to the disadvantaged and is the local successor to CSES and the subject of this portion of the chapter. It in turn subdivided into six sections: (a) client development services, (b) WIN, (c) employment service, (d) special

---

[2] The material in this section was prepared for the original study by Miriam Johnson.

services, (e) organization and management, and (f) CAMPS. This section is concerned specifically with the local office of ES.

The HRD Center

At the local level, the specialization of field offices according to whether or not they served primarily a disadvantaged clientele, which had been developing since 1962, was continued. On the one hand, there was the traditional ES office, as established by the Wagner-Peyser Act, that served the nondisadvantaged and sought to refer the best available applicant to fill an employer's job order. Its staff, mostly nonminority, had over the years remained approximately constant. On the other hand, the Human Resources Development Act created the HRD centers in place of most of the AOCs, YOCs, and state multiservice centers to concentrate on serving the disadvantaged. Their staffs, as of the beginning of 1971, were made up mostly of people from the ethnic minorities . . . 55 percent compared to 38 percent in the traditional offices. This tendency toward ethnic specialization was even more pronounced at the executive-managerial level, with 65 percent minority managers in the HRD centers compared to less than 10 percent in the regular offices.

Though the HRD centers were to specialize in services to the disadvantaged, they were organizationally separated from the administration of the federally funded programs having the same purpose. Responsibility for those programs was vested in the same person who was to be responsible for supervising the traditional offices. Thus the Northern California regional office was organized into three sections: The first, headed by the chief of staff services, was to provide technical assistance to all field offices. The second, directed by the chief of line operations, supervised the traditional offices, those YOCs that were not converted into HRD centers, the WIN and CEP installations, and the ES office maintained at the East Bay Skills Center. The third, under the supervision of the Northern California regional deputy director, was responsible for the HRD and state multiservice centers.

Because there were no intervening administrative layers between the deputy director and the HRD managers, indicative of their high status, they were to have higher civil service ratings and hence be paid more than the managers of the traditional offices. Whereas the former were to report directly to the deputy director, the latter were to deal with intermediaries. The HRD managers were to have more discretion in the conduct of their offices. The result of these arrangements was to exclude from HRD operations the older and more experienced personnel found in the line operations, and relatively to downgrade them, thus generating considerable resentment among the traditional personnel.

The mission assigned to the HRD centers was to provide comprehensive manpower services to DHRD eligible persons, defined as those whose family income fell below certain specified levels (though higher than federal poverty standards) and who, if unemployed, were "employable or capable of being made employable through available services." (The specified income levels were higher than those used to determine disadvantaged status for federally financed programs.)

The main thrust of the centers' activities was to be directed toward those persons who would be selected, according to criteria established by each center for itself, for comprehensive services. A person so selected was to become a "caseload client," and was to be assigned to a "case responsible person," either a rehabilitation counselor from the California Department of Vocational Rehabilitation or a job agent. The case responsible person, in consultation with the client, would draw up an "economic sufficiency plan," a blueprint of individualized services and steps necessary to move a person from joblessness or underemployment to permanent adequate employment which ostensibly would provide him a standard of living substantially above the poverty line.

The job agent or rehabilitation counselor would then become responsible for obtaining and evaluating all services provided to the client necessary to implement his plan. For the most part these services were to be provided through the federally funded manpower and poverty programs, or through the traditional channels used by local communities to provide social services.

The Local Office, 1960

Though the HRD center represented the greatest development (as of 1971) of the evolutionary process begun in 1962, the traditional local office was also affected. Thus an applicant entering the industrial and service office in San Francisco in 1960 would have encountered a different system from that of 1970. In the earlier year he joined the line, usually long, to see the receptionist, from whom he received a self-completing work application and an appointment with the completion interviewer. The latter reviewed the application, made corrections, filled in gaps in the chronology, and otherwise completed and clarified the information. His chief function, however, was to appraise the work history and education in order to assign a code to the application form from the *Dictionary of Occupational Titles*, the first step in the process of matching qualified applicants with job orders by the file search system.

The completion interviewer had a number of options. If immediately referrable — and there were job openings listed in the office — the applicant was sent to the placement interviewer, an employment security officer with some in-service training in assessing the occupational relevancy of handicapped persons and persuading employers to hire them. An older applicant might be referred to the older worker specialist who supplied his clients with information about relevant industry practice and acted as their advocate before the employers. Veterans concerned about their rights could obtain help from the veterans' employment representative. Furthermore, their application cards were colored differently from the others to facilitate giving them preferential treatment.

An applicant who was uncertain about his occupational choice, or who wanted to change occupations, was sent to an employment counselor (an employment security officer who became a counselor by virtue of a one-week, in-service training program). Here the applicant had his skills and potential abilities assessed, with the aid of a battery of aptitude tests, in light of the choices available in the market. An occupational goal was agreed upon, and a plan evolved that included recommendations for additional schooling, stopgap work, or a redirection of the search for work. If none of the above options seemed appropriate at the time, the applicant was then told that there were no jobs and that he would have to return within 30 days to keep his application active. Otherwise there was no advantage for him to revisit the office since it operated on the basis of a file search. In other words, "Don't call us . . . we'll call you."

Each placement interviewer specialized in a group of occupations (such as clerical) or in an industry (such as the garment industry). His primary function was to fill job orders, received from employers via the telephone, with qualified applicants by matching occupational codes. At his best, he was a skilled and knowledgeable job broker who could sell an employer and an applicant on each other. His most valuable asset, acquired from continuous exposure to his particular labor market, consisted of the insights he developed regarding variables within an occupation and the overt and covert hiring practices and preferences of his employers. At his poorest, he was a clerk who confined his activities to mechanically searching the job order and work application files for matching numbers. The nearest the 1960 office ever came to engaging in job development was when a placement interviewer occasionally attempted to develop an opening for an unusually salable applicant or when an effort was made to sell employers on the agency's services during the employer visiting program.

The scope of the interviewer's job was frozen into manuals. There were separate books for completion, counseling, order taking, selection, referral, supervision, clerical procedures, and each of the special applicant groups. Every contingency was provided for; moreover, a continuous flow of amendments kept the interviewer busy updating his manual, his "Bible," the source of all final wisdom and authority.

Next to violating the manual, the greatest crime the interviewer could commit was to bypass the supervisor and break the bureaucratic chain of command. Supervision, also prescribed by a manual, included such duties as examining all documents for preciseness, accuracy, and conformity to the appropriate manual, relating staff hours consumed to budgeted hours, analyzing various office statistics, and filling out reports for higher echelons of management. The goal of supervision was to ensure that the staff did precisely and exactly what the manual prescribed, as quickly as possible, with much attention paid to the burdensome and seemingly endless clerical aspects of the job. The ideal was a smooth, well-ordered operation. Innovations — shortcuts, new ideas, questions about the validity of any function, etc. — were neither invited nor encouraged.

No office statistic was more vital than placements because the size of the staff — people's jobs — depended upon it. Every person in the office, from manager to clerk, was constantly aware of this preeminent fact. Under such circumstances, little time was likely to be spent with, or many referrals made of the hard to place . . . today's disadvantaged or DHRD eligible persons.

The Local Office, 1970

When CSES got involved with the service to the disadvantaged, it soon learned that many of its traditional ways were inappropriate. For example, completing the work application — clarifying the work history, assessing for file search purposes, and coding it — made little sense for long-term unemployed persons of low skill. Their range of codes was narrow. Work histories contained little information of value. File search tended to be unproductive because of the frequency of address changes and the absence of a telephone at home. If completion accomplished anything, it was to teach the disadvantaged clients how to fill out application forms.

The placement interviewer soon found himself spending more time on the telephone hunting jobs for his clients than in file search. The employment counselor found that few of the disadvantaged were interested in exploring with him a range of occupational choices. First of all, the range for them was often exceedingly narrow. More importantly, however, their urgent need was for immediate employment — any job. If the disadvantaged could profit from counseling, it was most likely in nonoccupational matters, such as marital or legal problems, and hence beyond the training and experience of the employment counselor. Symbolic of the inappropriateness of the traditional ways, the manuals in the bay area's AOCs soon fell into disuse, and the amendments were consigned to wastebaskets.

Then followed an era of experimentation and innovation that produced new ways of doing things, even in the traditional, local offices. When an applicant entered the industrial and service office in 1970, his first stop might be at the job information center, a display (for the public to see) of all of the open job orders (except for domestic day work) arranged according to occupations. Only the employers' names and addresses would have been obscured. Had the applicant decided to pursue one of these leads, he would have been referred to a placement interviewer for advice and the necessary referral information.

Work applications were still being solicited, but now only from veterans, the handicapped, and persons who met either the federal or state criteria for disadvantaged. The completion interviewer was doing much the same thing as he did in 1960, except that now he could send disadvantaged persons to the HRD specialist. The latter would, if he deemed it appropriate, arrange needed social services for the applicant and help him find a job.

The employment counselor was now a person with a master's degree or 30 units of graduate study in counseling. More of his time was spent in motivational work than occupational selection. Even so, he might still not have felt up to his assignment. A large percentage of the applicants referred to him were alcoholics, drug addicts, recent discharges from mental institutions or prisons, mental retardees, and emotionally and mentally disturbed people of all kinds (whom he often referred for medical or other help rather than to a job or training).

Though manuals were still in evidence, little attention was given them. Supervisors seemed more concerned that applicants received their proper services than with evaluating documents. Interviews seemed to be conducted more leisurely; and many an applicant departed the office carrying a mimeographed handout which listed employers in the city who hire persons of his occupation.

Despite these obvious improvements, however, the same basic handicap that underlies all manpower programs for the disadvantaged remains unchanged: There are never enough jobs available, and no delivery system can deliver what it does not have. The California DHRD system is not a planning but an administering system. Its pattern is the vocational rehabilitation program with its one-to-one counselor-client relationship. The case-responsible job agent or counselor is expected to jointly develop with each client an employability plan and then put together the services to implement it. But there is a major variance from the vocational rehabilitation approach: The vocational rehabilitation counselor, to a substantial degree, has the opportunity to choose his own caseload and has, in effect, a blank check to purchase the necessary services. The DHRD job agent must accept applicants as they seek employment and is limited to the customary services of a public employment agency plus whatever slots are available in manpower programs. The form has changed and with it has come improvements.

SUMMARY

The bay area now finds itself with a number of new manpower institutions — primarily the three CEPs and a reconstituted ES. As new institutions, the CEPs have gone through some painful experiences. The most notable fact of the bay area CEPs is the obvious extent to which the public ES, first as CSES and then as DHRD, has been their mainstay. The public ES is clearly the most competent of bay area institutions on behalf of the disadvantaged. But even it has a fatal handicap . . . the objective is employment, and it has no control of the job to be dispersed.

Evaluating Bay Area Manpower Programs

11

As in the other metropolitan areas, it is convenient to divide bay area manpower programs for analysis into

(1) Those seeking to supply job skills to disadvantaged persons

(2) Those aimed at providing access to existing jobs for the disadvantaged

(3) Those seeking to develop or create jobs specifically reserved to the disadvantaged

In the bay area, more than in Boston and Denver, the manpower programs must be recognized as a minor addition to a plethora of training sources in secondary schools; junior, community, and state colleges; universities; proprietary schools; and apprenticeship. All of these were already in place before the start of manpower programs, but they did not necessarily serve the same clientele. The public ES has been the primary formal source of job information and placement for the public, but its role is small compared to the informal system and the aggregate of all formal company personnel systems. The particularized job creation function was new. This chapter deals briefly with an evaluation of training and job creation programs.

Skills for the Bay Area's Disadvantaged Workers

As in the other cities, MDTA and WIN were the only programs to attempt change in the basic employability of the disadvantaged worker by provision of job skills. Their clientele was different and so were the results. However, given the variety of linguistic and cultural backgrounds of the bay area poor, basic education and English as a second language (ESL) played an unusually large role.

The Manpower Development and Training Act Program

From the beginning, the breadth of MDTA course offerings in the bay area, especially for male workers, was limited by objections from organized labor concerned that union members not face increased competition for jobs and that the apprenticeable trades not be entered without going through the union-controlled apprenticeship program. A perusal of the minutes of the MDTA advisory committees on both sides of the bay indicates that rarely were union objections overridden. Courses for female and medical occupations — one and the same in many cases, e.g., nurses' aides and licensed practical nurses — were generally acceptable, as were OJT and preapprenticeship programs. As a result, the MDTA program in the bay area was more heavily OJT than elsewhere in the nation, concentrated in unorganized occupations, and largely for females . . . it was not until 1966 that males made up as much as 50 percent of the total enrollment.

In 1965, CSES proposed that a Skills Center be established to house the courses offered in Alameda County. This proposal was supported, with the promise of several million dollars from EDA which wanted to demonstrate what it could do in the way of urban development, and considered a Skills Center vital to its plan. It was also supported by the mayor of Oakland and the congressmen from the area. Only the unions, fearful that the proposal threatened their control over the apprenticeship program, objected. The MDTA advisory committee gave its approval in January 1966, and the Center was in operation a few months later.

The East Bay Skills Center seemed ill fated from the start. It was housed in an empty factory building requiring extensive alterations. Yet because it lay across their boundaries, four different cities had to approve its plans for remodeling, issue the permits, and make inspections. All of these considerations added to the expense of, and time consumed in getting into operation.

The original plan was to train 1,500 unemployed, male, heads of families in 30 occupations, emphasizing such fields as the automotive, clerical, building, and metal-working trades, and the repair and maintenance of office machines and home appliances. It was also planned to integrate basic education into skills training which the enrollee was to begin after five weeks or more of orientation sampling the various offerings of the Center.

Few of these plans were realized. Only 400 trainees were enrolled initially, not because of lack of applications but of money. EDA's contribution proved to be a mere $100,000, and the $4 million that was available from all sources was nibbled away by the high enrollee stipends fostered by California's unemployment insurance benefits, the requirement of the building lessor that two years' advance rent be placed in escrow, and the fact that remodeling costs were high and had to be amortized within a two-year period. The emphasis in course offerings proved to be in such occupations as the clerical trades, cashiers and grocery checkers, shipping and receiving clerks, dental technicians, cooks and pantrymen, service station attendants, and routemen, with a high proportion of women. Because of the huge demand for it, especially among the Spanish-surnamed, basic education, instead of being integrated into skills training, was taught in separate classes, and in fact became the Center's major offering.

Enrollment peaked at 1,000 and then declined as additional difficulties beset the Center. During 1966, the decision nationally to increase the emphasis on OJT at the expense of institutional training reduced its MDTA allotment. Federal officials, disturbed at the high initial training costs (approximately $5,000 per enrollee per year), imposed a ceiling of $4,000, limiting basic education to 24 weeks and the duration of total enrollment to 45 weeks. Other federal decisions eliminated courses for professional occupations (e.g., nursing) and those for the garment trades; and a state decision reduced female enrollment.

The advent of CEP the following year further reduced the MDTA funds available to the Center. It lost its basic education courses to OIC and to *Educacio para Adelantar*, and a portion of its skills training to the San Hidalgo Institute.

The Center had nonfinancial problems too. Its relations with OEDCI were poor; it had four directors in three years; it was beset by a succession of conflicts between students and the administration, and among the students between blacks and the Spanish-surnamed. And its fading public image was not greatly helped by a largely unsubstantiated newspaper story alleging narcotics problems and sexual promiscuity.

The Center halted its decline and stabilized during 1969. Its enrollment since then has hovered around 350, and its dropout rate has fallen from 45 percent in 1969 to 37 percent in 1970. Whereas only 46 percent of the enrollees who completed the program in 1969 were placed in jobs, 95 percent were placed in 1970, despite the softer labor market. Yet it may have achieved the better placement record, as any program whose performance is measured by placements is tempted to do, by concentrating more of its training in the high-turnover occupations rather than in those truly in short supply. Of the 13 occupations listed by DHRD office managers as in short supply, only two appeared among the 43 offerings of the Skills Center during 1969–71. Four were even listed as being in surplus supply. One area where it could clearly claim success was in reaching the hardcore unemployed of the disadvantaged population. Achievement tests administered by DHRD indicated that 22 percent of the enrollees tended to be nearly illiterate and that another 70 percent functioned below the 6th grade level.

San Francisco followed Alameda County's lead in 1968 and established a Skills Center, but without enthusiasm. The Unified School District preferred to continue giving MDTA instruction in its adult education and vocational training programs, and the HRD centers, which controlled the

MDTA slots, had a strong liking for individual referrals to regular vocational or technical education classes. As the number of positions available fell from 700 in 1969 to 408 in 1971, the percentage used for individual referrals rose from 29 to 38. The San Francisco Skills Center's chief customer proved to be CEP for language training and basic education.

Data available for MDTA trainees in the bay area who completed their training prior to January 1, 1969, revealed that 73 percent of the enrollees were employed at least 75 percent of the year following training, with another 16 percent employed at least 50 percent of the time. Before training, 32 percent of the employed institutional graduates experienced average straight-time hourly earnings of less than $1.50, and 42 percent earned $2.00 an hour or more. After training, that distribution changed to 7 percent at the lower figure and 73 percent at the higher; 61 percent of those who completed the course increased their earnings as against 32 percent who experienced decreases.

The MDTA enrollees in the 1970–71 follow-up study increased their average hourly earnings by $0.72, and the time that they were employed by 15 percent more than their postenrollment record.

A list was drawn up by the California Department of Employment to reflect supply and demand conditions in the summer of 1968, when unemployment hovered around the 4 percent level. Only eight of 47 MDTA occupations were included in the Department of Employment study. One was identified as a shortage occupation, two as surplus occupations, and five as those where demand and supply were in balance.

Another list compiled by the California Department of Employment to guide skills training in San Francisco provides telling insights into the policy being followed:

> In selecting occupations to be covered in the Profile, emphasis was placed on entry-level and volume occupations. "Volume occupations" means: those occupations where job openings are numerous, because of high turnover or the size of the occupation or both. Further, emphasis was put on occupations that could provide employment for the job seeker with few skills and on occupations for which training is feasible under the manpower programs available to the city's residents. Not all occupations meeting these criteria are in the Profile, but the more than 70 occupations or occupational fields that are discussed represent a sizable proportion of such jobs. Further, to put the occupations into perspective with the entire San Francisco job market, the jobs discussed represent a majority of the city's skilled, semiskilled, and unskilled jobs, over 50 percent of the clerical jobs, and most of the volume jobs found in retail trades and service occupations.[3]

---

[3] California Department of Employment, *Occupational Profile, City of San Francisco* (April 1969), p. 1.

The list contained 71 occupations, 25 of which appeared on the 1968 supply-demand list. Seven were shortage occupations, nine were surplus, and nine were those where supply and demand were in balance. Clearly, high turnover was considered important enough to override supply and demand conditions. On the evidence presented, it seems clear that the MDTA program in the bay area has succumbed to the temptation to schedule courses in high-turnover occupations, perhaps supporting the placement rate in the short run but reducing the long-run impact which must come through stable employment at good wages.

Despite this tendency, MDTA participation has been followed by the enrollees' substantially improved employment stability and higher hourly pay than that which they had before they were trained. In effect, people with sporadic work experience and low pay in the past move up to substantial improvement, but not enough on the average to eliminate their poverty status. Evidence is strong that MDTA institutional training in the bay area, after some early difficulties, enrolls disadvantaged people, concentrates on high-turnover rates rather than skill shortage occupations (primarily for budgetary reasons), but on the average results in substantial improvements in employment stability and earnings for its participants.

Basic Education and Language Instruction

The programs of orientation and basic education in the bay area resemble those in other regions of the nation. Most of the CEP and WIN enrollees received from two weeks to two months of orientation, which consisted of instruction in such matters as the proper mode of behavior to obtain and hold a job, the range of occupations available to enrollees, and the overall plan of the program itself. Basic education stressed improving the trainee's grasp of the basic tools of communication and reckoning. If there was anything unique in the bay area's approach, it was language instruction, sorely needed in the area because the chief barrier to employment for a number of residents, especially within the Chinese and Spanish-surnamed communities, was inability to speak English. Consequently programs of language instruction were established in several institutions: in San Francisco at the Skills Center, the Chinatown North Beach English Language Center, and the *Centro Social Obrero* language and vocational school (formerly the Mission Language Center), the latter two under contract to CEP; and in Oakland at the San Hidalgo Institute, the East Bay Skills Center, and *Educacio para Adelantar*.

Attempts to develop effective programs encountered difficulties. The program for the Chinese, for example, was hampered by inadequate educational materials and a dearth of bilingual instructors. On the other hand, though the supply of instructors for the Spanish-English programs seemed ample, the available educational materials were primarily for people of Mexican descent, and hence not entirely suited culturally for the large Central and South American communities in San Francisco.

A more fundamental problem, however, was finding the proper approach. During the first four years, basic English was stressed with little vocational orientation, and few of the graduates appeared to have sufficient fluency in the language to compete effectively in the labor market. Consequently, beginning in December 1970, the programs attempted to stress job-related English. Moreover in the two CEP-financed centers in San Francisco, language instruction was coupled with a work experience program. This approach has not been in effect long enough to assess the results at this time.

Because of the obvious need for the programs and their failure to produce the results hoped for, language instruction in the bay area was the subject of much controversy, mostly about the competence and validity of the teaching methods. Yet the most basic handicap was undoubtedly the scarcity of resources. Language instruction was supported by directing funds away from the already very limited amounts available for skills training and basic education. To stretch these monies over a significant number of people, courses of instruction were limited to a matter of a few months; and in the case of the two language centers, stipends were not paid to enrollees until December 1970, forcing many of them to interrupt their training to take short-term, almost always low-paying jobs or to attend class after a day's work. Yet despite all these difficulties, follow-up studies credit language training with major contributions to enrollee earnings.

The advent of WIN in 1968 did not "set well" with the local welfare departments in the bay area. These departments had run rehabilitation programs for the welfare populations under the Work Experience and Training and the Community Work Training programs and resented the implication that theirs had been an inadequate performance. The transfer of administrative authority to CSES, which claimed to be *the* expert agency in employment counseling, placement, job development, and other matters pertaining to the labor market, implied that the welfare departments were not so expert and hence were partly responsible for shortcomings of the earlier programs. (The welfare department in Contra Costa County had labored hard to create a fairly elaborate program under the earlier legislation and had a sizable staff whose jobs were now in jeopardy.) Moreover, instead of being totally relieved of responsibility, the welfare departments were called upon to do the selection, continue providing services, and pay a portion of the bill. They were to service what they felt should have been their program but which was controlled and operated by someone else.

As a rationale for their position, the welfare staffs pointed to the traditional employer orientation of CSES. Its chief concern, they charged, was to fill job openings with the best available people. WIN might force CSES to dip into the labor supply enough to place welfare clients, but it would be only to skim off the cream from among them. They felt that the responsibility should have remained with the agency that understood and would champion the client before he was subjected to training and educational institutions, employers, and CSES — all of which had hitherto resisted him.

Perhaps as a direct result of this attitude, referrals of eligible persons from the welfare departments barely trickled in. In defending themselves against charges that they did not want to refer their cases to WIN, these departments pleaded inadequate time to acquaint their vocational counselors, case workers, and other specialized personnel with the requirements of the program. Whatever the reasons, referrals began flowing into the WIN offices in October, two months after they opened. Then as the stream became heavy, CSES staff became concerned that the welfare departments were trying to swamp the WIN offices. The chief executive of one of the county departments boasted that this had happened, not because of any malicious intent on the part of welfare, but because of ineptness within CSES. Some of the WIN staff charged that they were being flooded with referrals of dead people, persons who had moved from the county, and otherwise ineligible individuals.

Aside from the petty sniping, there were at the outset real differences between the agencies in their interpretations of the eligibility criteria, resulting in a high proportion of the referrals being rejected by CSES as inappropriate. When these differences were finally resolved, that ratio declined except in San Francisco, indicating a possible degree of intransigency on the part of one or both of the agencies in that county. But as the flow of referrals picked up, so did the ratio of those referred who failed to show up for interview, one third of the total during 1968 and 1969. Of those who were referred, slightly more than half were enrolled in the program.

Together the three counties were allocated approximately $11,804,000 for the fiscal years 1969 through 1971 to finance 7,329 slots. As of December 1970, 6,571 persons had been enrolled in WIN in the three bay area counties. Of these, 3,261 had been terminated, 1,168 were in holding status, 1,318 were in training situations, and 468 were either working in entry-level or seasonal jobs or enrolled in other manpower programs. Only 20 percent of the terminations were listed as successful completions, 17 percent as dropouts, and 63 percent as terminating for other reasons. A total of 57 percent of all WIN enrollees were classified as "dropouts," terminating for "other" reasons, or in "holding" status, leaving the impression that a great many individuals entered the program but not much happened to them. Dividing the total WIN budget by the number of successful completions suggested a cost of $10,000 for each success.

The term "successful completion" had several meanings: It could mean that the trainee completed a training program but did not necessarily find work; that he was placed in employment and off the welfare role, or that he was placed in employment but continued to draw welfare benefits. Explicit data were not available, and welfare officials were vague in their guesses about the quantitative distribution among these meanings. Those who were willing to guess estimated that more than 50 percent of those who successfully completed the program were placed on jobs but continued to draw benefits. Information from one county indicated that only 9 percent of all terminees were being placed on jobs.

However, the one-year follow-up of a sample of those WIN enrollees actually engaged in basic education or skills training during the winter of 1969–70 revealed that 50 percent of them had some employment experience during the postenrollment year. True, the enrollees in San Francisco were on the average employed for only 26 percent of the available time; those in Richmond, 29 percent; and those in Oakland, 31 percent . . . nevertheless, that employment stability represented a nearly 50 percent increase over their preenrollment experiences. Moreover, if we combine gains in wage rates with improvements in employment stability, we find that the trainees gained an annual income equivalent of $860 in San Francisco, $1,760 in Richmond, and $1,620 in Oakland. The contrasting findings probably have three sources: (1) not all WIN enrollees received basic education and skills training, (2) the employment stability gains were for those who had some pre- and well as postenrollment work experience, and (3) despite the substantial income gains, many, depending upon the number of dependents, would still be eligible for welfare assistance. Given the small number of those who successfully completed the training, approximately 700, the most valid conclusion would probably be that those who were trained *and* entered the labor market after training profited substantially, but the impact on the welfare rolls, about 35,000 persons in the three counties, was insignificant.

JOB CREATION PROGRAMS

The bay area has been the recipient of all of the job creation programs — New Careers, MDTA-OJT, NYC, and NAB-JOBS — except Operation Mainstream, with the addition of a successful program for employment of the disadvantaged in federal civil service jobs.

New Careers

The New Careers program in the bay area was a combination of institutional instruction along with OJT and work experience in host agencies from whom the enrollees were expected to obtain permanent employment. The projects, all funded as CEP components, were as follows:

(1) The New Careers development agency conducted a project in Oakland that had enrolled 291 persons between its beginning in 1967 and April 1970, mostly in corrections and parole agencies. As of the latter date, 151 were still enrolled. Six of the early terminations, 43 of the graduates, and nine of those still enrolled had obtained permanent jobs with the host agencies. Of the 142 still

enrolled who had not as yet obtained permanent employment, eight were definitely succeeding in terms of advancement on the job and educationally, whereas none were clearly failing.

(2) When the San Francisco CEP was funded in 1967, it contained four New Careers components, one each with the California State Department of Corrections, the California State Department of Vocational Rehabilitation, the San Francisco Civil Service Commission, and *Arriba Juntos*, an organization of Spanish-surnamed residents of the Mission district. Furthermore, CEP versatile funds were used to finance a New Careers-type program with CSES. The combined San Francisco projects, including those operated by the state service center and CSES, had by April 1970 enrolled 258 New Careers people, of whom 77 were still in the program. Three of the early terminations, 52 of the graduates, and 52 of those still enrolled had obtained permanent jobs with the host agencies. Of the 25 still enrolled who had not as yet obtained permanent employment, 15 were definitely succeeding (in terms of advancement on the job and educationally), whereas two were clearly failing.

(3) The New Careers component in Richmond was started in 1968 and was administered by Neighborhood House. By April 1970, it had enrolled 120 persons, of whom 99 were still in the program, including 19 who had achieved permanent employment with the host agencies. Of the 80 still enrolled who had not as yet obtained permanent employment, 56 were definitely succeeding (in terms of advancement on the job and educationally), whereas one was clearly failing.

To summarize, 669 persons had been enrolled in New Careers-type programs in the bay area by the spring of 1970. Permanent employment with the host agencies had been achieved by 28 percent of the enrollees. On the other hand, 36 percent had left the programs, either by early termination (221) or graduation (17), without gaining permanent jobs with the agencies. The remaining 36 percent were still enrolled and hopeful of permanent employment. *Arriba Juntos* had the poorest record, with only 11 percent permanent placement and 73 percent failures, due in part to the fact that almost all of the host agencies were private rather than public. The San Francisco Civil Service Commission had the best record with 55 percent placements and 36 percent failures.

Mere permanent placement with the host agencies is not, however, a sufficient criterion for judging the success of a New Careers project. According to the ideology of the program, it is supposed to accomplish more. It is supposed to contain a promotional ladder that an enrollee can climb to achieve professional status with the host agency, to substitute work experience and OJT for formal educational requirements for mounting that ladder, and to rearrange job content so that paraprofessionals can do much of the routine work now performed by professionals. To test success by this criterion, data were gathered on the 69 ladders involved, on the personal characteristics of all of the enrollees, their academic and job performances with the program, and their postprogram experiences.

The only criterion that was not tested systematically was that of restructuring job content. Yet what was learned about the duties of the New Careers enrollees indicates that little restructuring occurred. For example, the 100 enrollees with CSES were job coaches. They were supposed to help disadvantaged workers placed in employment through CEP to hold their jobs by rendering them supportive, individualized, personal services not previously available. Examples were bailing enrollees out of jail, encouraging them to be punctual on the job, easing any tensions that they may have developed with their foremen, etc. Similarly, the 16 enrollees with Contra Costa County were performing tasks associated with the war on poverty that were not heretofore a part of any county employee's duties. In the extensive literature on the New Careers program, medical services are often singled out as a fertile place for restructuring. Yet the record of *Arriba Juntos*, which more than any of the contractors specialized in this occupational area, was exceedingly poor. For 44 of the 55 ladders for which such information was available, there were formal educational requirements, not only to obtain the top rung, but also to qualify for permanent status with the host agency. In fact 69 percent of the 55 ladders required some college (Table 11-1).

To meet the educational requirements of the ladders, the projects enrolled their New Careers people in local colleges to pursue their associate in arts degrees. To do this, enrollees were released from their jobs with pay for 20 hours per week. Provision was also made to provide high school equivalency certificates and remedial education where needed. Requiring the New Careers enrollee to work 20 hours per week and still obtain his associate in arts degree in the same two-year period normally prescribed for full-time, nondisadvantaged students (as did 28 of the 55 ladders) seems to be unrealistic. Either the enrollee would be likely to slight one or both of his responsibilities, or the contractor would select only those applicants who had demonstrated academic potential.

Yet the enrollees did surprisingly well, though their greatest difficulties were clearly with their college rather than their OJT performance. As Table 11-1 shows, success in obtaining permanent jobs was negatively correlated with the educational requirements, but the rate of early terminations showed only a mild correlation. Moreover, still enrolled in the 69 ladders were 38 New Careers people who were lagging in either their academic performance or job advancement, but not both; 34 of them were behind in school, indicating that success in college was the greater obstacle.

Table 11-1

Success as a Function of Educational Requirements in the New Careers Program for the San Francisco Bay Area (1967–70)

Grade Needed to Qualify for Permanent Status	Number of Career Ladders	Number of Enrollees	Completions		Early Terminations	
			Number	Percentage	Number	Percentage
None	11	158	46	29%	44	28%
12th grade	6	18	0	0	5	28
One year of college	10	179	24	13	57	32
Two years of college	27	233	16	7	69	30
More than two years of college	1	5	0	0	2	40
Total	55	593	86	15%	177	30%

An enrollee was judged to be lagging in his academic performance if either his grade point average was below 2.0 or his accumulated units were 20 percent below those called for in the design of the ladder. Grade point averages were available for 478, or 71 percent, of the 669 enrollees. Only 6 percent had averages below 2.0, indicating that, though college performance may have been a greater obstacle to gaining a permanent position than job performance, it was not beyond the abilities of most of the enrollees. Even those who had failed to complete the 8th grade did well — 62 percent of them earning an average grade of 2.5 or better. High school dropouts had the poorest record, with 10 percent getting less than 2.0. Yet even among them, 60 percent earned a 2.5 or better. Seventy-eight percent of the high school graduates and 90 percent of those with some college were able to maintain that high grade category.

Yet the foregoing grade point averages do not tell the complete story. The one modification the program was able to make in the educational requirements was to gain college credit for the work experience with the host agency. Usually this amounted to three units per semester. If the academic units alone are counted to the exclusion of work experience, the grade point averages are significantly lowered. Of the 463 enrollees who had earned credits in academic units, 17 enrollees who had 2.0 or better on all units earned less than a 2.0 on academic units alone, and four enrollees who earned 2.0 or better academically had their overall averages lowered below 2.0 by the work experience units. Nineteen enrollees failed to make a 2.0 on either criterion. Thus only 40 enrollees failed to do both jobs well, while 423 were successful, the majority of them earning 2.5 or better on academic units alone. Performance in college still proved to be more difficult than OJT, but most seemed able to handle both adequately.

Of course, every student knows how to keep grade point averages up by taking "incompletes" or "withdrawals" when a grade less than a "C" is threatened, and the New Careers enrollees did not fail to learn that lesson . . . 45 percent took 0.4 or more units of "incompletes" or "withdrawals" for every academic unit completed, and the more the enrollee's 2.0 average was threatened, the more he was inclined to take "withdrawals" and "incompletes."

By doing so, an enrollee ran the risk of falling behind the scheduled rate of progress contained in the career ladder. Yet only 34, or 12 percent, of the New Careers students still enrolled in the spring of 1970 for whom academic information was available had lagged academically, either having accumulated 20 percent less units than called for in the schedule, or less than 2.0 overall average. The evidence remains that most of the enrollees were able to perform satisfactorily in college.

One explanation of this success is the selecting of the enrollment. When the educational attainment of the New Careers enrollees was compared with that of the 625 trainees in the follow-up sample of those enrolled in other bay area manpower programs during the autumn and winter of 1969–70, it was discovered that only 39 percent of the 625 enrollees (compared to 74 percent in the New Careers program) had completed the 12th grade or higher. Selection of those among the applicants who had the best chance of succeeding academically limited the program as a vehicle for upward mobility for the disadvantaged population as a whole. New Careers, by its nature, is a program for the academic elite among the disadvantaged population.

Under the terms of the program, the subsidy to the enrollees and the host agencies was to end after two years. An ultimate test of the worth of the program is the number of enrollees it placed permanently with the host agencies on the career ladders at the end of the two-year period. As noted, 184, or 28 percent, had achieved permanent positions by April 1970 even though 98 of them had completed the two years on the career ladders. Another 67 of those who had achieved permanent status were still enrolled and doing well enough on the job and academically to expect positions on the ladders at the end of two years. In contrast, six enrollees had been placed in jobs not on the prescribed ladders, and one, in terms of his job and academic performances, could not expect to remain on his ladder. The remaining 12 enrollees who had achieved permanent positions were still enrolled but had such mixed job and academic records as to make uncertain their ability to remain on the ladders. Seventeen enrollees, 16 of them with *Arriba Juntos*, had completed their two years in the program without being permanently hired by the agencies.

In the record of achievement, 342 enrollees, having completed their stay in the program, could no longer be aided by it. Of them, 98 had achieved fully the objectives they had planned to reach after the two-year period. On the other hand, 238 of them (the 221 early terminees and 17 completers who had failed to obtain permanent jobs), or 70 percent, had failed. Six, though they failed to reach fully the objectives of the program, achieved partial success by obtaining permanent employment with the host agencies.

Still in the program were 327 New Careers enrollees, 28 of whom had been in such a short time that their progress could not be rated. Of the remaining 299 enrollees, 80 had achieved permanent positions and hence partial success. Of these, 67 were probably going to achieve full success, and one would most likely have to be content with a permanent job off the ladder.

Of the 219 enrollees who had not achieved permanent positions — either because of their shorter time in the program or the longer period required by their employers to gain permanent status — 162 were probably going to be fully successful. Twenty-six had mixed records of performance and 33 seemed headed for failure.

On the basis of the above record, it may be said that the program, as of April 1970, was succeeding fully for 51 percent of its enrollees, 98 who had already succeeded and 229 still enrolled who were on the way. In addition, it had assured permanent employment to another 19 enrollees. At the same time, it was failing 42 percent of the enrollees, including 33 who were still enrolled. Finally 25 of those still enrolled had such mixed records of performance that predictions about their futures in the program could not be hazarded.

MDTA-OJT

Terminating during the period January 1, 1966, and July 31, 1969, were 182 local MDTA-OJT contracts (including prime contracts with subcontracts outside the area) and 17 local subcontracts of four national prime contracts. Information was available on only 178 of the local contracts and 15 of the national subcontracts which had enrolled 5,451 persons.

Information about the program after mid-1969 was difficult to come by and consisted almost solely of authorized enrollments by contractors as of specific points in time. Thus at the end of 1969, there were six local contractors with 1,110, shrinking to 1,039 by the beginning of 1971.

The bay area Urban League was the largest OJT contractor in the area. It had been authorized 300 training positions in San Francisco for 1965 and 1966, using 1,050 in San Francisco and 700 in Oakland by 1969. However, after 1969, it ceased dealing directly with the Regional Manpower Administration and instead became a subcontractor to the National Urban League where its authorized enrollment was only 400 in 1971.

The Urban League chose to conduct its program with only the minimum of linkages to other manpower programs. In San Francisco, it failed, so far as is known, to place a single CEP graduate in one of its slots. In Oakland, the OIC, which did much of the placement of CEP graduates, from its beginning in the spring of 1967 to March 14, 1969, placed only 23 persons in OJT slots, ten of them with the Urban League subcontractors.

The reason for the Urban League's aloofness was the same that sparked the controversies described earlier between the job development and placement components of the CEPs, the job developers out to place the best and the placement people the poorer among the available clientele. The Urban League, instead, chose to bypass the CEP placement agencies, mainly CSES. It had developed a sufficiently large walk-in traffic in its field offices to fill all of its slots without the aid of other recruiting sources. Even then it had difficulty developing training positions with employers, filling only 913 of the 1,050 authorized in its second San Francisco contract, and 631 of the 700 authorized in Oakland. From its point of view, it would have done even less well had it accepted CEP enrollees as trainees.

Data available from DOL for the period between July 1, 1965, and December 31, 1968, indicate that 377 OJT completers experienced higher median earnings, $2.70 compared to the $2.25 pretraining median. Where 62 percent of the enrollees earn $2.00 per hour or more before training, 96 percent of them earned that amount during the posttraining year. Furthermore, they fared better than 562 more disadvantaged MDTA institutional graduates whose median wages improved from $1.80 to $2.35.

NAB-JOBS

The NAB-JOBS program in the bay area was divided almost equally in terms of money and slots between the Metro district in the East Bay serving Alameda and Contra Costa counties, and that in the West Bay covering San Francisco, Marin, and San Mateo counties. Each was funded at an annual budget of $5 million with planned slots at the close of 1972 and with an estimated enrollment of 1,732 and 1,987 slots, respectively.

The Lockheed Consortium

One unique feature of the bay area's program was the San Francisco consortium operated by the Lockheed Aircraft Corporation for the Management Council for Bay Area Employment Opportunity. The consortium was formed in 1968 to accept a contract for 41 companies to train and place in permanent employment 494 eligible persons at a cost exceeding $1 million.

An enrollee entering the program received four to eight weeks of institutional instruction at one of the two preemployment training centers operated by the consortium, followed by four to 12 weeks of OJT at the facility where he was to be employed. Pre-OJT instruction was restricted to classes of four to six persons, all destined (insofar as possible) for the same employer and occupation so that the course of instruction could be tailored to the particular needs of the job. The materials and equipment used in class were those that the trainees would work with when they joined their employers. Basic education was taught as an integral part of the skills training and was confined to these fundamentals necessary to the performance of the job.

Trainees punched in daily on the center's time clock and when late, could be sent home with the loss of half a day's pay. By the third week they were expected to arrive on time every day or face possible expulsion. Enrollees were paid $1.75 per hour while in pre-OJT training and then the entry rate of the individual firm, the lowest being $1.85 per hour, during the OJT phase.

While in pre-OJT training, the enrollee received a physical examination, counseling, and other supportive services to bring him up to job readiness. His counselors helped him with any problem, irrespective of its nature, that might impede his employability and remained in contact with him during the OJT phase. While the enrollees were in pre-OJT training, the company supervisors to whom each would report were given eight hours of sensitivity training.

NAB-CEP Relationships

The NAB-JOBS program was essentially a job development effort directed at private employers. The aim was permanent employment of the enrollee with the employer who had assumed responsibility for making him job ready. The preemployment training center was simply a device to institutionalize part of the process of preparing prospective employees. CEP, on the other hand, was a coordinating mechanism linking together a series of components aimed at recruiting eligible persons, making them job ready, and placing them in employment.

On paper, neither needed the other. Their only common bond was the fact that CSES recruited for both of them, except that some JOBS employers, especially those participating without the benefit of a government contract, preferred and developed alternative sources of recruitment. Yet, because all of the CEPs admitted that their job development components were not able to develop sufficient employment opportunities, it seemed reasonable that a linkage be established with the JOBS program. The gain to the employer would be the fact that CEP would assume responsibility for making the enrollees job ready. Such a linkage was clearly the intent of DOL's regulation giving preference to CEP in filling JOBS openings.

Yet very little real linkage was actually developed. CSES personnel at the CEP installations viewed NAB-JOBS and CEP as alternatives rather than complements. A person who was eligible for both programs was placed in *either* a JOBS opening *or* a CEP training or work experience slot. That person then became a CEP enrollee, even though his participation in the program was confined to being placed in a JOBS position.

Even more important quantitatively, most of the JOBS placements were not made by CSES. Like the San Francisco Chamber of Commerce, the job development unit of the Richmond CEP, and the Urban League, NAB-JOBS employers preferred to avoid CSES as a recruiting source, and for the same reason. Any attempted linkage would have been further strained by the fact that NAB-JOBS embraced a larger geographical area than did CEP. The important sources of blue-collar jobs were all outside of the CEP areas, none readily accessible to CEP enrollees by public transportation, and each with its own local poverty pockets.

Quantitative data were available for East Bay only. There, as of June 30, 1971, 562 firms had pledged 5,066 jobs since the beginning of the program, far short of the goal of 11,500. A total of 6,971 persons had been hired to fill these pledges, of whom 3,549 were still on the job.

Every bit as important as the number of pledges, hires, and retentions was the fact that these were jobs in the primary labor market. NAB-JOBS did not accept dead-end jobs identified as menial (e.g., service station attendants) nor those in low-wage industries. The numbers were fewer than desired but better than they might have been. How they compared with what would have happened in the absence of the program cannot be known.

Neighborhood Youth Corps

Eleven organizations, among them state and local public agencies, school districts, CAAs, and labor unions, have been NYC sponsors in the bay area. The experience can best be summarized by considering separately in-school, out-of-school, and summer programs.

In-School Programs

More than $4 million of federal funds were spent on in-school programs from their inception in 1965 through June 1970. This included over $3 million to pay allowances to approximately 12,500 enrollees.

The Oakland Unified School District was largest of the in-school contractors. It organized its program along the same lines as its work experience program, established under the state's educational code, whereby students work part time and go to school part time. They received academic credit and grades for job performances, and were otherwise subject to the supervision of the school while on the job. This means that when a student became an NYC enrollee, his class schedule was reduced. The school district interpreted the purpose of the in-school program (other than helping the enrollees to remain in school) to be that of providing students with an opportunity to learn firsthand about the demands and requirements of a job situation.

NYC coordinators, who, except for one, were regular school counselors, used the program for still another purpose — to encourage students to improve their academic performances. Thus one counselor emphasized the importance of keeping grades up to remain in the program. Another required his enrollees to take courses in mathematics and English and the girls to take typing. Moreover, he terminated enrollees who cut classes more than five times during a school year. Finally, all of the counselors provided their enrollees with a regular program of counseling, either individually or in groups.

Out-of-School Programs

As of December 31, 1970, $9.1 million of federal funds had been spent on the out-of-school program since its inception. Of this sum, $5.8 million went for allowances for 11,180 enrollees. All five of the February 1971 contractors — city, county, and CAA — had been major contractors since 1965 or 1966.

A number of other sponsors had succumbed to changes in policy or change of ineptness. San Francisco Unified School District had, at the beginning of NYC in 1965, a combination of classroom instruction and 10 hours per week work experience. Its objective was to produce office duplicating machine operators, auto mechanics, grocery clerks, janitors and porters, clerk typists, stenographers, and persons trained in industrial and technical skills. However, the project conflicted with the then current emphasis on work experience and low per trainee costs. The Alameda County Central Labor Council and Local #3 of the operating engineers also conducted an early program consisting of institutional instruction and no work experience.

The Alameda County Central Labor Council was the largest out-of-school contractor in the bay area until the end of 1967 when its inability or unwillingness to conform to the guidelines, as interpreted by the district office of the Bureau of Work Training Programs, ended its life as an NYC contractor. The public utilities commission was an out-of-school contractor continuously from December 1965 to March 1970. During that time it had often been criticized for the nature of its work stations, the attitude of its supervisors toward the enrollees, and its lack of supportive services. Its weaknesses in these areas made it particularly vulnerable under the guidelines for the new NYC-2 program emphasizing training, basic education, and supportive services.

The new NYC-2 guidelines placed greater emphasis on tailoring for individual enrollees a plan for their long-run vocational development, taking into consideration their interests and capabilities. The guidelines, if implemented as written, would radically alter a program which had, as a practical matter, emphasized the opportunity to earn a wage and to learn good work habits. Youth for Service, an agency whose reason for existence was aiding disadvantaged youth with their educational and vocational problems, seemed better suited to administer the new program, and San Francisco's two out-of-school projects were consolidated under its direction. The record of Youth for Service was better than that of the public utilities commission in terms of placements in full-time jobs, youths persuaded to continue their education, and the dropout rate. Youth for Service also conducted a program that seemed closer to the new guidelines than the commission's. Males newly enrolled in the commission's program were put to work with pick and shovel on the watershed owned by the city in nearby San Mateo County. Those who performed reasonably well there — mainly a matter of attendance, promptness, and obediance to instructions — were transferred to the machine shop at the Hunters Point Naval Shipyard or to the Airport School. At the shipyard, enrollees received 14 hours per week instruction in mathematics and English and eight hours per week in "test familiarization," training to prepare them to take the written examination for the position of helper in the shipyard. The Airport School gave the enrollees remedial education and trained them for the position of ramp servicemen with various airlines. Female enrollees were placed in clerical worksites, almost all of them at the shipyard, and received classroom instruction similar to that given the males enrolled.

The Regional Manpower Administration thought enough of the Hunters Point machine shop and the Airport School training to retain them in the consolidated program under Youth for Service, despite their high turnover rates. By the end of 1969, after three years of operation, 145 of the 250 enrollees sent to the machine shop either dropped out or were terminated for absenteeism or bad conduct. At the same time, 26 of the 56 females enrolled since the inception of that component in August 1968 were similarly terminated or dropped out. In fact only 92 males and 19 females could be counted as successful terminations during the lives of these projects. The record at the Airport School was similar; for example, during the last three months of 1969, there was more than 100 percent turnover.

The regional office blamed the public utilities commission for the high turnover rates, in particular its failure to provide adequate counseling, its rigid and stern attitude toward absenteeism, tardiness, and misconduct, and the fact that many of the enrollees placed in these installations had no interest in the type of training offered. In defense, the commission blamed its difficulties on the failure of the Bay View-Hunters Point YOC to fulfill its commitment to provide the project with counseling, job placement, and adequate selection. Youth for Service appeared to have had a more flexible attitude toward work stations and had developed a greater variety of alternatives. Nevertheless, the turnover rate at the machine shop actually increased under Youth for Service, though limiting enrollment to 16- and 17-year-olds may be an explanation.

Besides offering a greater variety of work sites, Youth for Service had an active counseling program, a full-time job developer, and an education program. It conducted intermittent remedial education at its various worksites and had its "Operation Minerva," a program to encourage enrollees to attend college, the latter having been successful with approximately 70 enrollees.

The public utilities commission was the only casualty of NYC-2, but all of the contractors interviewed anticipated difficulties with the new guidelines. The increased emphasis on skill training, education, and supportive services had increased the staff necessary to conduct a program for any given number of enrollees. The educational requirement was easily met by compelling enrollees to attend the continuation and adult schools that were ready at hand. The difficulty was getting youths who were already "turned off" by that kind of format to attend classes. Only Youth for Service, being more educationally oriented than the others, welcomed the change. It could now, more openly than before, select prospects who indicated motivation to resume their education.

In contrast, the skill training requirement caught all of the contractors off guard. Again Youth for Service was in the best position: It inherited the shipyard machine shop and Airport School from the commission. On the other hand, neither the city of Berkeley nor the Oakland CAA —

OEDCI — had developed a skill training program as late as December 1970. All of the contractors were disturbed that enrollees who had been receiving $1.60 per hour for a 32-hour week, or $51.20 per week, would now be paid only $39.75 per week.

The city of Berkeley and the OEDCI interpreted the new guidelines to require that an enrollee's week be equally divided among education, skill training, and work experience. The shorter hours for work experience, plus the fact that they must now recruit only 16- and 17-year-olds, according to sponsors, made it difficult for them to attract employers and caused them to lose several who had been cooperating.

Youth for Service interpreted the NYC-2 format differently. It took the view that an enrollee was to divide his time over the two years of his enrollment. Consequently, it often assigned enrollees full time to one or another of the categories. As of December 1970, five were fully employed in work experience, whereas most were enrolled in a program combining education and skill training. Nevertheless, Youth for Service, too, anticipated problems in getting employers to accept the 16- and 17-year-olds.

Summer Programs

From 1965 (when the first contracts were let) to the conclusion of 1969, more than $7 million in federal funds had been spent on summer projects, including $5.6 million in allowance payments to approximately 22,000 enrollees.

Because a summer program involves putting a large number of enrollees to work quickly, there is a tendency to employ youth in gangs in nearby make-work jobs. Examples are ways in which some of the enrollees were employed during the summer of 1970. One sponsor kept 22 enrollees busy by calling households on the telephone to remind them to register to vote. Another could not remember what his 50 enrollees did. A third created a special program, consisting of an art class and excursions, for its 30 enrollees. A fourth employed its 150 students on a house-to-house survey to determine the health problems of the 4,000 to 5,000 families in the immediate neighborhood, even though it had neither the resources nor expertise to organize and interpret the data gathered. A fifth kept its 35 enrollees busy clearing empty lots and painting old buildings. Summer programs suffer particularly from the fact that the size and timing of available funding are rarely known before the summer begins. Then youth must be recruited and assigned on an emergency basis with limited time to consider the usefulness and training contribution of the assignment.

The Work Stations

The work stations in the NYC program were supposed to provide the enrollees with "meaningful work experience" leading to "realistic employment prospects upon completion of enrollment." In the NYC-2 out-of-school program, "meaningful work experience" was to:

(1) Provide opportunities which may lead to other more advanced steps

(2) Provide for possible future employment at the worksite

(3) Provide a means of rounding out an enrollee's preparation for work

(4) Provide the enrollee with an understanding of the disciplines of work

The NYC job was expected to make the enrollee's subsequent work history more successful than it otherwise might be. However, this purpose would seem to be more important for the out-of-school program than the other two. It is designed for school dropouts, who, given that status, were currently or immediately potential members of the labor force. The in-school program was supposed to encourage students to remain in school rather than drop out. The summer program, by providing vacation jobs to school youth, was supposed to encourage the same thing and may have in addition served as "anti-riot" insurance. Presumably the jobs would serve these goals by merely providing income, irrespective of how else they satisfied the criteria of "meaningful work experience."

Next to putting money in the hands of the enrollee, the most important contribution of the in-school or summer work slot should have been for the enrollee to believe that the value of his performance to the employer was worth the income he was paid. This is what distinguishes productive work from make-work, earned income from a handout. Of the several criteria for meaningful work listed by the Regional Manpower Administration, that of work discipline would seem to have been the most relevant for in-school and summer work stations. It was probably necessary, though undoubtedly not sufficient, to require that the enrollee be prompt, obey instructions, etc., to convince him of the productiveness of his job. That this enhanced his understanding of employer expectations was important but secondary.

As a practical matter, however, the same kinds of work stations tended to be developed regardless of the type of project. If there was any difference, it was for summer slots. The urgency of placing a large number of enrollees quickly sometimes led to less well-defined jobs and greater recourse to work gangs. What difference did exist between job stations was more a function of the type of employer than the program. Where the employer was a traditional, established, governmental agency, such as the California State Department of Public Health or the Berkeley Unified School District, the work stations tended to possess the following characteristics:

(1) The individual enrollee worked among and in conjunction with regular employees rather than other enrollees.

(2) His job was well defined and structured in terms of the tasks to be performed and was relevant to the overall functioning of the agency.

(3) He was normally kept busy.

(4) He was expected to be prompt, obey the supervisor, and otherwise conform to what is thought of as normal work disciplines, and if he did not, he was removed.

(5) Little thought was given by either the contractor or the employer to what the content of the job, other than discipline, might contribute to the future employability and advancement of the enrollee.

(6) With the exception of the Oakland Redevelopment Agency (an OEDCI employer), the thought that the NYC job might lead to permanent employment with the employing agency was hardly considered.

Where the employer was an agency or organization already identified with protest in behalf of the poor or of the ethnic minorities, such as a CAA, neighborhood service centers, or an ethnic organization . . . whether or not it was publicly funded seemed to make no difference . . . the work stations were apt to possess the following characteristics:

(1) The individual enrollee's fellow workers were more apt to be other NYC enrollees.

(2) His job tended to be ill defined; in fact, he might himself have to find ways of keeping himself busy.

(3) He was not as busy.

(4) There was less concern with being prompt, following orders, or otherwise conforming to work disciplines.

(5) Little thought was given to the future employability and advancement of the enrollee or to his permanency with the current employer.

In general, contractors tended to locate their stations with agencies similar to themselves, traditional governmental agencies with traditional governmental agencies, protest- or reform-oriented organizations with protest- or reform-oriented organizations. The history of OEDCI as reflected in its work stations is an excellent illustration of these tendencies. OEDCI's origins were rooted in Oakland's traditional agencies, and it could hardly have been classified as a protest organization. By 1970, OEDCI which had pulled away from the city of Oakland had clearly earned the protest classification.

When OEDCI received its first NYC out-of-school contract in 1965, it was very much an instrumentality of the city government, whose agencies provided 63 percent of the work stations. When the second contract was consummated during the battle over the Police Review Board recounted earlier, the city's share of work stations fell to 57 percent and continued to fall subsequently until it was only 25 percent for the 1970–71 contract. Even within the city's share, the change was dramatic. During the first contract three very traditional agencies — the parks, recreation, and street engineering departments — provided 74 percent of the city's contribution.

By 1970–71, two other agencies, the Oakland Redevelopment Agency and the Dewey School, both more closely tied to the reformist movement than the average city agency — the latter being a "ghetto" school whose principal was active in the Spanish-surnamed community — were providing 87 percent of the city's share. The same trend is observable regarding the traditional private agencies. Whereas during the initial year of the out-of-school program they provided 32 percent of the job openings, by 1970–71 this was down to 3 percent. In contrast, reformist organizations (excluding OEDCI) increased their share from 0.5 of 1 percent in 1965–66 to 43 percent in 1970–71.

Paralleling the above trends was a tendency for OEDCI to provide more of its own out-of-school openings. In 1965–66, it contributed only 1.5 percent of them. This rose substantially to 21 percent during 1967–68, and by 1970–71 was 26 percent. The change in the composition of the employers is as noticeable for the summer as the out-of-school work stations. In contrast to its summer program, however, the OEDCI has apparently had difficulty from the beginning in filling its authorized enrollment. As of December 1970, it had enrolled only 73 percent of its authorization. The tendency for the OEDCI to provide an increasing share of its out-of-school slots would seem to suggest that a part of its problem was that of finding suitable job openings.

The fact that three employers, providing 43 percent of the authorized slots and employing 21 percent of the enrollees then employed, reported in December 1970 that 64 percent of their positions were unfilled illustrates the problem of recruiting enrollees. So also does the fact that the eight organizations, employing 44 percent of the trainees then enrolled, reported that their enrollees had on the average been on the job only 14 or 15 weeks. The advent of NYC-2, by aggravating the difficulties of recruiting employers and enrollees, probably worsened the figures for December 1970. Yet it is clear that the OEDCI had for several years experienced problems in filling its quota.

There is no evidence to indicate whether or not the NYC program made any significant difference in the subsequent lives of its enrollees. It provided employment and income to youths who were poor and unemployed. Whether or not that was sufficient justification for the program must, given the current state of knowledge about such things, depend upon the judgment of the observer. NYC-2 is a too recent development to judge whether its training and education emphasis will buy a more lasting and positive impact.

San Francisco Federal Employment Program

Through all of the government pressures upon private employers to hire the disadvantaged, seldom had government agencies examined their own hiring practices to determine the extent to which they did their share in the same cause. Since government personnel practices are ordinarily more structured than those of private enterprise, there was greater likelihood of "credential traps" and other unnecessary obstacles. This issue was particularly important in areas such as San Francisco where government was the largest employer. Yet that city saw only one major effort to open up federal civil service jobs. However, its experience was probably the most extensive of any city in the country.

The program was the response of the Federal Executive Board, a committee composed of the regional directors of the major federal agencies in the bay area, to the mayor's plea, following the Hunters Point riot of 1966, for more job opportunities for the poor among the ethnic minorities. Its development can be divided into two phases: the first year — when it was viewed as an emergency response to a crisis; and subsequently — when it was viewed as simply another component of CEP.

Following the riot, the immediate goal was to place as many disadvantaged workers as possible in federal jobs. Little thought was given to training or supportive services. Instead the concerns were obtaining the authority to hire, canvassing the federal agencies for job orders, and developing a mechanism that would ensure that the openings would be filled by the hardcore disadvantaged.

A total of 1,000 workers were placed in 700-hour and not to exceed one-year appointments. All of the major agencies except DOL participated, but data exist only for the 526 placed with the post office. These enrollees were given a year to qualify for permanent positions by passing the civil service examination . . . which they were to take once every 90 days or suffer separation. To increase the enrollee's chances on the examination, DOL funded an experimental and demonstration project aimed at improving their arithmetic and communication skills. Classes were held five days a week, two hours a day, at the worksites but outside regular working hours. At the end of the year, 276 of the enrollees had passed the examination.

At the end of the first year, the job performances of 489 of the disadvantaged workers were compared with those of 103 employees selected for the same positions from the regular civil service register. The retentions did not differ markedly for the two groups, nor did the rates at which the women in the two groups abandoned their positions or were terminated by their supervisors. However, the proportion of men who were terminated or abandoned their jobs was twice as high for the disadvantaged group who were also rated poorer performers by their supervisors. The younger, single males with the least education and those of both sexes who had arrest records were most likely to quit their jobs or be discharged. Those who made the comparison concluded:

> The distinction we are making between the success of the Control Group and the achievement of the Experimental Group is essentially that between the concepts of "selection" and "utilization." If the primary concern is *to select* the best available, the register is the place to go. But if we accept the responsibility to *utilize* segments of the labor force who heretofore would not have been considered, we see that many of these persons can perform satisfactorily in socially useful jobs.[4]

The post office's portion of the program was renewed in March 1968 as a component of the San Francisco CEP. Now, however, enrollees were given two weeks of orientation before reporting for duty; received such supportive services as legal aid, child care, and follow-up coaching; and took their basic education and preparation for the examination during working hours. At the end of 1970, 519 persons had been enrolled, and 242 had been promoted to career status as postal clerks or clerk carriers. Still in worker-trainee status were 41. Perhaps the best testament to the success of the program was that it became formalized as the Post Office Job Opportunity Program and was replicated in other metropolitan areas across the nation.

SUMMARY

The only significant test of the success of a training program is the degree to which the enrollees were able to obtain better jobs after the program than were available to them before. Both MDTA and WIN follow-up investigations support a favorable finding on this test. It can be only with more intensive follow-up that a definitive answer will be found. WIN has yet to produce sufficient enrollees who completed the program and who can be tested, but it is included in present follow-up interviews. With a total of 9,500 enrollees over four fiscal years in a labor market the size of the bay area, MDTA could be expected to have a significant impact on those trained but not on the labor market. Present examinations support the following four points:

(1) Per trainee cost restrictions have limited training to lower skilled occupations for which a plentiful supply of workers already exists.

(2) The "learning environments" need attention.

(3) The number trained is insignificant when related to the number who could profit from it.

---

[4] David Futransky and Donald Wagner, "On-the-Job Follow-up of Postal Clerks Hired in San Francisco without Employment Tests," report to the U.S. Civil Service Commission (July 1968), mimeographed.

(4) Those who enroll and complete training programs are substantially better off than before.

Little can be said for NYC in the bay area except that it provided some income for those poor youth who were willing to enroll at the prescribed wage levels. The in-school program was reasonably popular, but only out-of-school and summer slots were difficult to fill in competition with other alternatives, including idleness. MDTA-OJT has the standard difficulty in demonstrating that the enrollees were any different from those the same employers would have hired without the training subsidy.

Operation Mainstream was essentially a small adult NYC, but it provided opportunities to those with fewer alternatives and greater financial need.

New Careers apparently presented (for a selected group from the poverty population) opportunities of a type which would otherwise not have come their way. However, the program was largely limited to that select group who could successfully pursue simultaneous work and schooling. It made little if any headway in reducing credentialing requirements or substituting experiences for formal education.

The San Francisco Federal Employment Program was highly successful, worthy of emulation in the proposed Public Service Careers Program. It is probably also the model for later efforts to expand post office employment of the disadvantaged nationwide.

NAB-JOBS in the bay area requires further evaluation. The Lockheed consortium appears highly successful but on the basis of no quantitative measures of performance. To the extent employers are indeed changing their selection and training practices, the effort is salutory. There is currently reason to believe that this is happening to a large extent within the consortium framework and individual cases elsewhere, but not as a general rule. More often, employers appear committed to hire more minority workers so long as they are "motivated" and job ready. To this extent, the Lockheed consortium may provide the answer — an employer-connected training system for providing the job readiness.

Institutional Impact of Bay Area Manpower Programs

12

The bay area's manpower problems, with which all concerned wrestled so painfully during the 1960s, should have been evident from the 1950 census. There were already sizable areas in San Francisco, Oakland, and Richmond with continuous census tracts approaching 100 percent black populations. The dreary evidence of a high concentration of low income, unemployment, poor health, and inadequate education was there to be found. During intervening periods, the areas had widened as the poor flooded into the central cities and industry moved out, but the central characteristics had not changed . . . only the perception. What was portrayed as descriptive fact in the early 1950s now emerged as measures of pressing problems. During the earlier period, the problems were viewed as facts of life with little suggestion that improvements were possible or were the public's business. The 1960s were flavored by an air of optimism, as many had come to believe that problems of unemployment, underemployment, and poverty generally could be reduced or eliminated with appropriate strategies of intervention.

This chapter concentrates upon the impact of the manpower programs on the community institutions which operated them or were otherwise affected by them rather than the impact on those who were enrolled.

Community Impact and Response[5]

The introduction of programs, funds, and staff jobs into the bay area labor markets had substantial impacts upon political, social, and economic institutions of those communities. Organizational response varied in strength according to the extent each institution was directly involved.

---

[5] The material in this section was prepared in the original study by Dr. Curtis C. Aller of San Francisco State College.

Political Relations

Sporadic efforts during the 1950s were made by elements of the local Democratic Party, then largely out of power, to develop the ghetto areas as a source of resurgence. Both registration and voter participation remained low. Power lay latent as the manifest job needs of these areas, exacerbated by the recessions of the era, could not be linked to tangible formulations meaningful to the disadvantageds' everyday existence. The global images of the economist proved far too abstract for the political realities of these apathetic constituencies.

To the extent that race was a factor, the compelling political issues were fair employment and fair housing. Both were controversial, and their achievement absorbed the energies of those pressing for change. Activists, both white and black, were essentially middle class, and the political objectives they sought reflected a middle-class bias. Fair housing and employment were crucial to the further economic advancement of those blacks already in the employment system as well as representing rights to which they were entitled in terms of equity and citizenship. Neither was immediately relevant to the more pressing needs of the lower class who were but tenuously attached to the economic system.

In the 1960s the situation changed, slowly at first and then with a rush. National programs provided the stimulus and the resources. The bay area proved adept in securing its share of the new resources and often more. Oakland for a time was the special favorite of EDA which was endeavoring to show how much it could accomplish in an urban area by a concentrated use of its full authority. Both Richmond and Hunters Point became the locale of special demonstration activities under MDTA. The pattern for the poverty program was similar. Only in San Francisco for a time was there a failure to seize the opportunity for new resources provided by the model cities program.

As the civil rights movement reached its legal and legislative zenith in 1963 and 1964, its participants began the search for new activities. While some turned their attention toward employment issues, others struck out more directly for political power. One of the striking conclusions emerging from interviews with community leaders was the merely surface awareness and hence the token commitment to manpower programs. This was not where the action was thought to be, except in the case of those few who had carved out professional roles in the manpower arena. Clearly no viably consistent and broadly supported manpower strategy for the civil rights movement had been devised.

Community Organizations

In striking fashion the formless and apathetic ghettos at the start of the decade have come alive. Organizations and spokesmen seem to be everywhere. Yet fragility remains characteristic as neither permanence nor stability of leadership and organization has materialized. Leaders in search of followers have competed in terms of militance and rhetoric. Sporadic efforts to weld the various elements into coalitions and caucuses in pursuit of strength have met with indifferent success, and the process of fragmentation within and among ethnic groups continues unabated. All the established institutions — City Hall, schools, police, among others — felt the sting of this ferment and the often accompanying direct confrontations.

Some have asserted that national programs and in particular the poverty effort, by raising expectations, were the fundamental cause of this ferment. The exact cause and effect may never be known with certainty. In the bay area, there is no question that the energy and frustration of a new generation was beginning to be evident by 1960. At the most, poverty and related programs may have affected the timing and intensity of ghetto protest. The storm was already under way.

For a while at least, the poverty and more sharply the manpower programs lent form and tangibility. In this sea of discontent, programs offering jobs in some form as the outcome had an elemental appeal. Subsequent riots sharpened the efforts of governments to expand the manpower programs. To the establishment, these responses were patently disparate short-run efforts to cool the streets and thereby buy peace. Just as often perceived as such by the ghettos, they may have bred cynicism and hence were counterproductive in part. And yet they offered a way out for all parties. The presence of such a ready vehicle offering hope may by its very existence have prevented reliance on more negative repressive efforts.

There were some tangible outcomes deserving of mention. Some individuals secured new and different jobs and many had their income increased. One unrecognized source of new jobs turned out to be the poverty and related agencies. These together with new private organizations, OIC and Youth for Service among others, provided new leadership and management positions. The visibility of these positions in turn opened new opportunities in the established institutions, including business firms for those whose talents were revealed. Both activists and followers were co-opted through these new roles and jobs. Yet nowhere was the process complete even to the numbers required, and as we have noted, the effect may be faltering with the newer generation of militants.

The introduction of CEP brought into the open some significant differences in these three communities. In San Francisco, the San Francisco Central Labor Council proposed the creation of a tripartite commission, composed of the council, the Federated Employers, and a public member to be chosen by the mayor to sponsor CEP. When labor refused to allow the EOC chairman to be the public member, this proposal was rejected and EOC selected. Although EOC has gone through early turmoil, it is now becoming more stable and yet it remains fundamentally weak in important areas such as administrative capacity. ES as a consequence has to all intents and purposes become the dominant factor in CEP. The current mayor has displayed a knack for maintaining close relations with minority elements but without making any effort to become closely involved in program operations. Overall the city gives the appearance of accommodative skills sufficient to contain the existing tensions.

Richmond in recent years has had two black mayors with an intervening white mayor. The situation was favorable to the inclusion of CEP into the formal city structure through the model cities agency.

Oakland began the era with some advantages that seemed also to point toward city operation as the logical outcome. It had been the locus of a sizable Ford Foundation "gray areas" program. The agency and the leadership involved in this activity became the original home of the poverty effort. Two succeeding mayors were energetic supporters of manpower programs. The Oakland adult minority project and later the Skills Center were the products of unified efforts that included industry and labor. But by the time CEP arrived, the unanimity had disappeared, the poverty agency had been separated from the city, and strong conflict had broken out. The mayor lost in his bid to control CEP and received instead a consolation prize in the form of increased funding for the Skills Center.

Part of the explanation for the conflict can be traced to long history of conservative political control in Oakland. Other elements and in particular the black community never really became part of the decision-making process. OEDCI now stands as an outspoken citadel of militant minority expression. The cleavages are now deep and extend across a wide spectrum from the museums to the schools. A militant black caucus has the establishment more or less under continuous attack.

This intense polarization means that any attempt to shift CEP from one camp to another would add to the turmoil. More fundamental shifts in power will have to occur before unifying tendencies emerge again with the strength to provide the basis for program redesign.

The Business Community

When the black ghettos, previously quiescent, exploded — first in Watts and later in Hunters Point — there was a nervous certainty that Oakland was to be next. These riots and the fear of more set off shock waves in the business community. While never really opposed to manpower programs, business on the whole had been a passive participant. Now there was leadership commitment and a search for a viable business role was undertaken. The rash promises of the private sector in the wake of the Hunters Point riot never materialized into concrete achievements. The far-reaching recommendations affecting the private sector made by Mayor Shelley's task force report of December 1966 and supported by employer representatives produced no discernible results. A newly formed management council in San Francisco made a promising beginning and offered the prospect of more. However, it was not until the formation of NAB and the accompanying JOBS program that bay area business leaders acquired a vehicle for the expression of a commitment that was already there.

The response to NAB-JOBS was a ready one, but the experience proved once again that commitment by a company president will be followed by no more than faltering results unless there is sustained follow-through. To translate pledges into jobs and, more important, retention on those jobs, requires know-how and the devotion of specialized personnel. Hence one of the unheralded contributions of the NAB-JOBS program that emerged from employer interviews was the fact that government resources permitted the diversion of managerial talent and the acquisition of more time and energy that could be devoted to new tasks. The Lockheed consortium stands as a highly visible interindustry example of this thesis. But inside other firms, certainly those with contracts and some others as well, the same need to acquire personnel to apply any developed know-how was accepted.

The reason for this is not hard to explain. Basically, business firms have over a long period of time fashioned a personnel system compatible to their needs. Among other things attention was devoted to devising ways of identifying and thereby preventing the entry of high-risk personnel. Above all the objective was to secure the best so that productive efficiency in short- and long-range terms could be achieved. Hence the business firm asked to employ the disadvantaged takes on an unnatural task. To be able to do so without suffering counterproductive effects in terms of established values requires a high order of skill. It can only be done by those who know the complexities of an existing system and can devote time to devising suitable mechanisms for change. One measure of the difficulty, perhaps, is reflected in the comments of employers that more staff were required for existing and most certainly for additional commitments.

There is the attractive prospect that these efforts, although small in scale, will produce permanent modifications in hiring standards and other facts of personnel practices so that a smaller portion of those now deemed disadvantaged will require public attention. It is still too early to conclude with certainty that permanent change has taken place. In any event, too few firms have been touched by the JOBS program and even fewer have made the kind of special effort noted above for the effect in the aggregate to have much consequence in terms of numbers. For this reason alone several years' effort on an expanded basis will be needed. And precisely because it requires special effort, it would seem likely that private efforts will falter and disappear unless external pressure remains alive.

Labor Unions

The bay area is strongly unionized; collective bargaining has long since been considered mature. As important factors in the employment process, unions, like management, could not be ignored. At best they offered attractive prospects of support and participation and at the other extreme the danger of strong and successful resistance. Some unions — the operating engineers, laborers, teamsters, and the building trades in Alameda County — have, through projects of their own or as partners, become active contributors to the overall manpower effort, if by no other means than upgrading their own members. Other unions and the central bodies have been passive and more concerned with protecting vested interests. (There is no criticism implied here, as most unions do not control entry and few have spare staff around to devote to a new, challenging, and difficult task.) The introduction into this context of the labor-sponsored Human Resources Development Institute in Oakland has proved to be an effective mechanism in one very important respect.

The availability of specialized staff rooted in the labor movement has meant that union leaders could turn to a source in whom they have confidence for guidance when they are approached for assistance by one or more of the manpower programs. Prior to this, lack of information often led predictably into no action or opposition based on unsupported fears. By opening doors previously closed, more of the positive potential of the labor unions has now been tapped. Unfortunately, the San Francisco Central Labor Council has rejected the appointment of a Human Resources Development Institute man, mainly on the grounds that his loyalty would be to the AFL-CIO in Washington rather than to the San Francisco labor movement.

The Employment Service

Many public and private agencies have been actors in the combined manpower efforts of the decade. For ES, however, its involvement was central rather than peripheral to its function. Its growth, perhaps even survival, was at stake. The more significant finds are discussed below.

Changing Objectives

At the start of the 1960 decade, the California agency had recovered from its partial decimation in the 1950s resulting from an effort to divert its attention almost solely toward the discovery of fraud in the unemployment insurance program. It was a strong professional agency geared to its traditional function of selling its services as a provider of competent employees to a reluctant employer community. In keeping with the national pattern, it was endeavoring to strengthen its appeal by strong efforts to demonstrate competence in the field of professional employment. Separate offices to allow specialization had been established and an innovative effort to automate and improve the job-matching process for professionals called "LINCS-West" had been launched.

By the end of the decade, it was a vastly different agency. In the bay area, but not necessarily in the rest of the state, ES, by its own initiative and ready response to new national programs, now projects the image of an agency whose heart, soul, and identity are inextricably linked to the fortunes of the disadvantaged. While traditional functions have continued and their resource support remained steady rather than being diverted, they seem to be in a backwater. There are natural tensions between the proponents of the old and new roles, but the strains have not been severe. It appears that the most active, aggressive, and possibly competent staff went willingly into the new manpower activities. As later events proved, they were in the growth area, and their career prospects blossomed accordingly.

Staff Competence

Stability in the top leadership in the bay area throughout the decade was one favorable factor. This competent leadership willingly faced the challenges which it saw as opportunities of the period. Moreover there was professional in-depth strength and a capacity which the agency was willing to share by loaning competent people to DOL as manpower administration representatives, to the CEPs, and as staff support for NAB. Also, the agency devoted some of its best people to provide leadership and support for CAMPS efforts.

As new people were added and new programs arrived, ES at both the state and local levels devoted considerable attention to staff training. Its professional competence therefore has been maintained despite the growth and rapid change. The overall quality appears equal to the best that can be found anywhere.

Minority Staffing

The agency learned early that it needed to increase the proportion of minority employees at all levels but was unable to do so, and in part the failure may be due to its lack of vigor in pushing for changes in civil service practices. Although it was among the first to see the need of and use indigenous personnel in outreach activities, it was late in 1969 before approval of the state personnel board was secured for a new pattern designed to open up professional routes for these nonprofessionals. This recruitment task would have been difficult in any event because there was active competition for minority talent by the poverty programs, by private agencies, and in the latter part of the decade, by private employers. The most important achievement of the DHRD reorganization was elevating to top levels and permeating throughout the system black and Spanish-surnamed staff. In effect, two agencies have been created: one operated by whites for whites in the more prosperous areas and the other by and for minorities in the ghettos.

Interagency Partnerships

There is a dilemma posed by the institutional need for identity and the integrative requirements of a multi-agency activity which ES has never solved. Traditions, patterns of operations, and systems of control vary among the agencies. Jurisdiction is the lifeline of a public institution and therefore will be zealously guarded. Staff loyalty remains preeminently with the home agency — for it is there where career advancement is to be found.

ES acquired some early experience in one of the predominant patterns of the decade, the multi-agency project at Hunters Point in San Francisco beginning in early 1963. The program had begun in 1960 as the United Community Fund sought a more viable youth role. It stimulated the formation of a Committee on Youth, secured financial support from the city, and obtained planning money from the newly established President's Committee on Juvenile Delinquency and Youth Crime. Significantly, ES was not included at the start among the several private groups and seven public agencies on the committee. But the outgrowth in terms of a special project at Hunters Point included ES as a key participant among the 10 public and private agencies which provided administrative components.

There was interagency tension from the start. The Committee on Youth sought to retain full policy control and full administrative authority for its director. The record suggests that ES, with a detached staff at one point of nearly 20, attempted to cooperate. Yet it was criticized by the project management for failing to meet their needs for supervision and direction of staff. There was criticism, too, of alleged agency rigidities and inflexibilities. And for its principal task, job development and placement, it was judged to be sorely deficient.

For its part, ES drew a different set of conclusions. From Hunters Point it learned, it was thought, how to compensate for the inadequacies of other agencies and in a sense "to carry the ball" for others. As a training ground, it gave the central staff some valuable experience in learning how to evade or surmount administrative barriers at the state and national level, of which the basic education example was only one of many. Though it smarted under the criticism and was on occasion defensive, ES was thereafter heavily involved in interagency project activity. It initiated a few and never failed to enter others whenever it was expected to.

Surprisingly, the agency never sought to go beyond the partnership role. There were some opportunities, of which CEP was one. Its leadership, local and state, remained convinced that multi-agency skills and resources were required for any comprehensive effort. It sought neither an internal acquisition of such skills nor the overall management job of an interagency complex.

Failures in Job Development

Job development has been the Achilles heel of the manpower effort directed to the disadvantaged . . . and ES has shared in this failure. Job orders declined regardless of economic conditions and in spite of the increased efforts. This suggests that the conventional forms of job development — essentially job finding, soliciting orders, and endeavoring to find a taker for a particular individual — are fated to be inefficient and disappointing in their results.

Whatever the reason, and there are as many explanations as there are observers, ES lacks status with the real holders of job power. Among the top decision makers in business and labor, there is a plethora of criticism of ES and little awareness of its potential; they deal with it when they must and, even then, in a strictly limited fashion. In no leadership sector is there a willingness to lend support of institutions to strengthen the power, influence, and performance of ES in the job development arena. In the absence of such support, the agency has the never-ending task of establishing — one by one — contacts at the lower levels within business firms in the hope that a job order can be secured and a placement consummated. The employment process is not affected thereby, and the changes in the system — manifestly required if the disadvantaged are to be assisted in large numbers — occur, if at all, by accident rather than by design. It is no wonder, therefore, that ES, from the days of the Hunters Point project onward, had faced criticisms of its job placement performance. Both critics and apologists have focused solely on the symptoms. Rather than being the villain, ES is more likely the victim of a diagnostic failure.

The labor market, if one departs from the textbook abstraction, consists of innumerable separate markets that are highly variable from one to another in important dimensions. These markets range from high structured, organized systems to those seemingly without any structure. They are not impervious to change as economic, legal, and social forces are continuously affecting the behavior of these markets. ES in the bay area has always understood the diversity of this real world and has considerable organized knowledge of its complexity. Neither it nor any other institution has been able to use this knowledge to devise systematic changes in these labor markets. Yet such basic changes are necessary if ES is ever to provide suitable employment opportunities for the disadvantaged.

Other agencies in the closely related field of equal employment opportunity have learned through experience some lessons that could be profitably borrowed. They learned that individual processing of complaints was a costly low-yield affair. Therefore attention has shifted to a pattern-centered approach to a given industry so that it will affect discriminatory practice across a wide spectrum. The results are sometimes startling. When one important supplier of the U.S. Department of Defense was persuaded by the Department of Justice to adopt an affirmative action program, anonymous leaflets appeared on 14th Street in Oakland titled "Jobs" and giving the company name, location, and other details. Neither the distance and associated transportation difficulties nor the location of the plant in an all-white suburb proved to be barriers, and the company was overwhelmed with minority gate applicants. This incident proved once again the strength and effectiveness of the informal channels that so dominate the operation of labor markets. Individual job development efforts were not needed and might never have had much effect if they had been attempted. The system change was sufficient.

By working with an entire industry — such as that of printing in San Francisco — NAB was able to get acceptance of an arrangement that both expanded the number of jobs modestly and opened up an entry route for minorities. Also in San Francisco, the Human Rights Commission now has the backing of a strong antidiscrimination ordinance applying to all city contractors and suppliers. The full potential for change has not been tapped, however, as staff to work on its implementation have not been provided by the city. CEP denied a request for financial help on enforcement on the ground that the proposal lacked cost figures. Though negotiations are still being carried on, there yet may be an opportunity here for strategic intervention into the employment process with results far beyond those another training project would provide.

By now the term "disadvantaged" has in the bay area become a code name for minority employment. As it is already identified in this fashion, there may be untapped opportunities for ES to assist in, or become joined with, those agencies now in the business of a pattern-centered approach to job development. NAB may offer other unexplored possibilities. To the extent that ES still lacks entry into the top levels of business, it may be possible for it to persuade NAB to undertake more pattern-centered job development and to support such efforts with staff and other resources.

There seems to be little doubt that if public agencies by one means or another fail to move aggressively to open opportunities for employment of minorities in volume, direct action techniques will emerge as the alternative. In Oakland the poverty agency reflecting minority dissatisfaction with present methods proposed to take over job development for ES in the second year of the CEP programs and then to try to work out quota system contracts with employers. But DOL denied approval of this precedent-shattering plan by questioning both feasibility and validity of the approach. Yet there are fashions operative here as elsewhere. If "Operation Breadbasket" in Chicago, the picketing of construction sites in Pittsburgh (Pennsylvania), and similar activities elsewhere prove effective, the pattern is sure to spread quickly to the bay area. Negotiated change seems to be inevitable. The choice, therefore, is essentially between official and unofficial means. Herein lies the opportunity for ES to make an enduring contribution. If recent history is a relevant guide, the opportunity assuredly will be missed.

Upgrading Efforts

Closely related to job development are upgrading efforts which need more attention. Attention until now has been concentrated on entry-level openings. Though undeniably successful, the numbers have been small and the effort has faced a steady barrage of criticism of the dead-end nature of the jobs. Though this is a standard response, it cloaks at least two underlying realities: Far too often the jobs developed were comparable, if not identical, to those with which the target populations had experience and presumably could have found again on their own. Expectations, likewise, cannot be met by the income yield of a job at or near the minimum wage level. Many job developers, frustrated by the resulting low receptivity to these jobs, have simply stopped considering them. Overexpectation may be as much at fault as the failure to deliver jobs with built-in ladders since a high proportion of working careers are probably normally made up of a series of dead-end jobs, hopefully each at a little higher level than the last but not necessarily so.

Fundamentally this experience highlights a neglected aspect of the upgrading need. The initial effort has to be designed so that it will open up new channels for manpower flows from the unorganized underworld of the labor market to the higher opportunity sectors. Once this is accomplished, the second aspect of upgrading begins to loom larger. In many instances, those already at the entry levels must be moved up to make room for the newcomers. To avoid a new kind of dead-end phenomenon from emerging, special efforts for upgrading these newcomers may be needed.

ES provides a good illustration of this latter necessity. As with some other employers, it has made special efforts to secure more minority employees at the entry level, with new subprofessional positions created for this purpose. But systematic methods for accelerating their movement up the lob ladder within the system are only now beginning to be developed.

Innovative Responses to Opportunities

In other respects ES in the bay area has displayed a consistent capacity for innovation. Out of Hunters Point came the idea of YOC centers, and the Oakland adult minority employment project generated a network of AOCs. The bay area seems to have been in advance of the national pattern in these outreach activities. The agency moved quickly with the MDTA program in 1963 and 1964, pushed aggressively for expansion against some resistance, and was largely responsible for building a training capacity which has been unsustainable as money has been diverted to newer programs. It kept in step with each program as it was initiated, reflecting a ready acceptance of new concepts and the capacity to adhere to their spirit in operational responses.

When the HRD concept came out of Washington in early 1967 as the national administration's framework for reorienting ES, little adjustment was required in the bay area because it had for some time been functioning in accordance with these precepts. In similar fashion the changes decreed by the 1968 California legislature were accommodated readily.

In summary, CSES (now DHRD) in the bay area reflects the image of an institution that has learned to be comfortable with rapid change, able to stay in the mainstream of national currents (and sometimes in advance, thereby contributing to change), but still actively seeking its appropriate mission.

Militance in the Ghetto

Another factor which warrants separate attention is an underlying militance in the ghetto. Program focus is highly variable as are the leadership elements and groups. For the moment at least, activists apparently do not perceive manpower programs worthy of their attention. To them the action is to be found in the power and decision-making arenas. To a distressing degree, they seem convinced that manpower programs are too late and represent a cultural lag between their long-standing needs, the slow recognition processes of the "establishment," and the even slower problem-solving processes. The resultant gulf has been widening in the past two years and may be beyond closing by any governmental agency. The least likely candidate in terms of initial acceptance would seem to be ES. Yet some of the formal governmental avenues presumably developed for this purpose, such as the poverty and model cities agencies, appear to be moving out of touch. Only in Oakland is there any closeness between the poverty agency and the militants, and here the link is manifestly strong only for the blacks.

To find these militant elements is itself a challenge. To channel their energies toward fruitful participation in the manpower effort is even more challenging because a decision-making role is being sought and must be granted, at least in part, if the activist is to be won over. Though these actions are more easily accomplished in fiction than in fact, the program effort presumably directed to the needs of the poor will progressively lose its impact as the dialogue weakens and disappears. In some significant respects, ES seems farther from the real life of the ghetto than when it first ventured from its downtown headquarters five years ago in a less complicated, premilitant era.

Record Keeping and Reporting

There is a particularism in record keeping and reporting. In a sense this harkens back to an earlier era of a jurisdiction-conscious institution as the focus remains rather rigidly limited to the direct activities of ES. Less comprehensible is the drag of a traditional perspective that seems to prevent the ready and rapid inclusion of newer activities in the reporting system. For example, the certification of CEP eligibles for the NAB-JOBS employers is not reported even though the service is provided by ES.

On the positive side, ES has demonstrated a capacity for effective record keeping that is not yet matched by the newer manpower agencies. Reports are current and accurate, and the flow of operational information is increasing by the provision of more data on component activities.

Interrelationships in the Local Manpower System

CEP was an ambitious thrust toward creating a full manpower system for the disadvantaged. A new institution with such a complex assignment takes a great amount of time to build. As the CEPs in these three areas approach the third year of operation, there are encouraging signs that this basic building job has been completed. It is now possible to expect more attention and steady improvements in the quality of the internal operations. For example, the absence of planning has been deplored by many observers. Skillful and competent planning for the next refunding has already occurred in the San Francisco CEP. Even the record keeping and reporting activities, the absence of which has disturbed so many, is beginning to be mastered. Encouraging, too, is the degree of attention being focused on improving the linkages within the CEP system. These CEPs are now ready for, and will be able to use to the benefit of their own operations, the new requirement of DOL for systematic internal self-evaluation.

There are now several manpower systems at the local level, complete or partial, functioning more or less independently of each other. WIN is similar to CEP in terms of its comprehensiveness and the nature of its clientele. Yet the chain of command is different as is the exclusive responsibility of ES. WIN stands apart from CEP with a life of its own, consequently there is less integration than could be expected even in those activities performed for both by ES. The Skills Centers operated under MDTA and private efforts, such as the OIC and the Lockheed consortium, are also independent systems. They are less inclusive than CEP or WIN within themselves and are looked to as resources to be used by CEP and WIN.

The MDTA Skills Centers, as required by legislation, sharply divide functions such as those that occur between education and ES. These built-in jurisdictions seem fated to produce tensions and mutual recriminations. Since overall accountability for results cannot be pinpointed, a strategy for improvement cannot be devised when the situation is bad.

In San Francisco, where the relations of the Unified School District and ES have been reasonably harmonious since the start of MDTA, the newly established Skills Center is meshing well with CEP. But this is the product of long personal relationships among key individuals. In Oakland, the Skills Center, after a long period of mistakes and turmoil, may have achieved some inner stability; but in the course of its history, it lost community support and no longer relates well to CEP.

The NAB operation represents another independent, though partial, system. Linkages to other systems are weak. NAB is critical of these other systems as well, thus strengthening its desire for independence.

Proposed legislation may or may not ultimately compel a fusing together of all these parts. In the interim, administrative initiative may be helpful. For example, the creation of Regional Manpower Administration representatives to oversee local CEPs on behalf of DOL was an accidentally happy innovation. The lessons of this experience might be profitably scanned from time to time. In the bay area, the representatives were competent, strong individuals who proved to be an irreplaceable component in the evolution of the CEPs. They compensated for the weaknesses in executive management of CEP, and some thereby became deeply involved in CEP operations. As an independent force responsible for the exercise of DOL's contract authority, these representatives had the power to compel corrective action when they discovered deficiencies. Their full-time presence in the community gave them a degree of intimate oprational understanding that could not have been achieved in any other way. Though styles and degree of intervention varied among individuals, it is clear that effective monitoring was being applied.

The bay area experience supports the desirability of a single point of control through a federal presence at the local level. While many variants in application might be applied, some of the possibilities would be the following:

(1) If the level and complexity of activity is minimal, the authority of a federal monitor might be broadened.

(2) A variant of this that would also achieve the same objective would be extension of the CEP's authority.

(3) In any event, some local single point of control should be established so that the bifurcated nature of the existing system can be moderated by the influence of someone responsible for viewing the operation as a whole.

(4) As an alternative to the above, positions might be established for full-time attention to the linkages of CEP, WIN, Skills Centers, and other aspects of the local manpower system.

The fourth suggestion above requires elaboration: It can be argued that the RMA performs this function and in important respects this is true. Several factors, however, make the task difficult and thereby interfere with the officer's effectiveness. Because the RMA has a large territory, distance in itself serves to limit his knowledge of all programs. Because there are many different programs, a natural bureaucratic structure along program lines evolved but is now being replaced by generalists responsible for a particular state or other area rather than particular programs. The chain of command from region to state to locality is long and effectiveness in securing integration severely limited when the crossover points from one bureaucracy to another are limited at the top. In the best of circumstances, the time of the RMA is preempted by his many duties and absorbed in frequent crises which presumably could be prevented or solved and overall performance improved by developing a capacity to build bridges between elements at the local level. Yet in the San Francisco Bay area, as in other regions involved in this study, there is no management information system which automatically brings to the attention of the regional staff the condition of programs in their jurisdiction. Bits and pieces may arrive at their desks but provide no comprehensive overview. If the diverse information were to be centrally computed, time and interest would probably limit its usefulness. The vigor with which the representatives of the Regional Manpower Administration made DOL's presence more obvious in San Francisco and Oakland than it was in Boston and locating it in the metropolitan area have given this presence an advantage over that which has prevailed in Denver.

Some have seen in the CAMPS program a mechanism whereby linkages could be improved. To a limited extent this has happened, but CAMPS by its nature as a planning activity cannot go far in achieving integration where the need is the greatest — at the daily operating level. Moreover, CAMPS officials lack authority and often have been unable to secure information from or participation by all those agencies theoretically included. The RMA has authority through his control of funding. Just as the representative of the Regional Manpower Administration was able to use this authority effectively, so too could another local representative use it so that criticisms of ES by NAB (for example) could be investigated and solutions sought rather than leave the issue to fester in peoples' minds.

Although full integration will admittedly be harder to achieve than it has been in the CEP system (with its built-in advantages of a single prime sponsor with a purse-string control of subcontractors), others are totally different institutions with differing legislative authorities, roles, and traditions. From this fertile soil, there are ever-present bureaucratic rivalries, suspicions, and tensions. Difficulties would be immense, the required skills correspondingly high; nevertheless, any extension of the eyes and ears of the RMA to the local level would be followed by more effective use of the considerable power he already has and the further development of the overriding coordinating authority contained in little-used legislative enactments.

The Labor Market Impact

To understand the relative impact of manpower programs on the labor markets of the bay area, comparison of program enrollments and expenditures to the magnitudes of employment and unemployment there is necessary. (See Tables 12-1 and 12-2.) Although the San Francisco-Oakland SMSA encompasses the five-county region discussed in chapter 9, historically the bulk of the population and nonagricultural economic activity has been confined to the highly urbanized area along the shores of San Francisco Bay. Before we scrutinize the problems of the central cities and the contributions of the manpower programs undertaken in them,

TABLE 12-1

Total Expenditures for Completed Manpower Projects of San Francisco-Oakland Bay Area[a]
(Jan. 1, 1966, to June 30, 1970)

Program	Number of Projects	Calendar Year in Which Project Was Completed					Total
		1966	1967	1968	1969	1970	
MDTA institutional	296	$4,576,473	$3,609,623	$ 7,974,043	$ 8,806,140	$ 2,390,059	$27,356,338
MDTA-OJT	196	209,641	963,826	168,191	1,240,715	182,029	2,764,402
NYC in school	16	919,769	744,149	938,132		2,406,407	5,008,457
NYC out of school	19	1,845,921	1,861,561	3,055,019		3,666,373	10,428,874
NYC summer	20	1,054,915	1,775,085	1,994,912	2,697,360		7,522,272
New Careers	1		56,337				56,337
Operation Mainstream	2			211,333			211,333
Work Experience and Training	1	503,100	573,473	303,100	82,990		1,462,663
Work Incentive program	3				319,825	1,900,052	2,219,877
TOTAL		$9,109,819	$9,584,054	$14,644,730	$13,147,030	$10,544,920	$57,030,533

[a] A completed project is a contract or funding period that ended during the time beginning with January 1, 1966, to June 30, 1970. The data recorded in the table are for such completed contracts or funding periods. The one exception consists of NYC contracts that were ongoing as of June 30, 1970. The data for them, exclusive of the summer components for 1970, were recorded in 1970 per the cumulative reports that were available as of June 30 data. **Except for Work Experience and Training**, only projects involving funding through the U.S. Department of Labor were included.

Table 12-2

Actual Enrollment for Completed Manpower Projects of San Francisco-Oakland Bay Area[a]
(Jan. 1, 1966, to June 30, 1970)

Program	Calendar Year in Which Project Was Completed					Total
	1966	1967	1968	1969	1970	
MDTA institutional	2,616	1,893	2,164	3,070	717	10,460
MDTA-OJT	554	2,165	313	2,732	443	6,207
NYC in school	2,950	2,077	2,307		5,244	12,578
NYC out of school	2,684	1,414	3,337		2,522	9,957
NYC summer	3,137	4,685	5,540	7,839		21,201
New Careers		12				12
Operation Mainstream			42			42
Work Experience and Training	840	840	599			2,279
Work Incentive program				3,734	1,466	5,200
Total	12,781	13,086	14,302	17,375	10,392	67,936

[a] A completed project is a contract or funding period that ended during the time beginning with January 1, 1966, to June 30, 1970. The data recorded in the table are for such completed contracts or funding periods. The one exception consists of NYC contracts that were ongoing as of June 30, 1970. The data for them, exclusive of the summer components for 1970, were recorded in 1970 per the cumulative reports that were available as of June 30 data. Except for Work Experience and Training, only projects involving funding through the U.S. Department of Labor were included.

it seems appropriate that we get some concept of the economy of the entire area.

In the decade ending with July 1969, the five-county area experienced a 30 percent increase in employment to approximately 1.4 million workers, more rapid than the increase in population. All industrial sectors except the following experienced some growth: agriculture, shipbuilding, canning and preserving, other food processing, and a miscellaneous group of durable goods manufacturers that included lumber, furniture, stone-clay-glass, instruments, and aircraft and other transportation equipment. Exceeding the average growth for all industries were the manufacturing of electrical machinery, auto assembly, services, government, and finance, insurance, and real estate. By 1968, the major employers, in order of number of workers employed, were as follows: trade (with the heaviest concentration in retailing, services, government) and durable and nondurable manufacturing combined.

All five of the counties shared in the area's growth, though not evenly. The largest percentage of growth was experienced in the "bedroom" counties of Marin and San Mateo, and the lowest in the central city and county of San Francisco. Yet San Francisco and Alameda counties continued to retain their traditional roles as the major employers, accounting for 71 percent of the area's employment.

Opportunities for the Disadvantaged Worker

Because more data are available for Alameda County and its central city of Oakland, the impact of the manpower programs on the labor market is easier to assess there. Where available data permit, comparisons are drawn as well for the other central cities of San Francisco and Richmond.

Alameda County is second only to San Francisco County in the size of its employed labor force; and though its rate of growth in employment between 1960 and 1968 was the second lowest in the metropolitan area, it still experienced the largest absolute increase, 86,800 jobs or 34 percent of the total increase, followed by San Mateo County with 25 and San Francisco County with 19 percent. Furthermore, the outlook for Alameda County, locale of the tri-city industrial heart of the metropolitan area, was optimistic.

After surveying employers in mid-1966, the California Department of Employment projected a 15 percent gain for the county of Alameda in nonagricultural wage and salary employment to 1971, exceeding the projected rate for the United States. It was forecast that 67,000 new workers would be absorbed into employment, 57,000 into newly created jobs and 10,000 into jobs vacated by people leaving the local labor market. However, the rate of growth between 1966 and 1969 at 10 percent was ahead of that projected to 1971.

Translated into blue-collar employment, this growth meant job opportunities for disadvantaged workers . . . for blue-collar jobs (already more than one-third of the total in the county) would — contrary to nationwide trends — increase even more rapidly, thus reflecting forecasts of continued local growth in manufacturing and construction employment. This increase, the source of the projected growth in blue-collar jobs, was 18 percent between 1966 and 1969. The percentage of growth was higher in three other counties, 19 in Contra Costa, 21 in Marin, and 24 in San Mateo. Presumably, there was commensurate growth in blue-collar jobs. Only San Francisco experienced a decline in manufacturing and construction.

If we translate the growth in the county of Alameda into expanded opportunities for disadvantaged workers, we find that in July 1966, according to a study conducted that year by the California Department of Employment, there were 370,560 nonagricultural wage and salary workers employed in the county, of which 340,830 were in identifiable occupations. The employers of the latter group reported that 76,380 jobs were entry level (i.e., available to job seekers without prior experience) and that they expected the total employment to increase by 53,140 or 16 percent by 1971. To estimate how many of these jobs could conceivably be filled by disadvantaged workers, assume that the jobs would have to be entry level, with minimum educational requirements below high school graduation.

The above calculations nearly match the qualifications of the typical enrollee in manpower programs for the disadvantaged. Of the 731 enrollees in East Bay manpower programs interviewed for purposes of this study, all but two reported having some job experience. Yet that amounted to 12 months or less for 77 percent of the enrollees during the 36-month period immediately preceding enrollment. Only 8 percent reported employment of more than 24 months. Moreover, 33 percent were attending school prior to enrollment, thus their work experience probably consisted mostly of part-time and summer employment. Finally, 62 percent of the 565 enrollees had attained a maximum educational level of 11 years or less. The typical enrollee in a manpower program was a candidate for no more than an entry-level job with low educational requirements.

The California Department of Employment asked employers to list the minimum educational qualifications to fill their entry-level and other jobs. To estimate the number of jobs that might conceivably be filled by disadvantaged workers, we selected those occupations where 50 percent or more of the jobs could, according to the employers, be filled by someone who had completed no more than the 11th year of schooling and where there were entry-level jobs. When the 50 percent is calculated, the jobs for which no minimum education was indicated were counted as requiring high school graduation or better because this often meant an arrangement whereby work experience could be substituted for education.

In July 1966, employment in the occupations selected was 55,395 or 16 percent of the 340,830; of these, 21,014 were entry-level jobs. In addition, employers estimated that employment in these occupations would rise by 9,971 or 18 percent by 1971.

The Decline of the Central City

Much has recently been written about the relative decline of the central city, which is indeed true of Alameda County. Almost all of the growth in employment between 1960 and 1969 occurred in the southern portion. Former agricultural land was now the locale of 162,000 new residents and 87,000 new jobs. Furthermore, several durable goods manufacturers and wholesalers relocated there from Oakland. (Manufacturing and construction employment declined 16 percent in Oakland between 1958 and 1966.) Nevertheless, the decline of Oakland was only relative because overall employment during the period rose by 5 percent, and opportunities for the disadvantaged, measured by entry-level jobs with low educational requirements, by 2 percent.

San Francisco also declined relative to San Mateo County immediately south of it. Yet overall employment in San Francisco rose between 1958 and 1966 by 9 percent, and opportunities for the disadvantaged, measured by entry-level jobs with low educational requirements, by 1 percent. Similar data are not available for Richmond, but that the city has declined relative to the remainder of Contra Costa County is clear, while the most rapid employment growth has been white-collar jobs.

Population Changes

While employment opportunities in the metropolitan area were expanding (an increase of 24 percent between 1960 and 1968), so too was the population, though not so rapidly, increasing only 18 percent between 1960 and 1968. This relationship between growth in employment and population also held true for the central cities. Thus between 1960 and 1968, San Francisco's population grew by 1 percent, while its employment increased 10 percent.

The continued difficulty of placing disadvantaged persons in jobs in the face of such expanding opportunity, and hence the justification of manpower programs, is explained by the changing ethnic composition of the central city's population and the tendency of the suburban white commuter to fill the expanding job slots. The levels of education and skills and the quality of work habits of the Spanish-surnamed and nonwhite populations are lower than required to fill the jobs available in the city. Moreover, the changing occupational structure in the city tends to worsen that discrepancy, with the consequence that employers in the city rely heavily on commuters, and jobs that the disadvantaged might conceivably fill are more and more located in the suburbs.

Governmental employment was the only sector of the economy to show a net job growth since 1960 for unemployed Oakland residents. Among all other classes of workers, there were declines in the number of residents employed. The 7,000 new government jobs in Oakland since 1960 equal the number of additional Oakland residents who found jobs in the government sector during that period. When employment in Oakland is examined — irrespective of the residences of workers — there were increases in Oakland payrolls in transportation, communications, and public utilities; retail trade; finance, insurance, and real estate; and services as well as government. Nevertheless, opportunity per capita of population was expanding everywhere in the metropolitan area, as evidenced by the falling rate of unemployment (5.0 to 4.1 percent between 1960 and 1968) and the rising labor force participation rate (from 44 percent of the population in 1960 to 46 percent in 1968), including the central city and job opportunities for the lowly educated and inexperienced.

The task of the administrators of the manpower programs was to increase the competitiveness of those people who would otherwise be the last to participate in the expanding opportunity previously described. Supposedly, most of those people would, without the benefit of the program, be acceptable for the entry-level jobs with low educational requirements. They may, however, be less preferred by employers because of ethnicity, age, inability to speak English well, past failures with other employers, or personal styles and attitudes (different from the benevolent and comfortable middle-class people whom employers have sought and been willing to accept in the past). Manpower programs — through such activities as language instruction, work experience, prevocational training, and job development — may deal with some of these problems; or the program directors may seek to increase the disadvantaged population's area of competitiveness by increasing their geographical mobility so that they can bid for the entry-level, low educational jobs in the suburbs. No bay area program, however, contains such a component.

Finally, the area of competitiveness may be increased by upgrading the educational or skill levels of the disadvantaged workers so that they can bid for better jobs. Such components — general education development training, adult basic education, and skills training — are plentiful in bay area programs.

In the final analysis, the success of a program will be gauged by the number and quality of the placements it makes. To keep the number high, program directors might be expected to prepare workers for expanding occupations or occupations where employment is relatively large. Yet it is also possible that directors may be tempted to concentrate on high-turnover occupations, even though they are static or declining, thereby feeding what in essence is a pool of casual labor.

To test what had happened in the bay area, we examined the course offerings at the East Bay Skills Center for the period of July 1968 to November 1970 and in the San Francisco MDTA program for 1968 through 1970. Of the 47 occupations identified, 24 could be matched with those listed in the 1966 California Department of Employment study. Only one of the 24 — order clerks — was contained on the list of likely occupations for disadvantaged workers. This was as it should have been . . . the purpose of skills training is to qualify the workers for better jobs.

On a less optimistic note, however, the employers in 10 of the occupations reported in the 1966 study that they had no entry-level jobs and (in three) that they expected no growth in employment between 1966 and 1971. In fact, the ratio of entry-level jobs to total employment in the MDTA occupations was only 0.19:1 compared to 0.22:1 for all occupations, and 0.38:1 for the occupations with low educational requirements. On the other hand, the expected growth rate (21 percent) in the occupations for which training was offered exceeded that for all occupations (16 percent) and that for the occupations with low educational requirements (18 percent).

The list of MDTA occupations was also compared to one from the California Department of Employment to reflect supply and demand conditions in the summer of 1968 when unemployment hovered around the 4.0 percent level. Only eight of the occupations appeared on both lists. One was identified as a shortage occupation, two as surplus occupations, and five as those where demand and supply were in balance.

On the evidence presented, it seems clear that the MDTA program in the bay area has succumbed to the temptation to schedule courses in high-turnover occupations. A similar conclusion was reached by the California Department of Employment in describing a list designed to guide skills training in San Francisco:

> In selecting occupations to be covered in the *Profile*, emphasis was placed on entry-level and . . . "volume occupations" . . . those . . . where job openings are numerous, because of high turnover or the size of the occupation or both. Further, emphasis was put on occupations that could provide employment for the job seeker with few skills and on occupations for which training is feasible under the manpower programs available to the city's residents. Not all occupations meeting these criteria are in the *Profile*, but the more than 70 occupations or occupational fields . . . discussed represent a sizable proportion of such jobs. Further, to put the occupations into perspective with the entire San Francisco job market, the jobs discussed represent a majority of the city's skilled, semiskilled, and unskilled jobs, over 50 percent of the clerical jobs, and most of the volume jobs found in retail trades and service occupations.[6]

[6] *Occupational Profile, City of San Francisco*, p. 1.

The list contained 71 occupations, 25 of which appeared on the 1968 supply and demand list. Of these occupations, seven were shortage, nine were surplus, and nine were those where supply and demand were in balance. Clearly, high turnover was considered important enough to override supply and demand conditions.

In summary, the differences in magnitudes between total unemployment and the total enrollment of all manpower programs in the bay area are too great to manifest a measurable impact. Program enrollment has had a major influence on the lives and earnings of enrollees, but not of a magnitude to effect enrollment. Efforts to minimize costs have encouraged training for high-turnover occupations rather than those characterized by increasing demand and promising career opportunities.

Part 4
A Comparative Analysis

Iver E. Bradley
Garth L. Mangum
R. Thayne Robson

Analysis of the Impact
of Manpower Programs
upon Employment
and Earnings
13

The institutional impacts of manpower programs are important and worth examining. However, the only real justification for their existence is the extent to which they improve the employment and earnings experience of the enrollees. That in the final analysis can only be determined by some form of follow-up to compare postenrollment experience with some estimate of what would have happened in the absence of the program. This chapter summarizes the results of a follow-up study, comparing the pre- and posttraining earnings of enrollees in the programs having as their objective an improvement in job skills and basic education.

NATURE OF THE FOLLOW-UP SAMPLE

The follow-up sample for measuring the impact of training, remedial education, language, and orientation programs consisted of 1,709 enrollees in the Manpower Development and Training Act (MDTA) program, the Concentrated Employment Program (CEP), and the Work Incentive (WIN) program between October 1969 and February 1970. After enrollees were interviewed initially at the training sites, three subsequent contacts were made during the first, second, and fourth three-month periods following the initial interview. Of the original sample, 243 persons or 14 percent were still enrolled in manpower programs at the time of the fourth-wave interview. Another 329 or 19 percent were not found for interview after the initial contact. Of the remaining 1,137 enrollees, 821 or 48 percent completed their programs and were interviewed during the posttraining period, while 316 enrollees or 19 percent dropped out before completion. The sample for each of the four cities is summarized in Table 13-1. Available resources did not allow for a control group. "Before" and "after" comparisons are always suspect because of possible failure to

Table 13-1

Summary of the Follow-up Sample

Category	San Francisco		Oakland		Denver		Boston		Total	
	Number	Percent	Number	Percent	Number	Percent	Number	Percent	Number	Percent
Total enrolled	378		565		320		466		1,709	
Still enrolled at time of interview	48	13%	107	19%	32	10%	56	13%	243	14%
Pretraining interview only	75	20	88	16	62	19	104	23	329	19
Posttraining interview (those who completed)	192	50	210	37	173	54	246	55	821	48
Posttraining interview (dropouts)	63	17%	160	28%	53	17%	40	9%	316	19%

measure those changes that would have occurred in the absence of treatment. However, estimates of those effects were made, based on prevailing wage and employment trends, allowing an estimate of the net program impact. Unaccounted for is the tendency of young entrants to the labor force to experience an improvement in employment stability from the mere passage of time, a biasing factor for those programs enrolling a predominantly young clientele. While there are serious limitations which must be kept in mind when the survey results are assessed, they are not sufficient to explain away the generally favorable findings.

Objective Measurements

Comparisons were made between two different pretraining periods and the posttraining period. Period I is the full 36 months before enrollment in any of the manpower programs; Period II, the 12 months immediately preceding enrollment; and Period III, the entire posttraining period — i.e., the time elapsed when the enrollee left the program until final interview.

The employment and earnings impact was measured by wage differences between the weighted average hourly wage of the posttraining period and that of the pretraining periods and by employment stability and intensity measurements. Employment stability is defined (for those enrollees with work experience) as the percentage of time enrollees who held at least one job were employed during a given period. Employment intensity involves the total groups, whether or not they had held a job. It is defined as the proportion of available time worked by the entire sample during a given period.

The product of the average hourly wage rate and the employment stability resulted in an "earnings coefficient," a relative measurement of the enrollees' earnings from wages. For example, if a person works 75 percent of a certain time period at an average hourly wage of $2.00, his earnings coefficient would be $1.50. Multiplied by 2,000 hours, this person's annual earnings would be generated to $3,000 at the given wage rate and employment stability. Differences between the posttraining earnings coefficients and that for one of the pretraining periods provide an earnings difference.

With the above measurements, most of the analysis was directed to answering the following questions:

(1) What was the general effect of the manpower training programs upon the earning capacity and employability of the enrollees?

(2) Are there significant differences among or between the four cities in terms of the impact upon the enrollees?

(3) What training variables (such as content of program, occupation of training, or length of time in program) or socioeconomic variables (such as age, sex, number of children, etc.) are related to the success or failure of manpower training programs?

FOUR-CITY SUMMARY

When the follow-up study was planned, it was unforeseen that the initial interviews would occur just as national unemployment rates began to rise and continued to rise in a steadily slackening market. Despite the unfavorable economic climate, the impact of program participation across programs, service functions, and cities was surprisingly positive. Table 13-2 gives a summary of the average values of the measurements defined in the previous section.

On the average across the four cities, the mean hourly wage rate rose by $0.50 between Periods I and III and $0.42 between Periods II and III. The average hourly wage differences ranged from $0.30 in Denver to $0.76 in San Francisco. Any citywide wage difference exceeding $0.12 an hour was statistically significant at the 1 percent significance level. Although wages were rising during the period between the first- and fourth-wave interviews, there were no minimum wage increases and little unionization to boost the bottom of the wage structure within slackening markets. Since the midpoints of 36 and 12 months are a year apart, the $0.12 difference between the average hourly wage rates of Periods I and III may be an indication of the normal wage change in the tighter labor markets which prevailed between 1966 and 1969 and which included a substantial rise in the minimum wage. The normal increase during 1970 should have been no greater. Therefore, though the study included no control group to separate enrollment gains from those which would have occurred in the absence of the program enrollment, there should be no question that the impact of the programs on the earnings of the enrollees was substantial.

Improvement in average hourly wage rates measured only one dimension of the employment and earnings impact. The average enrollee who had work experience during Period I was employed 54.4 percent of the available time during that period. The average enrollee employed at any time throughout Period II had a job for 56.6 percent of the available time during that period. The average worker in the sample during Period III was employed 63.4 percent of the available time. An increase of 4.5 percent is necessary for statistical significance at a 1 percent level. Thus the improvements in employment stability were highly significant for San Francisco and Oakland. In Boston, the change in employment stability over Period I was significant, but that over Period III was at the margin of significance. The employment stability changes for Denver were not statistically significant, though the wage changes were.

The employment stability measurement compared only enrollees with some employment during the various periods. The employment intensity of the total sample, including those with zero employment stability, shows the same trends but at lower levels. The total groups were employed on the average 44 percent of the available weeks in Period I, 36 percent of the

TABLE 13-2
Average Wage, Employment, and Earnings Measurements

Category	San Francisco Hourly Wage	San Francisco Percentage	Oakland Hourly Wage	Oakland Percentage	Boston Hourly Wage	Boston Percentage	Denver Hourly Wage	Denver Percentage	Unweighted Four-City Average Hourly Wage	Unweighted Four-City Average Percentage
Period I:										
Wage rate	$1.76		$1.92		$1.79		$1.68		$1.79	
Employment stability		55.0%		45.3%		62.9%		54.4%		54.4%
Employment intensity		43.6		30.4		55.2		46.7		44.0
Earnings coefficient	1.00		0.95		1.20		1.13		1.07	
Period II:										
Wage rate	2.02		1.90		1.88		1.84		1.91	
Employment stability		47.0		49.4		68.2		61.8		56.6
Employment intensity		27.1		23.5		50.3		42.9		36.0
Earnings coefficient	0.99		1.08		1.35		1.28		1.17	
Period III:										
Wage rate	2.51		2.21		2.30		2.07		2.27	
Employment stability		63.3		60.2		72.6		57.2		63.4
Employment intensity		49.0		33.7		56.7		43.3		48.1
Earnings coefficient	1.60		1.43		1.76		1.26		1.51	
Period III differences[a]:										
Wage difference over Period I	0.76		0.40		0.50		0.35		0.50	
Wage difference over Period II	0.58		0.35		0.46		0.30		0.42	
Earnings difference over Period I	0.81		0.69		0.73		0.52		0.69	
Earnings difference over Period II	$0.81		$0.62		$0.62		$0.40		$0.61	

[a] Average wage and earnings differences are not necessarily equal to the differences in pre- and postaverages because differences are calculated for only those with *both* pre- and posttraining experience, while the averages are calculated for those with *either* pre- or posttraining work experience.

available weeks in Period II, and 48 percent of the available weeks in the posttraining period. Improvement in employment intensity was significant for all the cities except Denver, but only in Boston was the full postenrollment sample employed on the average of more than half the time.

The employment stability coefficient is the best measurement of the employment experience to the extent that those with no jobs were not seeking them and were therefore out of the labor force rather than "unemployed." If all persons without jobs were actually seeking them during a particular period, the employment intensity coefficient would be the relevant measurement. It would appear that the "true" measurement is somewhat between these two. For example, of the 342 persons who were never employed in posttraining Period III, more than half (53.5 percent) did not look for a job; i.e., they did not become members of the labor force. Interestingly, of those who did not look for work, 83 percent were women, and nearly 60 percent were in WIN programs. Thus many of the employment intensity coefficients are too low; i.e., there is a downward bias because many of the enrollees were not really members of the labor force. This is particularly serious for all WIN programs, and since the Oakland-Richmond area sample had a high proportion of WIN enrollees, the general level of employment in Period III is much closer to the employment stability of 60 percent than the very low employment intensity of 34 percent.

The difference between the earnings coefficients of Periods I and III was $0.69 an hour, while that between Periods II and III was $0.61. The average differences for Boston, San Francisco, and Oakland were all highly significant. Denver's earnings gains between Periods I and III were significant, but a slight drop in the earnings difference occurred between Periods II and III because preenrollment employment stability was enough higher to offset the hourly wage gain.

If we translate the above figures into annual earnings equivalents, we find that the average enrollee across the four cities would have gained $1,380 a year over Period I and $1,220 a year over Period II. Transformed into percentages, this means that there was an increase in earnings of 40 percent over Period I and 30 percent over Period II. However, the average enrollee who worked after training was still earning only at an annual rate of $3,000. Poverty had been made substantially more comfortable but had not been eliminated.

Comparisons of the results in the four cities show some substantial differences. Enrollee characteristics are compared in Table 13-3. There was little difference in median age, education, size of household, or number of dependents. The sex mix was significant: San Francisco and Denver had more than half male enrollees; Boston, slightly more female; and Oakland, overwhelmingly female. There were also substantial differences in the proportion of heads of households, with male-enrolling Denver and female-enrolling Oakland, in that order, at the top of the list. Oakland's

Table 13-3

Four-City Summary of Trainee Characteristics

Characteristic	San Francisco	Oakland	Denver	Boston
Average:				
Age (years)	28.1	28.6	27.3	28.9
Education (years)	10.5	10.2	9.7	10.2
Size of household	4.1	4.5	4.2	4.0
Number of dependents	2.6	2.8	2.6	2.2
Length of time in program (months)	8.9	10.2	6.2	5.9
Percentage of:				
Male	57%	33%	52%	43%
Head of household	69	71	77	61
Currently on welfare	43	76	42	40
Ethnicity percentage:				
Black	36	62	15	41
Oriental	18	2		
Spanish-surnamed	31	15	56	22
White	14	19	24	36
Other[a]	1%	2%	5%	1%

[a] American Indian and no response.

welfare proportion, combined with its female and head of household proportion, signals its major socioeconomic problem as well as the problem of its program administrators.

In ethnicity, Oakland's enrollees were nearly two-thirds black, with Spanish-surnamed and whites almost equally divided in the remainder of the slots. Boston's black and its white enrollees were nearly equal, accompanied by a smaller Puerto Rican group. San Francisco's black and Spanish-surnamed enrollments were roughly equal, as were Oriental and white enrollments. Denver's program enrollees were more than 50 percent Spanish-surnamed, 25 percent white, 15 percent black, and 5 percent other (primarily American Indian).

Of Boston's sample, 13 percent were still enrolled at the final interview, compared to 10 percent in Denver, 13 percent in San Francisco, and 19 percent in Oakland. Another 23 percent in Boston, 19 percent in Denver, 20 percent in San Francisco, and 16 percent in Oakland were not found for interviews after training.

Of those no longer enrolled but who were interviewed after training, 9 percent in Boston, 17 percent in Denver, 17 percent in San Francisco, and 28 percent in Oakland had dropped out before they had completed the programs, leaving 55, 54, 50, and 37 percent, respectively, as completions (see Table 13-1).

Of those with pre- and posttraining employment, the average hourly wage increase over Periods I and II, respectively, were $0.50 and $0.46 for Boston, $0.35 and $0.30 for Denver, $0.76 and $0.58 for San Francisco, and $0.40 and $0.35 for Oakland. Employment stability also improved substantially in the four cities, rising in Boston from 62.9 and 68.2 percent for the first two periods to 72.6 percent for the posttraining period. Similar calculations for other cities show, respectively, 54.4, 61.8, and 57.2 percent for Denver; 55.0, 47.0, and 63.3 percent for San Francisco; and 45.3, 49.4, and 60.2 percent for Oakland.

Comparisons of the wage and employment stability measurements can again be combined into one of earnings increases and equivalent annual earnings. For Boston, the earnings differences were $0.73 during Period I and $0.62 for Period II. As a comparison, the same figures, respectively, for the other cities were: Denver, $0.52 and $0.40; San Francisco, $0.81 for both; and Oakland, $0.69 and $0.62. Transformed into annual earnings equivalents, these figures show that the Boston enrollees on the average were gaining either $1,460 or $1,240 as a result of their decision to participate in the manpower programs. Comparable figures for the other cities, respectively, were $1,010 and $800 in Denver, $1,620 (both) in San Francisco, and $1,380 and $1,240 in Oakland — in all cases, a substantial gain for a low-income group.

In summary, San Francisco enrollees experienced a surprising increase in hourly wage rates. Boston's rate increases were next highest, those experienced in Oakland were substantial, with those in Denver modest but statistically significant. Boston experienced the greatest employment stability, but since the pretraining levels were also high, the improvement was modest and only marginally significant during Period II. San Francisco experienced the greatest improvement in employment stability with Oakland close behind, while Denver's was not significant.

However, the wage difference and employment stability measurements were for only those who had jobs. Fifteen percent in the Boston sample, 14 percent in Denver, 15 percent in San Francisco, and 30 percent in Oakland had no work experience in the posttraining period, representing particularly the high proportion of welfare mothers in Oakland. Including those with posttraining employment, Boston enrollees worked only a little more than half of the available time in the posttraining period; San Francisco enrollees, just under half; Denver participants, 43 percent of the available time; and Oakland enrollees, one-third of the available time.

Yet only Denver failed to experience significant improvement in employment intensity.

It is important to know which programs worked for whom and the conditions and locations of the programs. MDTA and WIN can be compared across the cities, with other programs more city-specific.

Manpower Development and Training Act Programs

There were no consistent differences in the enrollee characteristics among the various cities in the MDTA programs (as will subsequently be shown in Tables 13-4, 13-6, 13-8, and 13-10). In Boston, there were somewhat older enrollees and more females and whites than in other cities, more males in San Francisco, and more Spanish-surnamed in Denver. The Oakland sample contained few MDTA enrollees because of our inability to obtain a significant number of interviews in the East Bay Skills Center which handled most of the MDTA enrollment.

MDTA began with the handicap of relatively high preenrollment hourly wage rates and employment stability. Therefore, though the posttraining average hourly wage was relatively high in most cities, compared to other programs, and the posttraining employment stability was above average for the cities, the wage and earnings differences were not. Having started its enrollees at a higher level, MDTA found that improvement was more difficult for them.

Work Incentive Programs

In each of the four cities, differences between WIN and non-WIN trainees were, almost without exception, statistically significant, as shown by the following:

(1) Nearly all of the WIN enrollees were receiving welfare at the time of interview. Among the other groups, this proportion was rarely more than 50 percent, and usually between 20 and 30 percent.

(2) The WIN groups were predominantly female (70 to 85 percent). There were other programs with more females than males, but in general, the non-WIN trainees were more than 50 percent male.

(3) In addition to (2) above, WIN enrollees were significantly high in the percentage of heads of households and in the mean number of dependents.

(4) The mean age of the WIN group was higher than that of other groups, though mean years of formal education in the WIN group were generally about average for the city.

(5) The length of time in the WIN training program was considerably longer than for the other programs.

In San Francisco, Denver, and Boston, percentages of the total sample that were WIN trainees were, respectively, 27, 25, and 19 percent. In the Oakland area, this percentage was an overwhelming 64 percent; however, the citywide analysis of Oakland trainees is influenced by a two to one majority of WIN enrollees. The percentage of WIN trainees with work experience in the pretraining periods was usually lower than that for trainees in other programs. In the posttraining period, this percentage for the WIN group was always significantly low — leading to the assumption that few should actually be counted as members of the labor force.

Though it was not uniform across the cities, WIN tended to have low average wage rates and the lowest employment stability before enrollment. Its pretraining employment intensity was exceedingly low. Yet its wage differences and earnings coefficients were above the average in Boston, higher than any program in Denver, low in San Francisco, and about average in Oakland. Thus the program's greatest problem was that relatively few of its welfare mothers chose to seek employment after training. Its dropout rate was also exceedingly high. Yet for those who sought employment after leaving the program, the gains were substantial in some cities and significant in all.

Individual City Analysis

The remainder of the programs tend to differ considerably or be specialized by city. Therefore all of the programs are compared within each city.

Boston

Sampling in Boston included four programs, differing by sponsor as well as by content: WIN, run jointly by the employment service (ES) and public welfare; the orientation centers, run by the community action agency (CAA), Action for Boston Community Development, Inc. (ABCD); one orientation center, subcontracted to the Opportunities Industrialization Center (OIC); and MDTA training, provided by the Boston School Department. The mean length of time in training in ABCD and OIC (3.1 and 3.2 months, respectively) was less than half that in WIN (8.9 months) and MDTA (7.9 months) as shown in Table 13-4. As a subcontractor under ABCD's CEP contract, OIC was running the same 15-week orientation and skills program allowed by the prime contract, though its teaching emphasis and the sources of its enrollees differed somewhat from the ABCD-run orientation centers.

The MDTA trainees, as well as those of WIN, were significantly older than the ABCD and OIC trainees. There were other significant differences:

(1) The OIC enrollees were predominantly black, and the center gave major emphasis to technical training, specifically machine operation, engineering aide, and draftsman.

Table 13-4

Enrollee Characteristics and Training Content in Boston Training
Programs from Sample Survey
(1969–70)

Characteristic and Category	Total	WIN	ABCD	OIC	MDTA
Sample size	446	87	139	62	158
Average:					
Age (years)	28.9	30.2	26.8	26.6	31.1
Education (years)	10.2	10.4	10.1	11.0	9.8
Size of household	4.0	4.6	4.4	4.0	3.3
Number of dependents	2.2	3.0	2.1	2.0	2.0
Average length of time in program (months)	5.9	8.9	3.1	3.2	7.9
Percentage of:					
Male	43%	26%	65%	34%	37%
Head of household	61	84	45	52	66
Currently on welfare	40	98	35	19	20
Ethnic percentage:					
White	36	57	22	3	50
Black	41	37	47	80	21
Spanish-surnamed	22	6	29	10	29
Other	1	0	2	7	0
Training content percentage:					
English as a second language	14	2	17	15	18
GED and basic education	17	28	7	0	27
Clerical	26	9	20	0	51
Machine operator	16	7	20	59	0
Other technical	27%	54%	36%	26%	4%

(2) The MDTA training was almost void of technical training, with
approximately 50 percent clerical and the other 50 percent enrolled in English as a second language and basic education. The
MDTA racial emphasis was on whites and Spanish-surnamed,
with a lower proportion on blacks, most of the training occurring

in one Skills Center located in an area generally felt to be hostile to blacks.

(3) The ABCD group was the only one in Boston with more than half its enrollees male (65 percent), though it had the lowest proportion of heads of household. Training categories were broad, with relatively low numbers in English as a second language and basic education. Predominant racial groups in ABCD were black and Spanish-surnamed.

(4) Despite WIN's enrollment of 74 percent females, less than 10 percent of its trainees were in clerical training, with three of five enrolled in a variety of skilled manual occupations. The WIN racial mix was white and black, with few Spanish-surnamed.

In the city of Boston, the short-term (15-week) training programs conducted by ABCD and OIC were significantly more effective than MDTA and WIN, as measured by changes in earnings levels. The average hourly wage rate increase between Periods I and III was $0.64 for ABCD and only $0.35 for OIC, compared to $0.41 and $0.56 for MDTA and WIN, respectively (Table 13-5). However, OIC brought a large improvement in employment stability, while ABCD's was substantial. As a result, the difference in earnings coefficients over Periods I through II was $0.90 an hour for OIC and $0.91 for ABCD, compared to $0.45 for MDTA and $0.76 for WIN. Thus the average trainee in the ABCD and OIC orientation centers who found a job after training (as more did for ABCD and OIC than for MDTA and WIN) would have experienced the equivalent of an $1,800 increase in annual earnings compared with $900 and $1,530 for MDTA and WIN, respectively.

Employment intensity was also 65 percent for ABCD and OIC in the posttraining period, compared to 31 percent for WIN and 58 percent for MDTA. Because of the larger proportion of minorities (though no significant difference in education) in the former two programs, the achievements on the 15-week courses were impressive.

The advantage of ABCD and OIC over MDTA was not so much that the end result was significantly different, the posttraining average hourly wage rates and employment stability were similar, though the ABCD program had an edge of more than $0.20 an hour above the others. The primary difference was that the ABCD and OIC enrollees were farther behind before training and made greater gains. WIN was moderately behind in ending wage rate but farther behind in posttraining employment stability.

Though WIN was the lowest in pretraining employment stability, its gains did not equal those of the shorter programs, and it suffered the additional handicap that the average of its total enrollment (including those enrollees not obtaining posttraining employment) worked only 31 percent of the available posttraining time. Since ABCD and OIC training periods

TABLE 13-5

Employment and Earnings Impact of Boston Training Programs[a,b]

Category	Total Hourly Wage	Total Percentage	WIN Hourly Wage	WIN Percentage	ABCD Hourly Wage	ABCD Percentage	OIC Hourly Wage	OIC Percentage	MDTA Hourly Wage	MDTA Percentage
Period I:										
Average wage rate	$1.80		$1.77		$1.78		$1.91		$1.79	
Percent employed		88.0%		83.0%		92.0%		95.0%		83.0%
Employment stability		62.9		52.9		62.9		49.8		74.6
Earnings coefficient	1.20		0.97		1.15		0.95		1.44	
Period II:										
Average wage rate	1.88		1.78		1.88		1.89		1.93	
Percent employed		74.0		69.0		77.0		73.0		73.0
Employment stability		68.2		60.1		74.5		62.0		68.2
Employment intensity		51.0		41.0		67.0		45.0		50.0
Earnings coefficient	1.35		1.01		1.45		1.13		1.43	
Period III:										
Average wage rate	2.30		2.18		2.45		2.23		2.23	
Percent employed		77.0		48.0		86.0		90.0		80.0
Employment stability		72.6		65.2		75.8		71.8		72.2
Employment intensity		56.0%		31.0%		65.0%		65.0%		58.0%
Earnings coefficient	1.76		1.41		1.91		1.72		1.71	
Period III differences:										
Wage difference over Period I	0.50		0.56		0.64		0.35		0.41	
Wage difference over Period II	0.46		0.58		0.60		0.37		0.30	
Earnings difference over Period I	0.73		0.76		0.91		0.90		0.45	
Earnings difference over Period II	$0.61		$0.65		$0.68		$0.72		$0.50	

[a] Mean values.

[b] The postinterview sample size for each program is as follows: total, 286; Work Incentive programs, 54; Action for Boston Community Development, Inc., 93; Opportunities Industrialization Center, 41; and Manpower Development and Training Act programs, 98.

were only a little more than a third as long as those for MDTA and WIN and since ABCD and OIC enrolled a larger proportion of minorities, particularly blacks, they were clearly the better programs in terms of investment of time and money by the trainees and the sponsoring organizations.

Denver

Occupation of training and length of time in training, age and years of education of trainee, number of dependents, percentage male, percentage currently on welfare, and race were all program- and sponsor-dependent variables in the city of Denver (Table 13-6).

MDTA was the "star" program in Denver (Table 13-7). WIN produced a higher wage difference between pre- and postenrollment periods, but its employment stability and intensity were far less. Operation SER accomplished even less on the latter grounds, though it did better than MDTA on the Periods III and II wage difference. CEP achieved no significant improvement in wages or employment. MDTA and WIN contributed substantially in annual earnings equivalents to those of their enrollees who obtained jobs following training. However, only slightly more than half of the WIN enrollees had posttraining jobs, compared to 84 percent for MDTA.

The general results for Denver were positive but less favorable than in the other cities. The Operation SER sample was small but was drawn from a homogeneous group of predominantly young Spanish-surnamed. It provided only basic education and general education development (GED) equivalency for an average of 2.2 months' duration. It apparently did little to change their basic employability. More than 80 percent of the CEP trainees received only orientation and prevocational training, with a mean training time of 4.4 months. The WIN program group was primarily female heads of household, and 70 percent of them received only basic education.

Thus MDTA was the only Denver training program providing significant skills. Its enrollees were more than half males, 39 percent whites, and 46 percent Spanish-surnamed. Its average training time was 7.1 months; most of the enrollees received technical skills training in a community college Skills Center setting. There was a real opportunity for the enrollees to improve employability, and they profited from it.

San Francisco

For any sizable group of enrollees, MDTA paid off best in San Francisco as well; however, a series of smaller programs also did exceedingly well. A very small group — sponsored by the CAA's Economic Opportunity Council (EOC) — deserves some special comment. In a city where the success of the manpower programs can best be characterized as surprising, the EOC trainees achieved an even greater success. The initial EOC

Table 13-6

Enrollee Characteristics and Training Content in Denver Training
Programs from Sample Survey
(1969–70)

Characteristic and Category	Total	WIN	Operation SER	MDTA	CEP
Sample size	320	80	36	149	55
Average:					
Age (years)	27.3	29.7	24.5	26.6	27.5
Education (years)	9.7	9.2	9.1	10.0	9.9
Size of household	4.2	4.8	4.0	3.8	4.3
Number of dependents	2.6	3.3	2.3	2.3	2.7
Average length of time in program (months)	6.2	7.3	2.2	7.1	4.4
Percentage of:					
Male	52%	31%	53%	52%	82%
Head of household	77	87	81	72	71
Currently on welfare	42	95	39	19	25
Ethnic percentage:					
White	24	16	3	39	9
Black	15	24	0	9	27
Spanish-surnamed	56	58	91	46	56
Other	5	2	6	5	8
Training content percentage:					
Basic education	36	70	97	17	0
Orientation	14	0	0	0	84
Clerical	17	13	3	25	7
Skilled manual	33%	17%	0%	58%	9%

sample was 32, with only 20 interviewed after training. The mean length of training time was a short 3.2 months, about one-third of the training time for the WIN and MDTA groups. Racially, the EOC trainees were about one-third black and two-thirds Spanish-surnamed; the mean age of 24.6 years and the mean number of dependents (2.2) were both below the average for all programs (Table 13-8). Other than this, there was nothing obviously unusual or significantly different about the group. Yet the aver-

TABLE 13-7

Employment and Earnings Impact of Denver Training Programs[a,b]

Category	Total		WIN		Operation SER		MDTA		CEP	
	Hourly Wage	Percentage	Hourly Wage	Percentage	Hourly Wage	Percentage	Hourly Wage	Percentage	Hourly Wage	Percentage
Period I:										
Average wage rate	$1.68		$1.46		$1.79		$1.70		$1.77	
Percent employed		86.0%		63.0%		91.0%		94.0%		95.0%
Employment stability		54.4		46.4		66.7		54.2		56.6
Employment intensity		47.0		29.0		61.0		51.0		54.0
Earnings coefficient	1.13		0.97		1.43		1.15		1.01	
Period II:										
Average wage rate	1.84		1.73		1.76		1.86		1.88	
Percent employed		69.0		36.0		77.0		81.0		84.0
Employment stability		61.8		58.6		62.4		63.3		59.4
Employment intensity		43.0		21.0		48.0		51.0		50.0
Earnings coefficient	1.28		1.31		1.21		1.33		1.17	
Period III:										
Average wage rate	2.07		1.95		2.25		2.14		1.88	
Percent employed		76.0		54.0		73.0		84.0		86.0
Employed stability		57.2		47.9		32.9		66.0		53.4
Employment intensity		43.0%		26.0%		24.0%		56.0%		46.0%
Earnings coefficient	1.26		1.26		0.70		1.42		1.08	
Period III differences:										
Wage difference over Period I	0.35		0.48		0.33		0.40		0.12	
Wage difference over Period II	0.30		0.46		0.53		0.32		0.05	
Earnings difference over Period I	0.52		0.66		–0.04		0.65		0.34	
Earnings difference over Period II	$0.40		$0.48		$0.04		$0.51		$0.24	

a Mean values.

b The postinterview sample size for each program is as follows: total, 226; Work Incentive programs, 59; Operation SER, 22; Manpower Development and Training Act programs, 108; and Concentrated Employment Program, 37.

age wage increase was $1.16 over Period I and $1.19 for Period II. With 95 percent of the group obtaining jobs and working two-thirds of the available time, the earnings differences were $1.16 and $0.93 over Periods I and II, respectively, sufficient to add $2,300 and $1,860 to annual earnings (Table 13-9). Why such spectacular results in such a short time? The design of the program was to prepare for entry into the city fire department. The job was, in effect, guaranteed and the guarantee was fulfilled.

TABLE 13-8

Enrollee Characteristics and Training Content in San Francisco Training Programs from Sample Survey
(1969–70)

Characteristic and Category	Total	WIN	MDTA	EOC	Skills Center	Other[a]
Sample size	378	104	131	32	68	43
Average:						
Age (years)	28.1	29.3	28.4	24.6	30.1	24.5
Education (years)	10.5	10.5	10.5	10.2	10.2	11.0
Size of household	4.1	4.1	4.2	4.3	4.2	3.5
Number of dependents	2.6	2.8	2.5	2.2	2.7	2.3
Average length of time in program (months)	8.9	11.9	9.3	3.2	8.9	6.2
Percentage of:						
Male	57%	23%	71%	56%	78%	67%
Head of household	69	74	67	66	72	58
Currently on welfare	43	88	23	34	38	46
Ethnic percentage:						
White	14	28	6	3	12	14
Black	36	38	38	35	26	40
Oriental	18	10	24	3	29	14
Spanish-surnamed	31	24	31	59	33	32
Training content percentage:						
English as a second language	25	20	0	47	0	0
Basic education	10	20	0	47	0	0
Clerical	14	12	20	0	15	19
Auto mechanic	15	0	31	0	24	0
Nursing, dental, and medical	8	18	8	0	0	2
Other skilled manual	21%	28%	5%	0%	16%	79%

[a] Includes the following program sponsors and sample sizes: Concentrated Employment Program, 5; Youth Opportunity Center, 16; Adult Opportunity Center, 14; and Lockheed consortium, 8.

TABLE 13-9

Employment and Earnings Impact of San Francisco Training Programs[a,b]

Category	Total Hourly Wage	Total Percentage	WIN Hourly Wage	WIN Percentage	MDTA Hourly Wage	MDTA Percentage	EOC Hourly Wage	EOC Percentage	Skills Center Hourly Wage	Skills Center Percentage	Other Hourly Wage	Other Percentage
Period I:												
Average wage rate	$1.76		$1.97		$1.66		$1.89		$1.73		$1.79	
Percent employed		79.0%		61.0%		84.0%		65.0%		92.0%		85.0%
Employment stability		55.0		37.2		62.9		56.2		60.0		45.3
Employment intensity		43.0		23.0		53.0		36.0		55.0		38.0
Earnings coefficient	1.00		0.88		1.03		1.13		1.09		0.80	
Period II:												
Average wage rate	2.02		2.18		2.03		2.09		1.87		2.04	
Percent employed		58.0		29.0		73.0		65.0		63.0		50.0
Employment stability		46.7		51.6		54.1		48.8		38.8		25.5
Employment intensity		27.0		15.0		40.0		32.0		24.0		13.0
Earnings coefficient	0.99		1.31		1.11		1.06		0.78		0.63	
Period III:												
Average wage rate	2.51		2.30		2.56		2.84		2.55		2.29	
Percent employed		77.0		50.0		83.0		95.0		84.0		85.0
Employment stability		63.3		51.5		61.8		63.6		73.8		63.4
Employment intensity		49.0%		26.0%		51.0%		61.0%		62.0%		54.0%
Earnings coefficient	1.60		1.13		1.53		1.92		1.81		1.58	
Period III differences:												
Wage difference over Period I	0.76		0.55		0.76		1.26		0.84		0.46	
Wage difference over Period II	0.57		0.16		0.50		1.19		0.74		0.19	
Earnings difference over Period I	0.81		0.43		0.72		1.16		0.91		0.99	
Earnings difference over Period II	$0.81		$0.12		$0.60		$0.93		$1.35		$0.86	

[a] Mean values.

[b] The postinterview sample size for each program is as follows: total, 225; Work Incentive programs, 56; Manpower Development and Training programs, 94; the San Francisco Skills Center, 51; and other, 34.

There were two MDTA groups in the San Francisco sample: 50 enrollees from the San Francisco Skills Center and 94 in language centers and on individual referral to a number of schools in the area. Their wage differences were higher than any other San Francisco program except that of EOC, with the Skills Center achieving better than the individual referrals by this measure. Since the Skills Center also had a better record for increase in employment stability, its resulting earnings differential was nearly double for Periods II to III comparison and substantially higher for Period III compared to Period I. The non-Skills Center group had a post-training employment intensity record worse than any but WIN, marring its very substantial wage achievement for those with jobs.

The MDTA training in and out of the Skills Centers averaged nine months in duration and included a fairly wide spectrum of occupations. Forty percent of the Skills Center enrollees and 30 percent of the other MDTA enrollees received English as a second language (ESL) training only, most of them from Chinese to English. There were undoubtedly immigrants with substantial skills but impeded by language handicaps.

The programs listed as "other" were a combination of CEP, Youth Opportunity Centers (YOC), Adult Opportunity Centers (AOC), and the Lockheed consortium (National Alliance of Businessmen-Job Opportunities in the Business Sector, called NAB-JOBS), each of which were too small in number to analyze separately. The wage differences were not high for the group as a whole, but a very large increase in employment stability brought the earnings differences up to a level which would have increased annual earnings the equivalent of about $1,800.

The wage differences for WIN were about the same as for the miscellaneous group, but a very low level of employment stability representing no increase over the pretraining period resulted in a small, though significant, earnings difference. The employment intensity before and after training was exceedingly low. Despite all of these variations across program lines, the impact of the programs on enrollees in San Francisco who were overwhelmingly from minority groups and primarily male can only be described as spectacular.

Oakland

Nearly two-thirds of the Oakland-Richmond area sample were WIN enrollees (Table 13-10), and the Oakland analysis strongly reflects the character of that program. The enrollees were predominantly black in most of the programs — 62 percent citywide, 65 percent in WIN (for Oakland-Richmond combined), 81 percent in Richmond CEP, and 72 percent in OIC. The San Hidalgo Institute, a Spanish-speaking organization, was the only sponsor with no blacks. In addition to being characterized by a large proportion of black enrollees, Oakland was heavily female.

Table 13-10

Enrollee Characteristics and Training Content in Oakland-Richmond
Training Programs from Sample Survey
(1969–70)

Characteristic and Category	Total	WIN		CEP Rich-mond	OIC	San Hidalgo Inst.	Other[a]
		Oak-land	Rich-mond				
Sample size	565	172	179	88	47	34	45
Average:							
Age (years)	28.6	29.7	30.3	22.9	29.0	31.0	26.1
Education (years)	10.2	10.3	10.3	10.8	9.2	9.4	9.6
Size of household	4.5	4.7	4.7	4.7	3.6	4.0	3.8
Number of dependents	2.8	3.5	3.0	2.3	1.7	2.6	1.8
Percentage of:							
Male	33%	15%	21%	74%	34%	38%	67%
Head of household	71	82	78	51	64	59	56
Currently on welfare	76	98	97	50	53	24	24
Ethnic percentage:							
White	19	27	26	11	0	6	7
Black	62	59	69	81	72	0	37
Spanish-surnamed	15	11	3	6	13	85	47
Other	4	3	2	2	15	9	9
Training content percentage:							
Basic education	49	30	55	61	100	9	40
Clerical	17	34	13	15	0	12	2
Nursing and dental	10	10	15	3	0	18	0
Skilled manual occupations	24%	26%	17%	21%	0%	61%	58%

[a] Includes program sponsors and sample sizes as follows: Manpower Development and Training Act programs, 10; East Bay Skills Center, 17; and Holy Redeemer College, 18.

Oakland-Richmond WIN enrollees were 18 percent male, and only CEP in Richmond had more males than females (74 percent).

The nature of the WIN program and the results of its training have already been summarized; but since Oakland-Richmond were 65 percent WIN trainees, it is desirable to review this program in the Oakland area. For Oakland-Richmond combined, 98 percent received welfare, 82 percent were female, and 80 percent were heads of household. The mean length of time in training was nearly one year, longer than any other program in any other city, and the occupation of training covered a broad spectrum with emphasis on GED and basic education and the clerical-stenographic categories. Despite its handicaps, the WIN program proved effective for those who sought jobs after training. In the combined Oakland-Richmond WIN groups, the wage and earnings differences show substantial improvement from the pre- to the posttraining periods. The only negative aspect was that only 50 percent of WIN enrollees found jobs in the posttraining period.

Changes in wage rates and earnings levels were, without exception, significantly positive for all program sponsors, and not significantly different from each other (Table 13-11). Employment stability and employment intensity were both generally up from the pre- to the postperiod. In spite of this increase, however, employment intensity was very low for both WIN programs (29 and 30 percent) and OIC (31 percent).

Completer-Dropout Comparisons

For the entire four-city sample, 19 percent of the enrollees dropped out before completing their programs. Comparisons between completers and dropouts have been occasionally used as a substitute for a control group. In this case, however, there was no substantial difference, on the average, between the duration of enrollment for completers and dropouts, their demographic characteristics, or their subsequent employment and earnings experience. The highest dropout rate was for WIN, the program of the longest enrollment period, and these two factors interacted to extirpate most significant differences.

Only two consistent and statistically significant differences were observed: (1) the percentage of completers with work experience in the posttraining period was higher than that for the dropouts, and (2) the percentage currently receiving welfare was lower for the completers than for the dropouts. The first difference could lead to the possibly valid conclusion that completers found jobs easier to get because they completed the program or received more help in job placement. However, in view of the second difference, it seems likely that part of the poorer employment experience of the dropouts may be explained by the greater likelihood of their not actively seeking employment.

Boston experienced a dropout rate of only 14 percent, with a higher average postwage rate for the dropouts than for the completers. However, 80 percent of the completers had work experience after training compared to two-thirds of the dropouts, giving the completers the edge in employment stability and earnings gains. Denver's 23 percent dropout group experienced no significant differences in posttraining wages, employment stability, or wage and earnings differences from those of the completing group.

San Francisco had the unique experience of higher average change in earnings level for its dropouts who had work experience after training than

Table 13-11

Employment and Earnings Impact of Oakland-Richmond Training Programs[a,b]

| | Total | | WIN Oakland | | WIN Richmond | | CEP Richmond | | OIC | | San Hidalgo Institute | | Other | |
Category	Hourly Wage	Percentage	Hourly Wage	Percentage	Hourly Wage	Percentage	Hourly Wage	Percentage	Hourly Wage	Percentage	Hourly Wage	Percentage	Hourly Wage	Percentage
Period I:														
Average wage rate	$1.92		$1.88		$1.96		$2.16		$1.47		$1.87		$2.04	
Percent employed		67.0%		60.0%		60.0%		76.0%		75.0%		86.0%		87.0%
Employment stability		45.3		41.4		44.8		41.9		56.2		63.6		38.4
Employment intensity		30.0		25.0		27.0		32.0		42.0		55.0		33.0
Earnings coefficient	0.95		0.88		1.12		0.86		0.88		1.27		0.78	
Period II:														
Average wage rate	1.90		1.80		1.96		2.17		1.42		2.07		1.99	
Percent employed		48.0		35.0		39.0		63.0		61.0		71.0		74.0
Employment stability		49.4		43.3		50.2		48.1		53.5		68.4		44.0
Employment intensity		24.0		15.0		25.0		30.0		32.0		49.0		33.0
Earnings coefficient	1.08		0.95		1.19		1.09		0.81		1.53		1.01	
Period III:														
Average wage rate	2.21		2.00		2.25		2.45		2.15		2.11		2.42	
Percent employed		56.0		51.0		48.0		74.0		58.0		62.0		73.0
Employment stability		60.2		57.5		60.9		57.5		54.2		67.5		60.9
Employment intensity		34.0%		31.0%		29.0%		43.0%		31.0%		42.0%		44.0%
Earnings coefficient	1.43		1.51		1.40		1.49		1.25		1.39		1.40	
Period III differences:														
Wage difference over Period I	0.40		0.36		0.30		0.48		0.65		0.39		0.33	
Wage difference over Period II	0.35		0.36		0.21		0.49		0.51		0.14		0.34	
Earnings difference over Period I	0.69		0.81		0.63		0.70		0.65		0.41		0.74	
Earnings difference over Period II	$0.62		$0.89		$0.47		$0.66		$0.61		$0.23		$0.75	

a Mean values.

b The postinterview sample size for each program is as follows: total, 370; Work Incentive program for Oakland, 116, for Richmond, 121; Concentrated Employment Program for Richmond, 46; Opportunities Industrialization Center, 36; San Hidalgo Institute, 21; and other, 30.

for its similarly situated completers. Of the completers, 82 percent obtained jobs after training compared to 64 percent of the dropouts. However, of those with work experience, the dropouts enjoyed more posttraining employment stability than the completers. Completers spent nine months in program enrollment compared to 8.7 months average for dropouts. The dropouts, as compared to the completers in San Francisco, were characterized by a higher percentage of female heads of household and a higher percentage receiving welfare payments, again reflecting the importance of WIN. Inclusion or exclusion of the dropouts makes little difference in the manpower program analysis for the city of San Francisco as long as WIN is included.

The city of Oakland has already been described as the city of females and welfare. As such, it is also the city of dropouts, at 43 percent of the posttraining interviewed group. With the high proportion of female WIN enrollees, the mean length of time in training for dropouts was slightly higher than for completers. As in San Francisco, the percentage of the dropouts on welfare was significantly higher than for the completers; but, reversing the pattern in San Francisco, the percentage of males (23 percent) in the completer group was significantly lower than that for the dropouts. The median number of dependents for the dropouts was higher than that for the completers.

More than 80 percent of the completers in Denver were employed after training compared to 57 percent of the dropouts, yet the employment stability of the two groups was almost the same, while the employment intensity of the dropouts was much lower. In other words the dropouts were far less likely to seek jobs after training, but if they did, they were as likely as the completers to find and keep them.

The Effects of Training Variables

The sample included both those who were given skills training and those who received only orientation, basic education, language, or prevocational training. Nearly 100 persons in Boston, San Francisco, and Oakland (60 in San Francisco alone) were being taught ESL. Even though their posttraining wage rates tended to fall below the overall city averages, the wage differences and employment stability multiplied to substantial improvement in earnings. Apparently their skills were sufficient that the addition of language was all that was required for successful employment (Tables 13-12 through 13-16).

Basic education in Boston and Oakland and orientation and prevocational training in San Francisco resulted in good, though below average, improvements in wage and earnings levels. Nonskills training was less successful in Denver, with a combination of low wage rates and poor employment stability. Nevertheless, earnings differences were still positive. The

Table 13-12

Content of Training

Program	Denver No.	Denver Percent	Boston No.	Boston Percent	San Francisco No.	San Francisco Percent	Oakland No.	Oakland Percent
English as a second language, basic education, or orientation	74	43%	46	21%	75	38%	92	44%
Clerical	34	20%	72	33%	35	18%	48	23%
Other occupations	62	37%	103	46%	87	44%	67	33%
Total	170		221		197		207	

occupational emphasis was different among the four cities (see Table 13-12).

Many of the differences were accounted for in the sex mix (i.e., a high proportion of females in Boston and Oakland) and the racial makeup (a high proportion of whites in Boston, 54 percent Chicano in Denver, 62 percent black in Oakland, and 50 percent Oriental and Spanish-surnamed in San Francisco).

Clerical training resulted in below average wage rates but considerable employment stability. The construction and metal trades areas in Denver brought exceptional results. Generally, those who received nonclerical skills training were rewarded with above average posttraining wages and earnings even though the differences over their previous wages and earnings were below average.

Wage rates and earnings did not vary directly with the length of time in programs since the length of time did not dictate program content. Mean training time was 6.4 months in Denver, 5.3 months in Boston, 8.6 months in San Francisco, and 9.7 months in Oakland, the major determinant of length depending upon the relative importance of MDTA and WIN.

A short training program in Denver would of necessity exclude skills training, since MDTA and WIN were the only source for this. Yet inexplicably, the largest payoffs were for programs of three to six months and more than 11 months. The short-term trainees in Boston did exceedingly well. Shorter term enrollment meant training from ABCD and OIC rather than MDTA and WIN. The posttraining experience from MDTA was as favorable as that of the other programs, but it was based on higher pretraining wages and employment stability. In the bay area, the short-term courses were those which were basic education, orientation, or English but without skills training. The longest enrollments were for WIN. Therefore, the nature of the program was the critical variable with its length being coincidental.

TABLE 13-13

Mean Values of Posttraining Coefficients in Denver
(By occupation of training)

Occupation	Post-interview Sample Size	Post-training Wage	Wage Difference	Percentage of Employment Stability	Post-training Earnings Coefficient	Earnings Difference
Basic education	48	$1.76	$0.30	41.8%	$0.86	$0.14
Orientation	25	1.82	− 0.01	46.8	0.91	0.18
Clerical	34	2.01	0.54	67.6	1.47	0.89
Auto repair	7	1.84	− 0.09	61.0	1.21	0.24
Machine repair	3	2.21	0.09	38.0	0.75	− 0.05
Machine operation	7	2.08	0.36	62.1	1.42	0.64
Health occupations	4	1.35	− 0.12	40.0	0.75	0.60
Construction-metal trades	21	3.16	0.86	89.9	2.26	1.13
Engineering aide-drafting	11	1.98	0.16	63.4	1.36	0.31
Service work	4	1.38	0.28	46.0	1.00	0.46
Other occupations	6	1.76	0.27	65.2	1.25	1.01
TOTAL or average	170	$2.07	$0.35	47.2%	$1.26	$0.52

TABLE 13-14

Mean Values of Posttraining Coefficients in Boston

(By occupation of training)

Occupation	Post-interview Sample Size	Post-training Wage	Wage Difference	Percentage of Employment Stability	Post-training Earnings Coefficient	Earnings Difference
English as a second language	24	$2.21	$0.51	79.5%	$1.75	$0.91
Basic education	20	2.13	0.36	64.6	1.34	0.47
Clerical	72	2.27	0.49	76.3	1.92	0.65
Auto repair	12	2.43	0.37	62.8	1.66	0.46
Machine repair	4	2.56	0.30	81.0	2.03	1.08
Machine operation	49	2.14	0.45	71.2	1.70	0.87
Health occupations	4	2.97	1.42	60.8	1.50	0.83
Construction-metal trades	10	2.80	0.72	73.9	1.88	0.49
Engineering aide-drafting	16	2.59	0.58	71.7	1.77	1.12
Service work	6	2.06	0.66	66.8	1.88	0.02
TOTAL or average	211	$2.30	$0.50	72.6%	$1.76	$0.73

TABLE 13-15

Mean Values of Posttraining Coefficients in San Francisco
(By occupation of training)

Occupation	Post-interview Sample Size	Post-training Wage	Wage Difference	Percentage of Employment Stability	Post-training Earnings Coefficient	Earnings Coefficient
English as a second language	60	$2.47	$0.93	67.5%	$1.65	$0.76
Orientation	11	2.31	0.58	72.6	2.25	1.50
Clerical	35	2.13	0.60	63.2	1.38	0.90
Auto repair	25	2.67	0.38	62.4	1.64	0.69
Machine repair	10	2.73	0.85	72.1	1.81	1.29
Machine operation	8	2.28	0.48	61.2	1.46	0.76
Health occupations	14	2.78	0.49	60.4	1.48	0.47
Construction-metal trades	13	3.27	1.19	48.5	1.52	0.59
Engineering aide-drafting	7	2.86	1.05	68.4	1.89	1.33
Service work	4	2.56	0.84	66.8	2.25	1.58
Other occupations	6	2.54	0.75	44.0	1.08	0.48
TOTAL or average	193	$2.51	$0.76	63.3%	$1.60	$0.81

Table 13-16

Mean Values of Posttraining Coefficients in Oakland

(By occupation of training)

Occupation	Post-interview Sample Size	Post-training Wage	Wage Difference	Percentage of Employment Stability	Post-training Earnings Coefficient	Earnings Coefficient
English as a second language	14	$2.18	$0.64	71.9%	$1.65	$0.91
Basic education	73	2.24	0.53	54.4	1.44	0.69
Clerical	48	1.94	0.23	58.8	1.28	0.61
Auto repair	6	2.34	− 0.04	67.5	1.38	0.80
Machine operation	6	2.17	0.03	71.7	1.65	0.33
Health occupations	23	2.57	0.72	65.8	1.61	0.88
Construction-metal trades	7	2.86	0.64	56.6	1.32	0.70
Engineering aide-drafting	6	2.34	− 0.37	55.8	1.10	0.33
Other occupations	15	2.62	0.33	71.8	1.57	0.64
Total or average	198	$2.21	$0.40	60.2%	$1.43	$0.69

Demographic and Socioeconomic Variables

Since both pre- and postwage rates were higher for males than females, those programs and cities with the higher proportions of females tended to have the lowest posttraining wage rates (Table 13-17). However, because of their lower starting point, the females tended to experience greater wage and earnings increases. There were no significant sex differences in employment stability, but employment intensity tended to be lower for females, particularly in Denver and Oakland.

Generally, posttraining wage rates, employment stability, and earnings were higher for whites than for any other ethnic group (Table 13-18). Employment stability and employment intensity were lowest for blacks. There were no racial or ethnic patterns in the wage and earnings differences.

The language programs for Orientals appear to have had a particularly high payoff. It was apparent that many of the recent Oriental immigrants had skills which they could use when they attained a good command of English.

There was a tendency for the older trainees to develop higher earnings levels, but younger persons were more likely to achieve greater improvements in earnings. These were primarily due to the employment stability component rather than the wage component of earnings. Average hourly wage rates and average wage rate changes exhibited very little correlation with the age of trainees, except in Denver where there was a direct, but generally moderate relationship with age and both posttraining employment stability and the earnings level of the trainees. With the exception of San Francisco, the change in earnings level was inversely related to age.

In Denver, trainees with more education generally were better off. Employment stability, employment intensity, average postwage rates, average postearnings level, and the change in earnings were all generally increasing functions of educational attainment. In the other three cities, the group with the lowest education, 8th grade or less, had the maximum average postwage rate. In both Boston and Oakland, wage difference was maximum for this lower educated group and second only to the group with one year of high school in San Francisco. In the bay area (both Oakland and San Francisco), changes in wage rates were generally a decreasing function of educational attainment. However, those with high school education or better had the maximum employment stability, employment intensity, and earnings coefficient.

Consistent in all four cities was an increasing average hourly postwage rate with increasing number of dependents. Yet no consistent pattern emerged for employment stability and posttraining earnings.

Trainees Still Enrolled

Of particular interest is the 14 percent who were still in training at the end of the 12-month follow-up. Most of the 80 trainees were not in the

Table 13-17

Mean Values of Posttraining Coefficients
(By sex of trainee)

Sex	Post-interview Sample	Percentage of Employment Stability	Percentage of Employment Intensity	Post-training Wage	Earnings Coefficient	Wage Differences	Earnings Differences
San Francisco:							
Male	151	61.8%	49.0%	$2.67	$1.59	$0.79	$0.74
Female	104	65.7	48.0	2.25	1.63	0.66	1.00
Oakland-Richmond:							
Male	101	64.9	41.0	2.55	1.59	0.34	0.63
Female	269	58.1	31.0	2.06	1.32	0.43	0.72
Denver:							
Male	105	59.4	51.0	2.28	1.33	0.32	0.44
Female	121	54.7	37.0	1.83	1.16	0.38	0.64
Boston:							
Male	114	73.0	58.0	2.43	1.79	0.43	0.69
Female	172	72.4%	55.0%	$2.21	$1.74	$0.56	$0.77

TABLE 13-18

Mean Values of Posttraining Coefficients

(By ethnicity)

Ethnicity	Post-interview Sample	Percentage of Employment Stability	Percentage of Employment Intensity	Post-training Wage	Earnings Coefficient	Wage Differences	Earnings Differences
San Francisco:							
Whites	30	72.4%	48.0%	$2.53	$1.65	$0.75	$0.99
Blacks	85	55.1	38.0	2.48	1.47	0.35	0.68
Oriental	57	72.1	61.0	2.60	1.79	1.13	1.00
Spanish-surnamed	83	61.3	53.0	2.48	1.53	0.78	0.70
Oakland-Richmond:							
Whites	79	64.2	32.0	2.28	1.41	0.30	0.68
Blacks	225	56.7	33.0	2.24	1.41	0.42	0.70
Oriental	10	82.3	73.0	1.77	1.61	0.68	1.11
Spanish-surnamed	51	64.2	37.0	2.15	1.51	0.33	0.52
Denver:							
Whites	58	66.5	57.0	2.23	1.43	0.35	0.59
Blacks	38	51.7	29.0	1.87	1.29	0.30	0.73
Spanish-surnamed	123	52.8	40.0	2.04	1.17	0.36	0.42
Boston:							
Whites	103	75.4	59.0	2.38	1.89	0.55	0.72
Blacks	130	70.0	57.0	2.27	1.72	0.44	0.76
Spanish-surnamed	49	73.6%	46.0%	$2.19	$1.57	$0.60	$0.72

same training program in which they had been enrolled at the time of the initial interview. Many had transferred to college-level training — more than 25 percent in San Francisco, Oakland, and Denver.

The percentage of WIN trainees still enrolled was significantly higher than that of the original sample. These percentages for San Francisco, Oakland, Denver, and Boston, respectively, are as follows:

Percentage of total enrollees	*Percentage of enrollees still in training*
28	65
62	76
25	44
20	48

Not altogether unrelated to the tendency for WIN enrollees to continue in enrollment are the following:

(1) The percentage currently receiving welfare is significantly high for those still in training.

(2) With the exception of Boston, the average pretraining wages of those still enrolled were higher than those of the total sample.

(3) The percentages of female and of head of household are both generally higher for the still-enrolled group than for the total sample. Exceptions to this are in Oakland, where the percentage of females is the same for the total sample, and in Denver, where the percentage of females still in school is actually lower than that for the total sample.

(4) The average age of those still enrolled is generally higher than that of the total sample. The reverse is true in Boston.

(5) The percentage of whites still enrolled is higher than the average in three of the four cities; in Oakland the percentage of whites is low and the Spanish-surnamed percentage is high.

The prewage rates and employment stability coefficients are generally higher for the still-enrolled group than for the total sample. Though these differences are not significant, they are consistent among the four cities, indicating that some of those with the best work experience may have been those who chose to return to school to better themselves.

ATTITUDINAL CHANGE

Questions in the follow-up interviews were designed to test whether successful manpower program participation had any impact on the enrollees' attitudes toward: (1) the programs and the state ES, (2) the political system, (3) militant behavior, and (4) trust in other people.

Seven of ten respondents felt positive about the training they had received, with those who had completed training significantly more likely to have positive feelings than those who had not. However, there was no consistent relationship between those expressions and the extent of improvement in wages or employment stability. Attitude toward teachers was overwhelmingly favorable (in more than nine of 10 cases), with completers again the most favorable. Paradoxically, those with the greatest pre- and postwage difference showed the least favorable attitude toward teachers, while this attitude tended to improve with employment stability.

Two of three respondents had favorable attitudes toward manpower programs in general and toward ES. Completers did not change their attitudes, but those of noncompleters became more negative. In general, the greater the wage increase, the greater the improvement in attitude, but employment stability made no measurable difference.

Program completers did not tend to change their rather negative attitudes toward their ability to affect the political system, but noncompleters became even more negative. However, the greater the increase in employment stability, the more positive the attitude toward political efficacy.

Only one respondent of 10 favored militant activities, and the average was less favorable toward militant behavior after their manpower experience. Those in the bay area were the most militant and least likely to change. Both wage increases and employment stability increases caused movement in the direction of lessened support for militant behavior.

Bay area respondents were less likely than others to trust people. There was little difference between completers and noncompleters in the bay area, but in the other areas, completers were more likely to be trusting. Also in the bay area, there seemed to be an inverse correlation between wage increase and attitudes, with positive effect in Denver and neutral results in Boston. Increases in employment stability were accompanied by increased trust in others for Boston and Denver respondents, with no change in the bay area. On the whole, completion of manpower programs and improved employment stability tended to make more positive the attitudes of the enrollee toward himself and the society around him.

Total Impact of
Manpower Programs
14

Having explored the employment, earnings, and attitudinal impact of training programs of the enrollees, we now turn to constructing the enrollee impact of programs providing services other than training and to summarizing the impact of all programs on local economies, community institutions, and labor markets. This chapter reassesses the contributions of the various functional manpower services and explores the implications of the study for current manpower policy issues.

THE MACROECONOMIC IMPACT OF MANPOWER PROGRAMS

One direct impact of the manpower programs upon the cities in our sample is the number of staff jobs and the dollars expended for materials, services, and salaries in the operation of the programs. In the spring of 1971, more than 1,000 persons were employed in Boston as staff personnel in the administration of manpower programs. Nearly 100 of the federal staff had regional assignments, and 24 of the ES staff had statewide responsibilities; nevertheless, they were employed in the city of Boston. Part of the regional and state staff and the remainder of more than 900 people were required to administer the Boston manpower programs. An average of $12 million a year had been funded and was spent within the city for staffing and servicing the programs and the enrollees . . . a significant addition to the local economy.

For Denver at approximately the same time, the total manpower program employment figure was 418. The annual average expenditures for manpower programs in the local economy were $7 million, for a total of $35 million over eight years.

The San Francisco Bay area garnered $92 million for manpower programs over a 3.5-year period, for an average of $26 million a year. The total personnel for the programs in May 1971 was estimated to be 1,600 persons. In economic development terms, the advent of manpower programs was equivalent to a sizable export industry, drawing funds from outside the community for jobs within it.

The Impact of Community Institutions

Aside from the fact that manpower programs had an impact on the employment and earnings of enrollees, there are these questions: Have the programs wrought significant changes in the attitudes and institutional arrangements of the communities? Assuming that the persistence of poverty and low incomes reflects systemic as well as individual shortcomings, has the presence of manpower programs changed in any significant way the attitudes and capabilities of the prevailing local systems? The answer to both questions is clearly "yes." The important issues are how much and at what cost.

There are few quantitative ways of measuring the institutional changes that have occurred as a result of the manpower programs. Yet change can be assessed qualitatively by comparing systems at varying points in time and identifying significant differences. Judgment is then necessary to assign credit or blame to causes and contributing factors.

The Public Schools

It is a paradox of public policy that early success may be a prelude to later failures. Institutions particularly suited to their own time and circumstances may become so satisfied with that success and so entrenched as a result of it that they find it particularly difficult to change as new circumstances emerge. School systems of three metropolitan areas suffered to some degree from this phenomenon. Boston's was one of the first and most effective school systems in the nation, providing the classical education thought appropriate for social leadership in the 17th and 18th centuries. It "Americanized" the immigrants of the 19th and early 20th centuries but did not adapt comfortably to the demands of urban society in the last half of this century. Therefore Boston's school system and its "school committee" are widely known for their lack of innovation and their preservation of the status quo.

After long years of apathy and under considerable pressure, Boston's school system officials are now showing some signs of change in policy, but little can be attributed to involvement in manpower programs. Since postsecondary and vocational-technical education are the most likely to become involved through MDTA and adult education through WIN, these are the most probable components of the education system to have been affected. In Boston, however, the schools were shielded from change by parochial tradition-bound personnel with limited goals. They tend to oppose change and to denigrate vocational education.

An isolated Skills Center operated in an abandoned high school build-ing could have little impact on any school system, to say nothing of one of limited responsiveness. Even with another Center opened in the city, there is no evidence that MDTA courses or the Centers have had any impact on the Boston school system. Part of the reason is that much of the pressure for additional facilities for the minorities was alleviated when ABCD, because of the disinterest and generally poor reputation of the school sys-tem, was allowed to introduce orientation centers as part of its CEP. Two weeks of orientation was a universal component of the CEPs. But the term was a subterfuge in Boston. In fact, the 15 weeks of training allowed in these centers involved only three weeks or less for orientation integrated into the remaining time spent in skills training. In effect, little Skills Cen-ters were built outside the education system to serve the disadvantaged minorities. The decision was the right one for client service but minimized institutional change.

The successful period for Denver's schools was more recent and was largely measured in terms of the emphasis on college graduates over the past generation. The record of Colorado's schools, on behalf of those who pursue higher education within the state, is impressive. However, high average educational attainment only makes the competition rougher for those who lack it.

The manpower programs have had no noticeable impact on the ele-mentary and secondary schools but considerable impact upon at least one post-secondary (less than baccalaureate) institution. The Emily Griffith Opportunity School is an example of early success impeding change in future times. Dating back more than 50 years, it had an excellent reputa-tion for making skilled craftsmen of the sons of farmers and industrial workers. It was a no-nonsense institution with high standards and firm discipline. Teachers were strictly certificated and traditional. It was not prepared to cope with the cultural shock of ethnic minorities, unprepared in basic education and often with life-styles which were disfunctional in terms of the school's traditions.

When the Emily Griffith school proved unable to successfully help the disadvantaged, the federal and state officials began looking for an alterna-tive sponsor for MDTA. The timing was opportune because the state had just authorized a three-campus community college for Denver. An agree-ment was made to shift most of the MDTA institutional training to one of the three college campuses in the form of a Skills Center.

The Skills Center was given a separate management, as required by federal guidelines, but was otherwise completely integrated within the col-lege. Rather than take separate courses, MDTA enrollees shared the same classrooms with regular students. The result has been innovative for MDTA, but has probably had a greater impact on the college curricula. MDTA students for the first time were able to acquire college credit, and a few remained for an associate degree. The course offerings were broader than those normally available to manpower students, the facility was more attractive than normal, and there was added pride in being a college student.

MDTA Skills Centers had already developed open-entry/open-exit practices. Modular training made it possible for students to enroll whenever they applied rather than to have to wait for the beginning of a class-size unit, and this concept made it possible for an enrollee to leave when he had attained sufficient skill for a job. The necessity of basic education in MDTA established a base for remedial education for all students. Modular units and individualized instruction, also necessary under MDTA, became the norm for the school. A requirement for designation as an MDTA Skills Center is the sale of services to other manpower programs. As a result, the community college enrolls CEP and WIN as well as MDTA enrollees.

The Denver Community College with its integrated MDTA skills training is undoubtedly different from any other in the nation and is a much more effective servant of the community's educational needs than it would have been if there had been no manpower programs to establish a pattern. (The Emily Griffith school has also been affected by the experience but to a lesser degree.) MDTA courses exist in private schools but with little impact on the institutions and the remainder of the Denver school system. Higher educational institutions have felt little if any impact.

The emphasis of bay area schools was also connected with the vast expansion of post-secondary education in California. California schools were less oriented to college preparatory ambitions but more committed to post-secondary training. They have not been as guilty of racial and ethnic discrimination as many and have offered more second-chance opportunities to high school dropouts than most. Yet at the beginning of the manpower programs, they had not really plumbed the needs of the target populations of those programs.

One obstacle to employment for many who do not have formal training or who have high school-level vocational education was the abundance of junior college-trained mechanics and technicians. The competition continues for manpower program enrollees. The availability of training in the schools was one of the justifications for the labor movement's opposition to any training which might provide competition for union members.

It was ES, not the schools, which promoted the introduction of the East Bay Skills Center in Oakland. Because the local school districts responded negatively, the sponsorship was pressed upon a reluctant junior college district. The San Francisco Skills Center was sponsored by the San Francisco Unified School District, but both Skills Centers are in fact totally isolated from the schools and have no impact upon them. At the same time, substantial numbers have been referred individually to ongoing occupational programs in post-secondary vocational-technical schools and community colleges. In these cases, the MDTA enrollee must fit the curriculum rather than the curriculum suiting the enrollee.

The Public Employment Service

If the schools responded only marginally to the influence of the manpower programs, it was because the programs involved them only peripherally in post-secondary skills training, not in a major component of the education system. The state ESs were directly and centrally involved, and they experienced major changes as a result. Before the advent of the manpower programs, the goal of the most progressive ESs was to provide the best possible applicant for each employer's job order. The less progressive were likely to emphasize unemployment insurance administration. To ask them, in effect, to convince the employer to make do with the least prepared employee he could use was the complete antithesis of the traditional assignment. Yet in the five years since the commitment to the disadvantaged was made official and the Human Resources Development (HRD) program launched, an impressive metamorphosis has taken place.

Change came slowly in the Massachusetts Department of Employment Security (MDES), but it came. MDES showed no enthusiasm for the manpower programs, leaving a vacuum which ABCD, Boston's CAA, moved in to fill. The existence of ABCD in turn shielded MDES from much of the pressure to serve the disadvantaged. In many cities, the minor involvement of CAAs in placement and other traditional ES activities was a goad to change ES attitudes and practices. In Boston, few if any in MDES really cared. More were completely content to have ABCD shoulder a burdensome assignment.

The pressure that existed was internal and emanated from the bottom up rather than from the top down. Attitude and commitment were major obstacles, but administrative regulations contributed to the neglect of the marginal labor force groups. MDES had been criticized for an unimaginative, inflexible staff, unable to accept the purposes of a manpower program which contradicted the accustomed role of referring only the applicants who already possessed the skills and other characteristics preferred by employers. Having operated for 30 years under essentially the same policy guidelines, MDES found it difficult to adapt to the rapidly changing policies and added functions which characterized the advent of manpower programs. Performance had traditionally been measured by the number of placements, not their quality. None of the regular offices, even today, are located in the black ghetto. ES staff have not been neighborhood workers known to the disadvantaged or knowledgeable about the services available in manpower programs and how to attain them.

The advent of CEP was the beginning of change for MDES in Boston. In contrast to most other original CEP cities, Boston's CAA — ABCD —

had just imported a manpower-oriented staff from New Haven, who were capable of taking over the assignment with little assistance. Since ABCD launched its own neighborhood employment services, MDES did not become the "presumptive provider" of manpower services. However, as part of the CEP contract, MDES agreed to station in outreach centers employment interviewers in the neighborhood centers. These people soon became deeply committed to the welfare of their new clientele, and changed attitudes began seeping from them back up the ladder of ES.

The Denver experience was similar. The state ES there was no less traditional, though somewhat more aggressive than that of Boston. The chief executive of the Colorado Department of Employment was an outspoken "hardliner." He considered the growing emphasis on service to the disadvantaged to be a strategic mistake which would only alienate employers and dry up the source of job orders. It was his conviction, seemingly shared by most of his subordinates at the top level, that the disadvantaged would best be served by an ES which continued to emphasize referring the best available applicants to fill every job order. The officials viewed themselves as complying with federal directives but unenthusiastically.

In Denver, as in Boston, change began occurring at the bottom. Beginning with those involved in the YOCs and moving to those serving Denver Opportunity, Denver's CAA, and the Denver CEP, commitment to screening in rather than screening out the disadvantaged began to grow at the direct-contact level. However, it was WIN rather than CEP which wrought the greater change in Denver. Both the client and staff numbers were much larger, and the staff was forced to make individual employment plans rather than merely placements. Not only placements, but services to the individual — such as counseling, testing, training, medical and legal assistance, special schooling, rehabilitation, motivation, creating good work habits and job development, as well as job referral — were increasingly viewed as appropriate tools for ES.

Change came sooner in ES in the bay area because of earlier involvement on behalf of the disadvantaged youth and adults even before the advent of the manpower programs.

By the time CEP came on the scene in the bay area in 1967, the California State Employment Service (CSES) was already an experienced servant of the disadvantaged and became the backbone of the three bay area CEPs.

When the HRD concept was endorsed by the national office and spread across the nation, little change was required by CSES. With this experience base, it was a natural, through dramatic evolution, for California to reorganize its manpower service institutions into a state department of HRD, combining the State Department of Employment with other state agencies whose programs were funded by the Economic Opportunity Act (EOA) and the Department of Labor (DOL).

In effect, two separate ESs were created, a traditional one, serving non-poverty areas, and the HRD centers, serving areas with concentrations of disadvantaged people who are to receive priority for service. Minority personnel today staff these latter offices up to the top echelons. Most of the personnel increases which have occurred since the advent of manpower programs are assigned to the HRD centers.

Services have been transformed into a case-carrying concept modeled after vocational rehabilitation. A "case-responsible" staff member is accountable for each applicant. Frustrations are occurring because this case-responsible counselor lacks the "blank check" with which the vocational rehabilitation counselor purchases the services his clients need. With jobs and training slots scarce, it is difficult to find help to offer the applicants. Nevertheless, a new institution has been created on a broad experience base to serve the disadvantaged. Because of the background, the transition, traumatic in the remainder of the state, was a natural one in the bay area.

The Private Employers

Employing business firms were and are the major institutions of the labor market. They have changed less than ES but more than the schools as a result of the manpower experience. Yet the change in employer attitudes and practices has been more dramatic than either of the others.

Despite the relatively few employers directly involved in hiring manpower program enrollees, it is doubtful that any employer of a significant size firm in any of the cities is unaware of the effort, nor is he unaware that he is assumed to have a social responsibility to hire the disadvantaged. Consistently some of the most prestigious of the business communities serve in highly visible NAB positions and act as the conscience of the business community. Of those directly involved, few if any of the contracting employers can have avoided changing their recruitment, selection, hiring, training, and promotion practices. Most of those who have made and filled noncontract pledges are likely to have made some significant changes. There is no way of measuring quantitatively the amount and consequences of change. But there is no question that substantial change has occurred.

The Public Employers

Interestingly, the impact of the manpower programs on public employers has been far less than that upon private employers. There has never been a concerted effort to convince public agencies to change their recruitment, selection, hiring, and promotion practices. Because of merit system regulations, public employment is much more structured and thus more difficult to change. The concept of hiring by merit is a rationalization of intent to discriminate. The relatively low pay and the security of the merit system and civil service jobs is such that it is attractive to lower middle-class white workers with political influence.

As racial and ethnic minorities have learned the political ropes, they have been able to move into the lower level slots in public agencies, limited primarily to those who had the customary credentials such as high school diplomas. In 1970 the Public Service Careers program was launched for the purpose of opening up regular jobs in the public sector to disadvantaged persons without violating or abrogating merit service principles. The intent was to train potential employees, modify credentialing requirements, and otherwise make it possible for people with the potential, but blocked by artificial obstacles, to become employees of public agencies. The program was slow getting off the ground in each city, and was only beginning at the close of this study. However, without the carrot of wage subsidies or the stick of enforced involvement, there was no reason to expect substantial change.

The Unions

Until recently, unions played no significant role in Boston and Denver manpower programs, while their influence in the bay area was negative. In the former two cases, they appeared unaware of the programs' existence. In the bay area, unions prevented MDTA from training in occupations where there was a reasonable expectation of employment . . . for fear the occupations would become overcrowded and create competition for the jobs of union members. Exceptions in the bay area were the marine cooks and stewards and the operating engineers unions who each ran training programs under federal contracts, though primarily for upgrading their own members.

More recently, it has been the much maligned building trades which have made the greatest contributions. In Denver, this help consists of a successful apprenticeship outreach program to bring minorities into the building trades. In Boston, it consisted of a more extensive effort, through union-management negotiations, to add upgrading for present employees and to recruit and train partially skilled journeymen for skilled productivity. A similar though smaller program exists in Oakland.

On the whole, unions have probably been greater hindrances than helps in manpower programs of the bay area but a mildly positive influence in the others. In turn, the programs have had a slight influence on the handful of unions involved.

The Political Structure

The impact of manpower programs upon the political structure must be viewed in the context of the number of forces increasing the political power of the poor and the minority groups. None of the cities have the concentration of a single self-conscious minority group — typical of a Newark, Cleveland, or Gary (Indiana) — leading to political dominance by that group. Boston and Denver remain predominantly white, despite growth of their minority populations. Boston's blacks are becoming politically conscious, but the governmental structure there requires a citywide and therefore white or multiracial following for successful election. Denver's Spanish-surnamed minority has never been politically conscious and unified, despite efforts of the Crusade for Justice and the Black Panthers to generate militancy. The minorities of the bay area are too splintered ethnically and racially to exploit the power of their members. For example, a black-brown political alliance could become dominant in Oakland if it could get out the vote.

In Boston, a black city councilman has survived for two terms and in his reelection, gave evidence of citywide white support. He remains aware of the manpower programs as a focal point of racial concentration but has no control over potential patronage from the programs. Politics of the Boston manpower programs is primarily internal, generated within the ABCD governing board and the area planning action councils which guide the neighborhood employment centers. Ethnic politics have always been exceedingly important in Boston, but significant power has never shifted to the blacks and Puerto Ricans, and the manpower programs and the "politics of poverty" do not yet appear to be a contributor to such power.

There is no significant politics of poverty in Denver. The small Denver CEP continues almost unnoticed within the poverty community. The governor's office has taken a hands-off role for manpower in general and for Denver in particular. The city government has been willing to sponsor programs in the past when it was necessary to attract federal dollars, but has ignored them in practice. Initially the mayor's office and the CAA in Oakland struggled over the original CEP assignment, and the mayor lost. Yet the CAA then subcontracted the CEP action without using it for a patronage and power base. There is a great deal of militancy in the community not yet coalesced into organized political power. The black and brown militants, predominantly young, appear almost contemptuous of manpower programs as a symbol of subservience. However, the recent veto of the CAA's refunding by the governor and its sanction by DOL may signal a return of some of the manpower action to the mayor in accord with the recently expressed principles of decentralization. If so, manpower cannot avoid influencing and being influenced by city politics.

In San Francisco, a mayor with a labor movement background became involved in employment and manpower affairs following the 1966 Hunters Point riot and was politically burned. His successor has stayed at arms' length. The Spanish-surnamed community in the bay area, stemming from some 24 Latin American nations, has never coalesced within itself or with the blacks. The politics of poverty has been influential but has not included manpower programs, perhaps in part because the major responsibility for manpower has rested with the essentially nonpolitical ES.

New Institutions

Each of the study cities was a recipient of a number of new labor market institutions emanating from the manpower programs, some of which can now be found in every city of equal size and some of which only happened to occur in these particular cities. In addition, a number of institutions emerged which are peculiar to the particular cities. A CAA, a NAB group, and a Cooperative Area Manpower Planning System (CAMPS) office are a uniform consequence of size. Although each city was the recipient of a Skills Center, a CEP, an OIC, and a DOL Regional Manpower Administration office, the particularized institutions were, in all but one case, ethnically oriented and dependent upon each community's racial and ethnic structure.

Skills Centers

The MDTA Skills Centers were a major contribution nationally. In the four study cities, only one was typical of the national group, and it was a latecomer on the local scene.

Boston's Skills Center in the Daniel Webster School was an early effort that emerged before priorities had shifted clearly to the disadvantaged. Its location in a part of the city that is difficult for blacks to reach, probably not a deliberate discriminatory step, illustrates an insensitivity to minority problems. The Daniel Webster School has become primarily an institution of clerical training for white lower class girls and basic education and language training for Puerto Rican immigrants. Its enrollees have profited consistently in employment stability and earnings, but since they started from a higher level, the difference between their pre- and postsituations has not been so dramatic as that which occurred in other training institutions in the city.

The East Bay Skills Center in Oakland suffered at the outset from an unfavorable location in an undesirable facility, a negative response from the local school system, failure of one of the sponsoring agencies to meet its financial commitments, and union opposition. Nevertheless, an institution had been created which, though troubled, was clearly by and for minority groups and the disadvantaged; and despite its difficulties, the completion and placement rates have risen steadily.

The San Francisco Skills Center avoided most of the trauma of its East Bay counterpart. However, as a latecomer, it has operated in a milieu of extremely limited resources, amid an environment wherein ES prefers individual referral projects in the regular schools. It is making a substantial contribution in providing ESL to Chinese immigrants.

Denver's Skills Center is unique in the nation and may have set a pattern for the future. Skills Centers in general have had their problems including second-class facilities, deteriorating equipment, narrow occupational offerings, uncertain funding, and fluctuating enrollment. These institutions, established especially to train the disadvantaged, are socio-economically segregated and cut off from the mainstream of post-secondary training and the labor market they serve. To cope with the problem of dropouts increasing per capita costs of training, Skills Centers had adopted the practice of filling empty slots by bringing in new enrollees while a course was under way. To do so required modular training and individualized instruction. An advantage was that an underprivileged person needing training was not forced to wait until a new course was ready but could move into an empty slot in an ongoing course. If an enrollee could enter at any time, he could also complete his training individually and leave whenever he was ready. This lent itself to open-ended as well as open-entry courses, with a ladder of skills allowing an enrollee to leave with a salable skill at any point along the way. "Dropout" was an obsolete concept.

With Denver's Skills Center integrated into the new community college, regular courses soon took on a Skills Center coloration . . . open entry became standard. The presence of basic education and prevocational orientation for MDTA enrollees made the same services available to others. Thus from MDTA there emerged in Denver an institution committed to and capable of serving the disadvantaged, but avoiding segregating them and stigmatizing them as second class. In the doing, Denver got a different community college, but one which fits the progressive mode that two-year, community-serving, post-secondary institutions are supposed to fulfill.

Concentrated Employment Program

It is difficult to imagine five institutions with a common origin and funding which have so few characteristics in common as the CEPs of the study cities. ABCD comes nearest to the original concept of an umbrella agency which could unite disparate programs and agencies into an integrated and concentrated attack on the manpower problems of a limited target area. However, the CEP program cannot take credit for ABCD's creation. ABCD's nature had already been determined, and CEP was merely a source of additional funds. Despite ABCD's conformance to the desired pattern, its independence, self-sufficiency, and political strength brought initial suspicion from DOL officials and other agencies in Boston. Fortunately, those relationships now appear to have improved substantially. ABCD's performance has probably been as good as might have been expected, given the internal political struggles of the emerging minority community, the lack of staff and managerial experience, and the still-limited availability of the final objectives — good jobs within the reach of disadvantaged people. Clearly, no other agency in Boston has equal capability and commitment.

The first year of the Denver CEP saw it constantly upset by internal organizational problems. However, it managed to survive its initial problems to become an effective manpower unit. Even though it has the capability to manage efficiently the programs it directly operates, it is unlikely to become an effective coordinator and concentrator of manpower efforts. Though it is a city agency, its director has had no place within city government to report; thus in effect, it operates as an autonomous, independent unit.

Oakland's CAA, the Oakland Economic Development, Inc. (OEDCI) program, became a sponsor of the Oakland CEP after a sharp political struggle with the office of the mayor and a city government which also had manpower aspirations. Yet when it got control, it used the CEP only as a contracting entity, subcontracting all the action programs to independent organizations. The OEDCI director doubled as CEP director. There were no separate offices, and only the CEP central records unit staff were full-time CEP employees. Even the ES staff assigned to CEP were part of the staff of an ES project long housed in OEDCI neighborhood service centers. The job development unit was a device for the OEDCI target area advisory committees to get a piece of the CEP action. All other functions were subcontracted to other community-based organizations or to public agencies. In contrast to the concept of CEP as an umbrella agency for unifying separate manpower programs and the ABCD approach which used CEP money to turn itself into a comprehensive manpower agency, OEDCI uses CEP as one of several sources of money to support a variety of separate community programs, some of which are manpower oriented. With the governor's recent veto of OEDCI funding, an entirely new situation must now emerge in CEP, probably with the mayor's office as sponsor.

The official sponsor of the Richmond CEP is the model cities agency, but CEP is completely independent of its sponsor. It has its own staff, facilities, and even a CSES unit devoted totally to CEP activities. The CEP central staff are all city employees, and the program services are for the most part supplied by public agencies, making the Richmond CEP very much an establishment organization. Residents of the target community supposedly have a voice through the model cities neighborhood board; but if they do, it is a muted one. CEP is essentially an outside agency placed in their community to serve them. Yet strife within the target groups has not been a serious problem. Perhaps job development has been such an overwhelming obstacle that it has limited the number of people involved and dwarfed every other problem. More people than could be handled have always been available at intake without outreach efforts, but the jobs available for placement have always been few.

The San Francisco CEP is under the sponsorship of a CAA; EOC and the mayor appear to prefer it that way. Yet EOC appears never to have taken a deep interest in its CEP responsibilities. Administrative performance was so bad that CEP was once placed on probation by the U.S. Office of Economic Opportunity (OEO) and DOL and was later pressured into subcontracting much of the program services to hopefully more competent agencies. Admittedly, the heavy load of non-English-speaking clients created a special problem. Nevertheless, an administrative vacuum existed into which CSES gradually moved and provided what strength CEP had.

Since CAAs are the presumed sponsors of CEPs, it seems expedient to comment here on the effectiveness and impact of these institutions. In Boston, CEP and CAA are identical. CAA became a manpower organization and absorbed CEP funds to carry out its intents. In Denver, CEP authority was given to the composite city-county government, despite the fact that Denver Opportunity, the CAA, already had five neighborhood centers in the target area. Denver Opportunity had not been manpower oriented and showed no competence in putting together a CEP proposal. Thereupon, the regional manpower administrator (RMA) informed the city that there would be no CEP in Denver unless the city-county government sponsored it. CAA therefore became only a minor subcontractor in the Denver CEP activity and gained no significant foothold in manpower. CAAs in the bay area are too strife ridden by black-brown conflicts to effectively participate in the delivery of manpower services and are more interested in community politics than in becoming manpower service agencies.

All of the CEPs are burdened by the internal conflicts and the community political struggles which are part of the birth pangs of emerging political organizations being attracted by patronage available for the first time to that particular city's population from manpower and antipoverty funds and staff jobs. The only differences among the five are that the internal ABCD struggles are among black individuals, while the political battles in all the western cities have coalesced along black-brown racial and ethnic lines.

As a new program with no history or tenure and without the defense of assignment to a long-established stable agency, CEP and its survival are always uncertain, and CEP personnel are concerned about their futures. The staff is inordinately preoccupied with budgetary matters and the uncertainties of annual funding. Each CEP has gone through a series of two or three directors as part of the strife, and high turnover has been typical. Yet much of this turnover carried people from the target neighborhoods through CEP staff positions upward into other public agencies or industries. Operationally, the major shortcoming is lack of employment opportunities for enrollees. Outreach is unnecessary, and intake must usually be restricted to prevent flooding the system with eligible people in search of services. There are simply never enough training slots and, beyond that, enough jobs to match the intake with successfully trained enrollees.

As umbrella agencies — their original purpose — these five CEPs have functioned primarily as devices to bring more funds into the target areas. Only in ABCD has an integrated manpower program resulted, but the comparison is marked more by the administrative deficiencies of other

CEPs and other agencies than by any remarkable competence of ABCD. The CEP concept itself seems to have made no appreciable difference in the quality of the services available. Enrollees still find themselves in a program which has slots available rather than in one which fits their particular needs. Each program still runs as a separate unit, with little coordination or communication among programs. CEP has created an agency which has more ready access to the target population than in the past, but its inability to provide the ultimate objective — good jobs — has been its fatal weakness.

Cooperative Area Manpower Planning System

The CAMPS experience, fairly uniform in the four study cities as well as in the nation, is useful as a communications system for manpower programs. Those operating in the same jurisdiction and territory and serving an overlapping clientele should know what each other is doing. Coordination is desirable, but equals cannot coordinate equals. With no power to allocate funds by vote, the participants have nothing to gain by being in the program or to lose if they are not.

With no common power to whom they can report, there is no reason to concede when concession is necessary for cooperation. Only in Boston has there been a serious attempt to turn CAMPS into a true planning operation. The mayor's representative who undertook the task had authority over none of the participants and only his individual persuasiveness as a weapon for change. In the midst of his efforts, he resigned for a Washington position, leaving Boston's CAMPS effort in limbo. There is no present indication in any of the cities that CAMPS makes a significant difference in program administration, but coordination cannot be made worse by communication.

National Alliance of Businessmen

The local arms of NAB are probably a temporary institution in each city. The concept involves "on loan" business executives who contact their fellow employers for job pledges, after which ES obtains job orders, makes placements, and negotiates contracts for those who want them. The commitment of these executives was substantial during the early period of presidential push and initial enthusiasm. That enthusiasm is clearly waning; and ES, except in Boston, is assuming more and more responsibility for employer contacts as well as placements.

The Boston scene differs somewhat because the NAB metro director is a salaried professional brought in from outside the city with no attachment to any business firm. His high degree of energy has been devoted totally to the NAB-JOBS program; and he is now supported by a full-time staff of 10, hired primarily from ABCD as part of a DOL-funded pilot project to supply technical assistance to interested employers. In effect, Boston's NAB now has its own ES.

In Denver, there is little likelihood of NAB's being a permanent part of the scene, even though it preceded the national program. Enthusiasm within the city's business community has been low, and the role of the chamber of commerce as sponsor has not increased the commitment. Turnover of metro chairmen, metro directors, and loaned staff has been high. In San Francisco, one company (Lockheed) has been primarily responsible for nearly the entire effort . . . which will probably survive so long as Lockheed underwrites it. Oakland's NAB has been moderately active and successful, but is unlikely to survive as a permanent institution.

The Regional Manpower Administration

As it turned out, the three metropolitan areas chosen for this study became the locations for offices of DOL's Regional Manpower Administration. Because they are located in the study cities, the regional offices play a somewhat larger manpower program role in these cities than in those which do not have such offices. Though it is difficult to assess the reasons for this, it is evident that an awareness by state and local agencies of their source of funding undoubtedly causes them to conduct themselves differently from other program sponsors. There is also a more thorough knowledge of local conditions and performance which increases the realism of contract negotiations. More program monitoring occurs, formal and informal, than is likely or even physically possible at a greater distance.

Community-Based Organizations

In addition to the above official agencies, a number of organizations have emerged in each city — either coming into existence autonomously and then seeking manpower funds or organizing specifically to receive manpower funds and deliver manpower services. Typically, they have specific racial or ethnic commitments. An OIC exists in each metropolitan area. Boston's OIC functions primarily as a CEP contractor and has been very successful as a recruiter, trainer, and placer of blacks. With the base of CEP support to operate one of the orientation centers with their 15-week work curricula, the Boston OIC has been able to undertake unfunded evening training programs and training for specific employees. It is well regarded by the community and by Boston employers. Denver's OIC is an illustration of the necessity of base funding. Without a federal contract of any kind, it has never been able to raise sufficient money locally for a meaningful program. The Oakland OIC has become primarily a basic education subcontractor for CEP. It seems to do an effective job, but because it is somewhat isolated from the other manpower agencies of the community, there is no unity with skills training or other functional services.

The two Denver programs, Operation SER and La Rasa, and *Arriba Juntos* and *Educacio para Adelantar* in the bay area are more important as training grounds for minority staff and outlets for energies and contacts into the larger community than as actual deliverers of manpower services.

The language centers in the bay area are not really community based, but are exceedingly important adjuncts to the education system in an area heavily impregnated with immigrants.

Reorienting Agencies

There is no question that manpower program participation has brought about some reorientation in the objectives and practices of existing public agencies in the communities, as well as creation of new institutions. ES in the bay area has changed greatly, in Denver moderately, and in Boston very little.

The public schools have been changing for other reasons; their manpower programs have been instrumental in providing basic education and language and skills training, but modifications in their regular functions are negligible. The extent of public school cooperation in each city followed the same hierarchical delineations as those of ES.

Yet mild as these changes were, they had no direction. Agencies were given new assignments without relinquishing the old. They were never given a specific set of objectives . . . nor were they told that their new assignments were more important than the old. Reward systems were not explicitly changed to provide clear incentives for performing new tasks. No explicit strategies were developed to use the many leverages available in a directed effort to achieve reorientation. Those individuals given assignments solely concerned with the welfare of the disadvantaged did implicitly have their responsibilities, objectives, and reward systems changed, and they responded accordingly. The same was not true of agencies as a whole.

Much of the uncertainty of the period was ambivalence between building on the experience and resources of existing agencies, but reorienting the objectives, or starting again with new, inexperienced agencies but with reward systems directed toward new objectives. The CAAs were the latter; the CEP, an uncomfortable marriage of convenience between both. Neither the originators nor the operators of the CAAs in Denver, Oakland, and San Francisco were sure whether their role was to bring pressure for reorientation on existing agencies, provide services to target groups, or organize the poor. The strength of ABCD was that in responding to available sources of funds, it clearly opted for the second role and was never confused as to its objectives.

The ABCD experience suggests one other principle about reorientation agencies: Training institutions can dodge ultimate responsibility for results so long as they receive other people's recruits and hand them back for placement. Their reward system requires only enrollment and course completion, not job placement. Outreach and placement agencies can lay the blame on the schools and elsewhere when jobs do not follow. ABCD has the responsibility of recruiting, training, and placing. The same is true of the Lockheed consortium. Obviously, failure to achieve the final objective clogs up the system, and unplaced people become excessive "inventory." The same principle holds true for ES. Presently, there is no cause and effect relationship between willingness and efficacy of an ES in serving the disadvantaged and the resources made available to that agency. A reporting system which requires recording the number of disadvantaged who are served will increase awareness of the assignment, but no real breakthrough will occur until budgets, positions, promotions, and other rewards in the system are tied directly to achievement of the priority goals.

Community Attitudes

In none of the four cities have the manpower programs become central to the politics of poverty, and also in none is poverty a central issue in city politics. The patronage that usually fills staff jobs has not proved attractive as a source of power, nor does it provide irresponsible freedom to attack the establishment. Perhaps program responsibility cannot serve as a power base so long as success is elusive. At the citywide level, the poverty community — in terms of effective political organization and votes — still represents too little of the total for a mayor or other city official to base his administration on a war on poverty. In a tenuous situation where fear of a riot is strong yet sympathy for the poor has not been destroyed, it is questionable whether a holder of a citywide office can profit from aid to the minority poor.

Nevertheless, the existence of the programs and the constant criticisms — on the one hand from those who resent their presence and on the other from those frustrated at their ineffectiveness — have increased awareness that society is far from affluent, that unrest exists, and that some action is necessary, whether it be solution or containment. It is true that the unrest (more than the programs) has built this awareness. Yet though the manpower programs are not central to poverty politics, it is doubtful that self-conscious political groupings among the poor would have emerged to the extent that they have if it had not been for the initial impetus of the antipoverty programs, including those with manpower objectives. In part, awareness has engendered sympathy; in part, special efforts on behalf of the minority poor have fomented resentment. One way or another, community attitudes have been affected, and the issues can no longer be ignored.

LABOR MARKET IMPACT

Since the goals of manpower programs are steadier and more satisfying employment and higher earnings for their enrollees, they are certain, if successful, to have an impact on the local labor markets. Among the possible impacts are: (1) increased labor force participation and therefore a larger labor supply, (2) improved skills among those in the labor force, the importance of the latter depending upon the meshing between the skills supplied and those in demand, and (3) a reduction in labor market frictions because of the increased exposure to and familiarity with its institutions as a result of program enrollment.

Those program enrollees who find themselves more steadily employed after enrollment may have filled jobs which would have been taken by others, or they may reduce unemployment either by filling otherwise vacant jobs or by reducing the frictional period between job opening and placement. There appears at the moment to be no means of measurement. Even if a job vacancy series were available for all occupations and industries in each labor market, the present magnitude of program enrollment is probably too small in relation to the total size of the labor force, employment, and unemployment to have a measurable impact.

For example, more than 72,000 persons were enrolled in bay area manpower programs which were completed between January 1966 and June 1970, with an additional unknown number enrolling in programs still in progress. From 20,000 to 25,000 a year as an average enrollment is enormous, but the bay area labor force averaged 1,400,000 persons in 1969, of whom approximately 1,000,000 are employed in the study area. Unemployment would have averaged 70,000 for the standard metropolitan statistical area (SMSA) and 50,000 for the study area. In more than three years' time, approximately 21,000 people were enrolled in programs which could have been expected to make a basic change in their degree of employability.

The message from the bay area labor market is repeated in the other cities. Boston's labor force is approximately 240,000, with 20,000 unemployed. The CAMPS 1971 estimate of the universe of need is 113,000 — 20,000 of them unemployed, 9,200 involuntarily part-time employed, 66,000 employed full time at incomes below the poverty level, 2,600 out of the labor force for unexplained reasons, and 15,000 youth needing part-time or summer jobs. Program enrollment averages less than 6,000 per year. The Denver SMSA has a labor force of 540,000, an unemployment magnitude of 17,800, and an average annual enrollment of no more than 2,500 in manpower programs.

This is not a criticism of the programs or a suggestion that there was no impact. The data measuring the very substantial impact of program participation on the employment and earnings of the individuals involved dispel that notion. It is simply a recognition of the fact that the programs have had the resources to enroll only a fraction of those eligible and an infinitesimal proportion of the labor market participants.

Therefore a better measure of the extent to which the programs have served the needs of the labor market is a comparison between the occupations for which training has been provided and the occupations in demand in the labor market. What is happening in manpower training is painfully clear. To meet the "reasonable expectation of employment" requirement while keeping per capita training costs low, MDTA administrators have chosen to train for jobs where openings occur because of high turnover, whether or not they are characterized by rising demand. Two occupational areas happen to be characterized by both high turnover and rising demand: health occupations and clerical occupations. These comprise 70 percent of all female MDTA Skills Center enrollments. As a result, females are given good employment opportunities even if they are forced into narrow occupational limits. Beyond these two areas, most expanding occupations require a training duration beyond that possible within the informal per trainee expenditure limitations imposed. Thus 76 percent of MDTA Skills Center enrollments are limited to seven occupations, only the above two of which are expanding rapidly. This occupational distribution is also probably true of other training programs.

The Mix of Services and the Universe of Need

A major contribution of manpower programs has been development of a variety of services found to be useful in various combinations in aiding the employability and job access of disadvantaged individuals. The quality of such services varies widely, and the criteria for deciding which individuals could profit most from what combination of services have never been discovered. How useful each manpower service turned out to be in the four-city experience is instructive.

Outreach, Recruitment, and Selection

Part of the mythology of manpower programs has been the image of the disadvantaged individual lacking knowledge of services available to him and distrustful of all public agencies. To be served (it is supposed), these individuals must be searched out in bars, poolrooms, or wherever, and enticed to come in to receive available services. If there are such people in the four cities, the number who are alert to opportunities and quick to demand services is so much greater than the resources available to provide them with these services that the existence of the alienated has never been tested. The task in all cities has been to limit intake to some manageable relationship with the program slots and the job opportunities available. Only where a program was unpopular, as in the Boston Neighborhood Youth Corps (NYC), was there a need to "beat the bushes." JOBS employers sometimes complained that referrals to fill their pledges were slow in coming, but agency efficiency not enrollee availability was apparently the reason.

Just as there was no evidence of significant outreach and recruitment efforts, there was also no indication of any particular effort to select those eligible persons who could most likely profit by certain services. The more appropriate task of starting with an individual's needs and then putting together a package of services to meet his needs was not possible under the present program structure. Selection was purely a process of filling available slots with eligible people with little concern for the appropriateness of the match. The exception was the assignment to basic education of those who had serious educational deficiencies or to language training for those of foreign origin with serious language handicaps.

Orientation and Prevocational Training

Boston and Oakland CEPs have incorporated orientation into prevocational skills training and basic education. The others maintained separate two-week orientation programs, but choosing who would or would not sit through them tends to be somewhat haphazard. The Boston-Oakland view is that certain subject matter, such as filling out application blanks and role-playing to gain self-confidence in employer interviews, is useful but more acceptable if integrated with other training activities. Experience with WIN enrollees suggests some unwillingness on the part of these clients to (as they see it) "mark time" and be identified as deficient in grooming, etc. So far as is known, there is no evidence to either support or disprove any positive influence of orientation on retention or employment. From observation, only a tentative judgment can be expressed that integrating the orientation in training or education, having more obvious relevance to jobs, should make it more acceptable. Actually, most CEP clients are different from the Chicago "gang kids" for whom the YMCA's Jobs Now program first designed a two-week grooming and transportation orientation effort.

The definitive meaning of prevocational training is less than clear. It originally began in the MDTA Skills Centers as an occupational "tryout" or "work evaluation" period. Those with inadequate experience and knowledge in the labor market and not satisfactorily testable by existing culturally biased tests were given an opportunity to try out — for a few days each — a number of skills training courses before choosing one in which to train. A new meaning appears to have grown out of the OICs. Courses in minority group history and similar subjects are designed to promote racial and ethnic identification and pride. There is no evidence which leads to the conclusion that placing people in prevocational training makes any difference one way or another.

Basic Education and Language Training

Those who need basic education and language training need them badly. Indeed the follow-up data, though mixed with orientation and prevocational training, strongly support this observation. Whether or not the techniques in use are the best would require an intensive and specialized study. It appears that the greatest contribution from the paired services emanates from ESL. There are many Spanish-surnamed and Chinese immigrants who have substantial skills which can be applied only after language competence has been achieved. The returns on this effort have been great despite considerable weaknesses in the techniques used.

Skills Training

The follow-up data provide a resounding testimonial for skills training. In the four-city study, those who obtained skills training showed better employment stability and earnings than those who received only nonskills training. However, no comparison was provided between institutional and on-the-job training (OJT) or work experience. Occupational comparisons were scarce, but male occupations showed higher wages — but not necessarily greater wage differences and improvements in employment stability — than those of the females. Generally, the greatest earnings gains are found in the more technical occupations.

Boston offered an interesting comparison between the results of MDTA skills training of nine-month duration and ABCD orientation center skills training of a three-month average. Posttraining wages and employment stability were nearly identical. However, because those with the shortest training were the most disadvantaged and had started the farthest behind, their gains were much greater. Evidently, the after-training jobs were approximately the same despite enrollee characteristics and training duration.

Skills training is the most familiar of manpower services but not the easiest to assess. Its contribution in comparison to OJT experience is a highly debated (and debatable) matter. Essential problems are those of the level of jobs and the duration and quality of training. Most of the training given under MDTA and WIN is entry level; i.e., it assumes its enrollees have competitive handicaps and for the most part attempts to prepare them for entry into jobs which those without the competitive handicaps could have obtained directly without training. Employers are not likely to face labor shortages in these occupations unless the jobs are unattractive. Therefore, some commitment from the employer is necessary, or the completer is still faced with tough competition and poor job prospects.

For those who receive more substantial training, competition will depend on the availability of training opportunities for others in the community. For example, California MDTA graduates must compete with junior college graduates in clerical, metal working, and mechanical and other skilled occupations. NAB-JOBS was to provide a solution for this problem by making the job commitment first and supplying whatever training was necessary while the trainee was on the payroll. So far, few employers have been willing to accept the responsibility for hiring, and fewer have provided any meaningful training.

Many of the people whom NAB-JOBS hired merely needed an opportunity and, once hired, were as productive as other job incumbents. But these placements require jobs of a certain nature as well as people of a certain caliber. The Lockheed consortium is a substitute for the abortive MDTA coupled relationship. DOL has apparently not been enthusiastic about promoting the consortium approach. Educators, in general, prefer a training duration longer than needed for an entry-level job and longer than most adults are willing to limit their incomes to stipends. Comparisons of Skills Centers with ad hoc training courses in "moonlighted" facilities strongly support the former. However, the MDTA centers are caught between this bias in favor of longer training and the necessity to keep their per enrollee costs down. The Boston orientation centers are specific and of short duration. It has been charged that the jobs could have been obtained without the training. The best defense on this point is that MDTA placements, following training courses three times as long, produce almost the same earnings. The preferred solution would appear to be a two-level system. Those unwilling to take longer term training should be given short-term, specific, entry-level basic education and skills training, augmented by a job guarantee from cooperating employers. For others — the young without heavy financial commitment — the alternative would be the full 104 weeks of the MDTA authorization in the equivalent of a remedial community approach leading to technical- rather than entry-level jobs.

Counseling

Counseling in manpower programs for the disadvantaged seems to bear little resemblance to the usually nondirective principles of professional counseling. Less of the successful counselor's time appears to be spent helping the client understand himself and make his own decisions based on resolution of his own inner conflicts. Rather the effective counselors seem to be those who help the individual directly in the solution of personal problems — intervening in legal processes, mediating marital disputes, appealing to creditors, loaning money, bailing clients out of jail. Professional counselors can provide these services as well as anyone, but rapport rather than professional training seems to be the critical factor. There are biases in the professional credentialing process which prefers those without the necessary rapport; e.g., the bias in favor of white middle-class female counselors for minority youth often suffering for lack of male role models. Certainly requiring professional credentials would rule out effective nonprofessional indigenous counselors.

Promotion and Subsidization of Employer Involvement

The NAB-JOBS approach was clearly desirable, but experience in the four cities suggests that it will never enroll enough employers or employees to have more than a minor impact. In all but Oakland, responsibility for promotion has ultimately settled down to a full-time employed staff rather than "on loan" executives. The comparison opts for the full timers, so long as the staff can be fairly flexible and unimpeded by bureaucracy. If the latter can be accomplished, whether the staff are on public or private payrolls, would probably make little difference. There is a need for promoters and job developers to match those job applicants and jobs which need or require no formal training. There is also need for institutional training facilities, again publicly or privately run, to bring the remaining trainees, once on the payroll, to levels the employers can and are willing to use without extensive "processing."

Job Development

There is no question that the critical bottleneck in all programs in all cities is the lack of jobs to which people can be referred when they have completed the preliminary stages. Despite relatively tight labor markets in all of the cities, there simply were no employers hungrily waiting with attractive jobs in easily accessible locations which they were willing to offer to manpower program participants. That the more able and aggressive of the residents of the target areas managed to find jobs, get to them, and hold them is beside the point. The objective of the manpower programs has been to "make a connection" for those who had not been able to do this without help. It is also true that, justifiably or not, there were jobs available in the cities for which there were no takers. Welfare recipients with families of any size simply could not afford these jobs. Others had developed overexpectations which are difficult to eradicate.

The exact definition of "job development" is also not clear. In general, it seems to mean "give the job to my client rather than someone else." There was no evidence of any restructuring of jobs to fit the applicant. The existing approach to job development is a competitive one which cannot provide the answer for all. Jobs are not created except by increased purchases of goods and services, and job developers can do no more than try to win slots away from others for their clients. There was surprisingly little complaint from employers interviewed about the number of people engaged in doing exactly that.

There seems to be no other way to solve the job development dilemma than to (1) use the most aggressive, pattern-centered measures to assure equal access to jobs, then (2) take on the long, arduous task of bringing the noncompetitive worker to the point that he can win for himself his share of the jobs, and (3) provide some temporary or permanent subsidized private employment, public employment, or income maintenance holding or transition stage.

Placement

Assuming the job development phase is such that job orders are on file and the outreach or recruitment stage bringing in job applicants, placement is largely a function of (1) information and (2) priorities. Undoubtedly, automatic means of paper shuffling could help, but the critical issue confronting the placement officer is the latter — who has priority, the employer or the applicant, and who among the various groups of applicants?

Some have complained that placement only finds for the applicant a job no better than those he has held in the past. A primary and secondary labor market with an impervious wall between them has been hypothesized. The comparison of pre- and postplacement earnings does not refute this view, but it raises interesting questions about the location of the boundary between the primary and secondary markets. It identifies a tendency to escalate the earnings of the poorly paid but to leave the better paid unaffected. The implications are that those with the lowest level jobs get better ones but that there is a ceiling on the quality of jobs referred to ES so that the better paid return to jobs that are no improvement.

Coaching and Follow-up

The actual amount of job coaching done appears to be less than that paid for. Yet the function appears to be useful when properly applied. The difficulty most often observed was the tendency of coaches to identify so closely with the coached that they often reinforced rather than ameliorated the latters' weaknesses. The coach must understand the trainee's problems, but if he is going to help him settle into a job, he must convince the trainee that it is necessary to accept discipline and be productive rather than the two of them doing no more than agreeing on the shortcomings of the employer.

The limited amount of follow-up occurring in all the programs has coaching as its sole objective. There is no meaningful follow-up occurring for feedback purposes. Therefore, any learning and program improvement based on knowledge of the trainee's subsequent experience is based on accident. Follow-up for the latter purposes will undoubtedly have to be done by other than program operators and is more effectively and economically done on a sampling basis.

Supportive Services

Child care is an obvious necessity for the participation of mothers, yet there are no adequate facilities in the study cities. Buying the service from private or public sources rather than undertaking the function as part of the manpower program might be preferable. Health care, both medical and dental, appears to be a necessity to successful programs for the disadvantaged, as does legal assistance. Transportation was less often mentioned as a necessity. Though access to suburban jobs was emphasized as a serious problem, little effort was addressed to solving it.

Agency Interrelationships and Linkages

All agencies showed a remarkable facility for separatism, even in running different programs within the same agency. For instance, ES organized and ran WIN with no connection to MDTA administration, except when MDTA slots were desired for WIN clients. CEP might be an umbrella over the various programs, but the programs tended to remain sharply segregated under the umbrella. It is not surprising then that there has been so little intercourse between, for example, CEP and NAB-JOBS. So long as separate staffs, budgets, and titles are maintained, the separateness will continue. In a comprehensive manpower program, a strong supervisory hand will still be necessary to enforce unity, linkage, and differentiation, based only on the needs of particular applicants. In none of these four cities (and by implication, in no other area) is there any central source of planning and coordination. There is no point in the metropolitan manpower system at which problems can be identified, objectives determined, resources marshaled, and any kind of comprehensive or integrated attack begun. Federal, state, and local agencies and private manpower organizations respond to the presence of federal funds and within the limits of national directives. There is also no point at which the question — how can available resources, including those from the federal manpower programs, best be used in solution of this community's manpower problems? — can be answered.

Upward Mobility for Staff

The manpower programs have been a means for identifying able individuals among target groups, testing them in the crucible of experience, and moving them up through the ranks and out into other programs or other public or private employment. Though no number can be put on the amount of upward mobility engendered, it has been one of the main byproducts. However, the upward motion has been greatest in communitybased organizations — CAAs, CEP, OIC, etc. Merit systems may allow hiring indigenous personnel, but they usually place an impenetrable ceiling on how high they can go in the system. Even New Careers has not been able to pierce these ceilings. A major change in merit system practices will be necessary to move people upward based on nothing but objective performance. One universal need is for training — initial preparation and, more important, both short-term, in-service training and longer released time for pursuit of formal education. But the principles of manpower program administration are not yet sufficiently identified to give much value to formal classroom training alone, unmixed with OJT experience.

Work Experience and Job Creation Programs

NYC, Operation Mainstream, New Careers, NAB-JOBS, and MDTA-OJT must be appraised without the advantage of quantitative data. There are no data on MDTA-OJT, and NAB-JOBS employers were reluctant to share information on employee progress even if they had it. There is some useful information on New Careers: The work stations of the two work experience programs were examined for the quality of the experience offered, but there were no data on the subsequent progress and no expectations that employability was enhanced; thus the appraisal of their impact is largely judgmental.

A review of the NYC work stations shows some of them to be good jobs with useful work experience, but for the most part work crews seem to be assigned to menial tasks with little supervision or discipline. There are indications of progress in making the work experience more useful in addition to building up the education component . . . the income has been needed and the experience has been better than none.

The desirability of NYC depends heavily upon the answer to the question: If there were no NYC, what alternatives would be provided poor youth to earn and to a limited extent, to learn? Before and after comparison of NYC enrollees is very difficult since few of them have a meaningful job market "before." Since the program has been without clear objectives, it is hard to know if it is achieving them.

Operation Mainstream and equivalent work programs are easier to evaluate. In some cases they have been temporary "parking lots" while the enrollees await entry into other programs. Beyond that, the goal has been some modest self-esteem and income for alcoholics, elderly men, and others unlikely to make it in the regular labor market. Although it is a last resort, many are enrolled in such programs.

New Careers has been a disappointment largely because of its high expectations. It has provided access to white-collar employment for the most capable and best prepared of the disadvantaged population. Agencies and professionals have been reluctant to offer real subprofessional ladders into more meaningful careers. The concept has great promise, but it has never been successfully accomplished in practice. One mistake appears to be the failure to provide the tutoring and similar support necessary to make it possible for disadvantaged people, no matter how intelligent, to simultaneously hold down a job and attempt to obtain educational credentials. If the credentials are to be required, then high support efforts must be provided as well.

NAB-JOBS must be declared a positive influence on the individual, the labor market, and the employers. At worst the enrollee gets a job he could have obtained without the program. At best he gets upgraded into a regular job and continues to progress upward in the employing system. If the former, the taxpayers pay contractors for a product they do not receive, though noncontract pledges are cost-free to the government. MDTA-OJT is but a cut-rate version of JOBS.

Summary

Each functional service has its role under various circumstances, but the data and observations are relatively clear on which has the most value in the general case. Which are the greatest of manpower obstacles, those inherent in the individual which reduce his employability, or those in the institutional arrangement which block his access to jobs? This issue has never been adequately settled. There is evidence for both obstacles, but the only services which received solid statistical support from the follow-up study were those that changed the enrollee's basic employability with the prize going to those services which changed it most. Therefore, the service functions with the most statistical support appeared to be basic education, language training, and skills training. Skills training appears most vital, with the others as necessary prerequisites.

There is also statistical support for those training courses with the most technical content. Training does not create jobs, and logic and experience emphasize the need for job development and job creation. The NAB-JOBS effort, with growing reliance upon full-time ES contact men, is well worth continuing. Public service employment is needed and can be useful if the aura of "real jobs" can be created. To fail to do so would be to repeat the poor performance of current work experience programs. Basic education, ESL, and skills training with a job guarantee either through a private employer (subsidized or unsubsidized) or through a public agency is the best route to success in manpower programs. Public service employment jobs should be structured into the regular state or local government merit system to make the jobs meaningful and real.

CURRENT POLICY ISSUES

The intensive study of manpower program administration in the three metropolitan areas offers some enlightenment on the three major current national manpower policy issues: (1) the advisability of decentralizing the administration and decategorizing the funding of the manpower programs, (2) the need for a public service employment program, and (3) the employability of welfare recipients.

Decentralization and Decategorization

Legislation introduced in 1969 and still before Congress in 1972 would delegate to governors and mayors many of the decisions now made at the federal level and would eliminate or reduce the number of specific program categories, allowing funds to be distributed functionally — based on approved state and local plans. Specific proposals differ in the number of categories and the relative roles of federal, state, and local governments. What can be learned from the workings of present approaches in the three metropolitan areas? It is first necessary to repeat that there is currently no planning for manpower programs in any of the three areas. Planning involves a setting of objectives, an examination of alternative routes to those objectives, a choice and implementation of plan of attack and monitoring, evaluation, and feedback for determination and improvement of results. In none of the metropolitan areas studied does that occur.

The California Department of Human Resource Development (DHRD) shifted the priorities of CSES more specifically to the disadvantaged. There is no planning element in the system which merely runs the federal programs as federally prescribed. There is no mechanism for considering the appropriateness of those programs to the local environment nor for changing the program mix if the existing pattern does not fit. Even the CEPs, which could vary the uses of their CEP versatile monies to some extent, rarely see reason to do so. In Denver, every program operates autonomously and no instrumentality of state or local government has overview responsibility or concern. The same can be said for state and local government in Boston. However, CEP provides a somewhat broader manpower umbrella than in other cities. It does some planning in the formulation of its proposals and delivers a variety of ·services with considerable internal coordination.

The only significant experience with decategorization in the study cities is that of ABCD in running the Boston CEP. Its NECs are its own employment service. In its orientation centers, it has run the equivalent of an MDTA Skills Center. It has adapted its Operation Mainstream funds to the special needs of an otherwise neglected group. It has worked effectively with and used productively the efforts of other nonprofit organizations such as OIC. However, when it has launched a program and assigned a staff to it, there is no indication that it rethinks priorities and develops new programs for new circumstances. There is some evidence of willingness to abandon an unproductive effort, but none of reallocating funds just because something else might work better, or because other needs might become more pressing. Unless some special effort or requirement is introduced to force and guide reconsideration, a permissive decategorization would most likely leave agencies doing the same things in the same ways for a substantial period in the future. Only if the decategorization resulted in a redistribution of power, causing one agency to replace another in the delivery of services, would change in the mix of services be likely to occur. Even then, under the circumstances, the reallocation would likely be in the direction of those services most familiar to the new power holders.

The major issues in decentralization are: (1) to whom to decentralize and (2) how much authority to relinquish how fast. A consensus has developed that planning and policy-making responsibility below the federal level should rest upon the chief elected official in a state or city rather than upon more impersonal and nonpolitical agencies. It is assumed that nonmetropolitan areas are the governor's responsibility. There also appears to be agreement that above some size, it is only politically realistic, if not desirable, to charge the mayor with planning and decision-making responsibility. Differences exist over the size of the city to which this passthrough of authority and funds should apply. Given the aggressive lobbying of the mayors and the apathy of the governors, the tendency has been for the size of city, allowed to have its own autonomous manpower budget and responsibility, to shrink as new legislative proposals are introduced.

Three considerations complicate the issue. First, search for some means of welding chief executive officers of cities or counties together into a labor marketwide planning unit has been unsuccessful. Given the concentration of disadvantaged persons in central city areas, mayors tend to have within their jurisdictions the bulk of manpower program eligibles. The good semi-skilled jobs which could lift from poverty people without substantive skills and education have fled to the suburbs, and no labor marketwide political jurisdiction exists. The governor's scope encompasses the suburbs . . . but as part of the entire state, and state governments have not been responsive to specific populations, particularly those in urban areas. On the other hand, the only meaningful, experienced delivery systems for manpower services are in the hands of state agencies. The need for a governor-mayor partnership is obvious but the means for achieving it is not.

Second, the assumption is that decentralization accompanied by de-categorization would lead to planning for resource allocation and service provision according to localized and changing need. But no one at federal, state, or local levels has any experience with manpower planning. Congress and administration guideline writers have designed programs with only the vaguest notions of the nature and needs of the target population and the realities of the labor market. State and local agencies have responded by running the federal programs according to federal rules. Management information data systems are inadequate. Little is known about what services work how well for whom under what conditions. Developing planning techniques will be a lengthy trial-and-error process. To be implemented effectively in the reasonable future, all of the considerations will require technical assistance which no one presently knows how to give.

Third, it is a rare state or city government that can claim any substantial manpower expertise. After all, it was only 10 years ago that a few people were "drafted" from other related or unrelated activities as the core of a manpower cadre. After nearly a decade, a body of reasonable competence has developed at the federal level. At the state level, personnel of agencies administering federally funded and designed manpower programs have developed capability to do the job they were assigned to do. The time lag between changing assignments and changing attitudes has been amply illustrated by efforts to reorient existing agencies.

Only a handful at the state level have any experience at the broader planning tasks. At the city level, there are only a few community action staff, a small proportion of whom have any manpower experience. There are almost no training programs for manpower administrators, and there is no agreed upon body of knowledge and skills about which to organize a training program. To speak lightly of decentralization without recognizing the long period of technical assistance and staff training necessary to reach a moderate level of competence is to evidence naïveté. Planning is much more difficult than administration, and at the local level there is now the competence to do neither. The funding of CAMPS secretariats for mayors and governors has brought a lot of eager new people into the manpower field, but unless better methods of skill acquirement are found, they will require the same decade-long trial-and-error experience as the federal staff.

The three study areas illustrate the problems. No manpower planning agency exists in any of the states or cities. Nor does any of them possess any form of central coordinating unit for manpower policy. The Colorado governor's office gives no indication or recognition that manpower programs exist, and if forced into recognition, would undoubtedly turn the assignment to the state ES. Massachusetts had evidenced the same disinterest until it recently began organizing a series of new departments, at least two of them with manpower responsibilities. California, between the Democratic assembly and the Republican state administration, formed DHRD but gave it no planning responsibility and authority and limited resources. The DHRD contribution was to divide the CSES between a traditional placement agency for all and a minority-run agency committed to serving the disadvantaged. However, the resources to do the latter job were not provided, and even the continuance of the experiment appears to be in doubt.

There is even less manpower capability at the city level. Boston's mayor had on his staff one manpower expert, now departed to Washington. Denver has sponsored NYC and CEP programs without giving their directors someone in city government to whom to report. Oakland's mayor once tried to assume manpower responsibilities but after losing out in competition to administer the CEP, abandoned the interest and disbanded the staff. The recent action of California's governor in vetoing refunding for the Oakland CAA and the DOL approval of the action may signal a return of manpower responsibility to the mayor's office, but there is no staff there now to receive the assignment. San Francisco's mayor has never assumed manpower responsibilities since his predecessor was politically burned by unfillable promises made at the time of the Hunters Point riot. He now has on his staff an exceptionally knowledgeable manpower expert, sequestered from CSES, but as yet with no authority. Before a "passthrough" to the mayors of these cities is endorsed, it should be clarified as to who will receive the passthrough and what he will do after receiving it.

Decentralization is not completely hopeless because decategorization requires it, and both put a premium on planning. The four-city message is more likely that it can be achieved with patience and a gradual extension of responsibility, if accompanied by technical assistance, staff training, and time.

Public Service Employment

The experience of the four cities includes solemn testimony of two related facts: (1) it is unlikely that there will ever be enough acceptable jobs for the central city disadvantaged without some form of public employment guarantee, and (2) no set of programs are more difficult to administer effectively.

Throughout the three years of this study, in tight and loose labor markets, every manpower program faced dual pressures in never having enough program slots for all the applicants and never being able to place enough of its enrollees. The structure of the central city labor market persists — white-collar and minimally paying, insecure service jobs. Well-paying, semiskilled jobs continue to draw away to the suburbs. Jobs (even those without skills) in city government are popular and have substantial waiting lists. Their security and fringes tend to offset low wage rates. Cities are strapped for funds, and there are untold needs not now filled in the public sector.

On the other hand, the message of NYC, Operation Mainstream, and similar programs is that so long as employment takes priority over production in program design and administration, no one — enrollee or supervisor — will take the assignment seriously as jobs rather than excuses for income maintenance.

The San Francisco federal employment program, especially as it involved the post office, provided regular jobs by reducing artificial barriers. The disadvantaged people hired not only took the jobs seriously but performed more productively and with more stability than the regular employees. New Careers has had, under the best of circumstances, a similar tendency. Public Service Careers has only begun to try to work around merit system barriers.

The message of this experience for the new Public Employment Program introduced by the Emergency Employment Act of 1971, depends upon the objective of that Act which was passed as a countercyclical weapon against general unemployment not specifically aimed at those disadvantaged workers who experience difficulty even in times of high economic activity. Given its general nature, there should be no difficulty finding governmental units willing to accept what is essentially free labor from their viewpoint. There are ample useful public services to be performed. There are also far more job seekers than the limited budgets can absorb. But the jobs will probably go to the best prepared among the unemployed. The impact upon the target groups and locations of this study will be minor though positive.

The great need for such areas is a public employment program addressed specifically toward those central city residents among whom unemployment and low income have been concentrated. It is for such a program that the experience with NYC, Operation Mainstream, and New Careers contains lessons. Make-work jobs are easy to make, but "real" ones are not. Such activities are taken seriously only as sources of income maintenance. They are helpful, but do little to put disadvantaged feet upon the ladder leading to the labor market mainstream.

Manpower programs in general have paid too little attention to the way the labor market works. They have concentrated upon the pathologies and too often ignored the lessons that examination of the successful routes might have provided. Training programs have prepared enrollees for occupations wherein formal institutional training was not the usual means of entry without asking why the program participants needed the training for those same occupations. Work experience programs have given little thought to how that experience was to lead to regular employment.

A successful public service employment program for the disadvantaged must offer to them regular employment status. Major reforms in merit systems and other public personnel systems will be required. Expansion of public service activities requires only the infusion of federal dollars. The inclusion of those persons formerly excluded as public servants will require far more.

The Employability of Welfare Recipients

As the employment and earnings section testified, the WIN program has been overwhelmingly characterized by female heads of household with multiple dependents. The males were few and their numbers easily exhausted. Females were demonstrably available for project participation. Few presented themselves for employment following training, but those who did experienced substantial increases in wages and employment stability. The issue to be faced comes through clearly from the four-city study: There is a tremendous number of capable women on welfare, but they are hampered in training for and finding jobs by their family responsibilities and the lack of day-care and other facilities. Only by providing these facilities can we test the full motivation. But the next step would be extensive training to make it possible for these working mothers to earn at a level above their current assistance levels.

The legislators who dream of reduced welfare roles are doing just that — dreaming. Because the rhetoric tends to mislead even those who know better, it is necessary to be reminded that the real purpose for which welfare reform was first proposed was to provide income supplements to the working poor, not to put significant numbers of recipients of welfare, almost all of whom are mothers, to work. The evidence seems to be that most of them would prefer to be self-supporting and, where feasible, they should have that opportunity, but no one should expect a significant impact on total numbers. The strains placed upon the family structure in urban America and the perverseness of the labor markets, not the willingness or unwillingness of people to work, are at issue.

In short, the four-city study recommends caution and a step-by-step approach to decentralization of manpower program planning and administration. It demonstrates the need for public service employment but also the necessity and difficulty of making the jobs real for the disadvantaged, and it casts serious doubts on the employability of most welfare recipients.

Summary and Conclusions

The message of this study of the total impact of all manpower programs on the enrollees, economies, and labor markets, and the institutions of three major metropolitan areas are sharp and clear on some points, dependent upon informed judgments in others, and subject primarily to conjecture on a few. Nine specific considerations are spelled out below.

1. Across all cities and programs and despite unfavorable economic conditions, the average enrollee in an institutional training program was substantially better off in terms of employment stability and earnings because of his program participation. The lower the pretraining wage rate, the greater the wage and earnings gain was likely to be. Relatively few female WIN enrollees chose to enter the labor market after training, but those who did profited about as much as enrollees in any other program. Skills training, on the average, paid off better than nonskills training such as basic education and language training. Yet nonskills training alone also had significantly positive employment and earnings impacts, and some of the language training brought spectacular results as it freed technically skilled immigrants from their communications handicaps.

2. Placement services alone, unaccompanied by any service designed to improve employability, had a generally positive impact on the earnings of those with low preplacement wages but was generally neutral in impact for others.

3. The impact of work experience and OJT programs is less certain. NYC in general has supplied income maintenance and menial activities, but the quality of the work stations appears to be improving. Operation Mainstream has been useful as a source of income, a "drying out" place for alcoholics and a "parking lot" while awaiting slots in other programs. New Careers has been a disappointment because of high expectations, but has been a positive force in getting the better prepared among the disadvantaged into entry-level, white-collar jobs. Data are most lacking on NAB-JOBS, but these programs do represent real jobs, and the net contribution is almost certain to have been positive.

4. The programs and their budgets have added significantly to the jobs and payrolls of the community. Staff jobs have been important ladders of upward mobility within the minority community.

5. Measuring the impact of manpower programs on the community is exceedingly difficult. Enrollments are so small in contrast to the size of the labor force that any impact is unlikely to be measurable. If we com-

pare training occupations to demand occupations, it is obvious that the tendency has been to train for those jobs characterized by high turnover rather than those in expanding demand.

6. Existing community institutions have been reoriented in their attitudes toward the disadvantaged and their capability of providing service in direct ratio to the degree of their involvement. Thus the schools have been changed little, ES greatly, private employers moderately, public employers less, and unions hardly at all — all with only limited political impact.

7. The Skills Centers have been useful new institutions, the CEPs less so, and CAMPS has been a useful communications but not a planning device. Manpower funds have sparked the emergency of a variety of community-based, minority-oriented organizations, more important as incipient power bases than as deliverers of service.

8. Of the available manpower services, outreach has been mythical, job development rare, orientation and counseling useful, and supportive services necessary. In general, the most vital and most productive have been basic education and language training for those who needed it and skills training for most of those who have received it. If it were necessary to cut off all manpower services but three, these would be the three to keep.

9. The four-city study supplies important insights on current manpower policy issues. Decentralization must move cautiously, accompanied by large doses of technical assistance and staff training. Public service employment is the most needed but the most difficult to administer of all programs, if its objective is jobs for the disadvantaged. Prospects for moving welfare recipients off the welfare roles and onto payrolls are severely limited.

Bibliography

California Department of Employment. *Occupational Profile, City of San Francisco.* California Department of Employment, April 1969.

Cronin, Joseph M., *et al. Organizing an Urban School System for Diversity: A Study of the Boston School Department.* Massachusetts Advisory Council on Education, October 1970.

Fried, March, *et al.* "A Study of Demographic and Social Determinants of Functional Achievement in a Negro Population." Final Report. Boston: Institute of Human Sciences, Boston College, January 1, 1971.

Futransky, David, and Wagner, Donald. "On-the-Job Follow-up of Postal Clerks Hired in San Francisco without Employment Tests." Report to the U.S. Civil Service Commission, July 1968. (Mimeographed.)

Johnson, Miriam. *The Workshop: A Program of the San Francisco Adult Project Office.* California State Employment Service, September 1967.

Levin, Murray. *The Alienated Voter.* New York: Holt, Rinehart and Winston, 1960.

Schrag, Peter. *Village School Downtown.* Boston: Beacon Press, 1967.

Shannon, William V. *The American Irish.* New York: The Macmillan Company, 1963.

Thernstrom, Stephan. *Poverty, Planning and Politics in the New Boston: The Origin of ABCD.* New York: Basic Books, Inc., 1969.

Zubrow, R. A., *et al. Poverty and Jobs in Denver: A Study of Employment, Unemployment and Job Vacancies in the Denver Labor Market.* Economic Development Administration, U.S. Department of Commerce, June 1969.

Index